# Google, Amazon, and Beyond: Creating and Consuming Web Services

ALEXANDER NAKHIMOVSKY AND TOM MYERS

Google, Amazon, and Beyond: Creating and Consuming Web Services
Copyright ©2004 by Alexander Nakhimovsky and Tom Myers

ISBN (pbk): 1-59059-131-3

Printed and bound in the United States of America 12345678910

Technical Reviewer: Jeff Barr

Editorial Board: Dan Appleman, Craig Berry, Gary Cornell, Tony Davis, Steven Rycroft, Julian Skinner, Martin Streicher, Jim Sumser, Karen Watterson, Gavin Wright, John Zukowski

Assistant Publisher: Grace Wong

Project Manager: Sofia Marchant

Copy Editor: Nancy Depper

Production Manager: Kari Brooks

Production Editor: Laura Cheu

Proofreader: Linda Seifert

Compositor: Diana Van Winkle, Van Winkle Design

Indexer: Kevin Broccoli

Artist: Joan Howard

Cover Designer: Kurt Krames

Manufacturing Manager: Tom Debolski

Distributed to the book trade in the United States by Springer-Verlag New York, Inc., 175 Fifth Avenue, New York, NY, 10010 and outside the United States by Springer-Verlag GmbH & Co. KG, Tiergartenstr. 17, 69112 Heidelberg, Germany.

In the United States: phone 1-800-SPRINGER, email orders@springer-ny.com, or visit http://www.springer-ny.com. Outside the United States: fax +49 6221 345229, email orders@springer.de, or visit http://www.springer.de.

For information on translations, please contact Apress directly at 2560 Ninth Street, Suite 219, Berkeley, CA 94710. Phone 510-549-5930, fax 510-549-5939, email info@apress.com, or visit http://www.apress.com.

The source code for this book is available to readers at http://www.apress.com in the Downloads section.

*To our children, who will be users of*
*Googles and Amazons for decades to come:*
*Toby, Emma, Paul, Peter, and Tamsin (tjm)*
*Isaac and Sharon (adn)*

# Contents at a Glance

# Contents

# About the Authors

 **Alexander Nakhimovsky** received an MA in mathematics from Leningrad University (1972) and a Ph.D in linguistics from Cornell University (1979) with a graduate minor in computer science. He has been teaching computer science at Colgate University since 1985. He is also the author of books and articles on linguistics and artificial intelligence—the foundational concepts of the Semantic Web.

 **Tom Myers** studied physics in Bogota and Buenos Aires before receiving his BA from St. John's College, Santa Fe (1975) and a PhD in computer science from the University of Pennsylvania (1980). Recently, he has been working on Java and XML projects, especially database work in Java using J2EE. He is also the author of a book and several articles on theoretical computer science.

# About the Technical Reviewer

As Web Services Evangelist for Amazon.com, **Jeff Barr** focuses on creating developer awareness for the Amazon software platform. He has a longstanding interest in Web Services and programmatic information interchange. Jeff has held development and management positions at KnowNow, eByz, Akopia, and Microsoft, and was a co-founder of Visix Software. Jeff's interests include collecting and organizing news feeds using his site, www.syndic8.com. He holds a Bachelor's degree in computer science from the American University and has done graduate work in computer science at the George Washington University.

# Acknowledgments

As always, we are grateful to the excellent editorial staff at Apress, to our families, and to the people who came up with all this new stuff for us to learn and write about.

# Introduction

## What Is This Book About?

This is a book about Web Services. Web Services are still more like a movement than a mature technology. The movement is motivated by a vision of a semi-automated Web that can support long chains of interactions between autonomous agents. There are three important components to that vision. One is interoperability: a service can have clients (agents) from any platform, in any language. Another is autonomy: an agent can discover the services it needs from their published descriptions that include both *what* the service can do and *how* it does it (the interfaces of available actions). The third is (semi) automatic code creation: one description can be used by a development framework to automate the creation of code for clients and by the services themselves. As of today, interoperability is close to full realization, with only occasional glitches; autonomy is a distant vision; code creation is useful but it still has problems. Interoperability has been achieved in part by using an XML-based high-level protocol (SOAP) for message exchanges between clients and services. As long as the client can produce messages in the right format, it doesn't matter what language they're written in or on what platform they run.

The first three chapters of our book show how to write platform-independent Web Services clients in Javascript and Java running from within a browser (IE6 or Mozilla). The services to which our clients connect are for the most part from Google and Amazon, the first companies of substantial size to open access via Web Services to their proprietary information and functionality. To illustrate the generality of approach and possible integration, we use the same techniques and the same clients to connect to other services as well, combining the results in a single application.

Chapters 4 and 5 continue with the idea of integration, but this time we develop a service of our own (a local Book Club) and show how it can be integrated with other services (like Amazon). Chapter 5 adds some security to our service but it also introduces an important new topic: Web Services without SOAP. There is a large movement and a well-motivated argument that SOAP is not a good idea, and that the same benefits of interoperability can be achieved using just HTTP. The movement is generally known as REST (Representational State Transfer), and you'll find out about it in Chapter 5 when we present a REST version of our Book Club service. (We are helped here by Amazon's wise decision to offer both SOAP and REST interfaces to their Web Services.)

In Chapter 6, we introduce a great tool—XSLT—and show how it can be used to process the output of a Web Service. Chapter 7 continues with REST, showcasing another great (and greatly under-utilized) tool called WebDAV. DAV stands for Distributed Authoring and Versioning; it's a set of extensions to HTTP that allows people both read and write access over the Web. In Chapter 8, we use WebDAV and XSLT to develop a framework for collaborative authoring of a store of documents. The documents in the store are automatically cross-linked and searchable by very complex queries, even though the people who create the documents can use such widely known tools as Microsoft Word.

Finally, in Chapter 9, we take a look at the current state of Web Services' description and automatic code generation. We show how it is supposed to work and does work in simple cases, but also how it doesn't quite work in more complex cases that require a good understanding of the description language (WSDL, Web Services Description Language). Chapter 9 explains WSDL, and develops a WSDL description of our Book Club service. The description is then used to generate client code for the service. This is where the vision collides with reality and the still unresolved problems become apparent. We are at the cutting edge here: the WSDL specification is a working draft and undergoing rapid development.

## Who Is This Book For?

If you have programmed in any language, this book is for you. Whether you are an experienced programmer or a weekend hobbyist, you will find something here that is useful and, we hope, fun. There aren't many computer users who have not done a Google search or bought a book at Amazon, and the ability to invoke those services (and others) from your own little program or script creates a world of opportunities for your imagination to explore. Our Javascript code is very readable and easy to recast in your favorite language; our Java code is extensively commented and can be understood and reused with very little Java background.

# What Do You Need to Use This Book?

All the supporting software is free. You will need the following:

- A current browser: IE6.0 or Mozilla 1.4

- Sun's Java Development Kit (JDK) version 1.4.1 or later

- Tomcat web server and the Axis Web Services framework from Apache

- Tidy HTML-to-XML converter from SourceForge

- The code archive for this book from Apress

Detailed installation instructions are given in Appendix A.

# The Book's Code

This book's code is available from the Apress web site, http://www.apress.com. Please understand that our code is there to experiment with—it's not production code. When given the choice between a simple approach and one that handles errors well, we often choose the first. Even more important than simplicity is transparency; we want you to see both XML and HTTP go over the wire. In your own code, you may want to hide them.

We do not reuse code as much as a production version would. At times we've actually copied Javascript functions and Java methods from one file to another so that a file can be read as a self-contained text, whereas for production code we would avoid such copying. We do develop some small libraries that are reusable, however, both in Java and Javascript.

Most of our Javascript code is in .js files, invoked from normal HTML files. The top-level HTML files are usually framesets with one control frame for user interaction and one or two data frames for results. We know that frames are disliked by some users and deprecated by W3C, but we found that our cross-browser frameset solutions were easier to follow than equivalent IFRAME structures, especially when we have XML in one frame and HTML in another. Both of our browsers allow convenient frame-based debugging.

Now that you know what to expect, download, unzip, and enjoy!

# CHAPTER 1

# Defining Web Services

THIS BOOK IS ABOUT consuming, creating, and deploying Web Services. To "consume" means to use a client that communicates with a Web Service. What are Web Services, and how do their clients communicate with them? Most generally, a Web Service is a distributed application that exposes public procedures whose input and output conform to a standard, language-independent and platform-independent protocol. The key feature of Web Services is interoperability: they can be invoked remotely over the network by client programs written in different languages and running on different platforms.

In this book, you will see Web Service clients written in JavaScript and Java, running from a Web page, a command line, or off a server via JavaServer Pages (JSPs). Figure 1-1 illustrates.

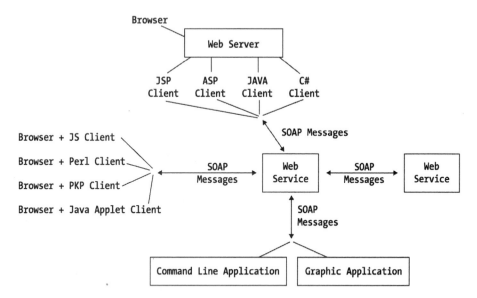

*Figure 1-1. Clients all around*

This impressive interoperability is possible because the communication protocol of Web Services is based on XML and usually carried over HTTP, both of which are open, platform-independent standards.

> **NOTE** *We assume that you are familiar with XML basics. If not, start with* `http://directory.google.com/Top/Computers/Data_Formats/Markup_Languages/XML/` `Resources/FAQs,_Help,_and_Tutorials/`. *Read, then return here.*

In addition to interoperability, an important requirement of the "Web Service vision" is that Web Services must be self-describing. There are two aspects to this requirement. First, the description of a Web Service must enable a client looking for a specific functionality to find the Service that provides that functionality. Additionally, at the lower Application Programming Interface (API) level, after the Service is found, the client must be able to connect to the Service and use it. This is summarized by the well-known diagram shown in Figure 1-2.

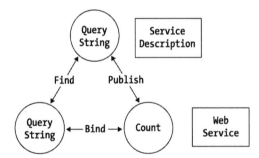

*Figure 1-2. Publish, find, bind*

In this diagram of ideal Web Service usage, *Publish* is the first step and that action is performed once: a Web Service publishes its description in a Service registry. After that, a customer looking for a service of that type can find it in the registry and use information to bind itself to the Service. A productive exchange of services (and, in many cases, funds) takes place.

For Web Services to work, at least three specifications are needed: a communication protocol, a Web Service description format that is in sync with the communication protocol, and a registry format. All three specifications are still in draft form, in various degree of readiness.

- The communication (or messaging) protocol is called SOAP. The name began as an acronym for Simple Object Access Protocol but the latest version of the specification, SOAP no longer stands for anything. (See `http://www.w3.org/TR/soap12-part1/#intro`.) SOAP was initially developed by a small group of companies, including Userland (prominently featuring Dave Winer), Microsoft, and IBM, but has since been adopted for further development and standardization by the World Wide Web Consortium (`w3c.org`), the same organization that is responsible for developing HTML and XML standards.

- The proposed Web Services description language is called, reasonably enough, Web Services Description Language (WSDL, pronounced Whizz-Dill). Also XML-based, it provides a description of both how to connect to the service (the access points) and how to use it (the interfaces). WSDL is backed by a powerful industry consortium and it is embedded in Web Services toolkits from Microsoft, Apache, and others, but it has not been adopted by W3C, probably because of a potential conflict with its Semantic Web project. We explain the issues involved later in the book.

- The format for online Web Service registries is called Universal Description, Discovery and Invocation (UDDI). It is less well-developed than the other two, possibly because there aren't many Web Services to register yet.

**NOTE** *In this book, you will see a good deal of SOAP, beginning with this chapter. In later chapters, you will also see WSDL. UDDI is not used in this book at all. We'll now take a brief look at history and evolution of Web Services.*

# The Evolving Web Services Vision

Web Services started as a vision of a "web of applications" that could find each other on the Internet, establish communication channels, and exchange information and services without human intervention. As is often the case with visions, it was a bit too ambitious, and it remains a distant goal even today, after a couple of years of intense effort.

However, that effort generated interesting technology with exciting possibilities, and during 2002, some of those possibilities began to materialize. Current Web Services applications, although quite different from the vision, opened accumulated technologies to individual innovation.

## *Area of Application: Service-to-Service Interactions*

There are two main areas of a "peer-to-peer" symmetrical Web Services application.

- Automatic service discovery and invocation on the Internet by software agents that construct long chains of interactions without human intervention

- Legacy data and application integration

The first area has received by far the most attention and is a frequent subject of media discussions and futuristic scenarios. (The word "hype," which we try to avoid, may be appropriate here.) Consider the standard example of a travel reservation service. Currently, a person finds a reservation service on the Web and uses it to connect to a database and view the options. After an option is selected, another process, again initiated by the human user, results in booking and online payment. After that, the same overworked user has to start all over for hotel reservation and car rental. Web Services would theoretically automate much of this: the user supplies the parameters of the situation to an intelligent agent of some sort that initiates a chain of interactions among several specialized services, such as airline booking, hotel reservations, and car rental, based on the user profile and previous history.

Scenarios like this determine much of the content of SOAP and other specifications. This is not surprising; a specification has to be future-oriented to avoid being obsolete on arrival. However, a careful analysis suggests that in this case, the specifications may be aiming too far ahead. Futuristic scenarios of the kind we've just described are very distant because they involve two kinds of difficult issues. One is more technical: for software agents to cooperate, the problems of security, quality of service, payment, and enforceable contracts among Web Services have to be resolved in some standard, interoperable ways. The corresponding specifications are barely on the drawing board, except perhaps for security where the well-understood TLS standard (Transport-Level Security, also known as HTTPS) can be used.

The other difficult issue is not even technical yet; it is still conceptual: cooperation among human agents is based on deeply shared context that several decades of Artificial Intelligence have been unable to formalize. The notion that Web Services will suddenly succeed where previous long-term efforts proved fruitless doesn't seem to be based on any solid ground. We highly recommend two recent articles on XML.com that discuss these issues in great detail.

```
http://www.xml.com/pub/a/2002/02/06/webservices.html
http://www.xml.com/lpt/a/2001/10/03/webservices.html
```

Web Services' use for legacy data integration is a much more realistic proposition. Web Services wrap all their data exchanges into a standard XML format that is understood by any Web Service client, including other Web Services. To bring legacy formats into a distributed application, one only has to write a Web Service that encodes those formats as SOAP messages. If the application is intended to run within the "shared context" situation of a single enterprise, the problems of Internet interaction can be kept under control. The semantics of lexical items can be agreed upon, Web Service interfaces can be stabilized and changed in sync, and problems of security and payment will be either nonexistent or at least solvable with current technologies.

## *Area of Application: Client-to-Service Interactions*

The initial Web Services excitement was generated top-down by big companies that seemed to believe there was a lot of money to be made on the automated, service-to-service Web. Rank-and-file developers remained largely unaffected at that stage because there wasn't much for them to do. An individual developer cannot very well create a massive Web Service of general interest, and in the absence of services, the technology was just spinning its wheels. The situation changed when two Internet innovators, Amazon and Google, put out Web Services that provided programmatic access to their massive data stores. The access was and remains bandwidth-limited and carefully controlled, but even so, it has generated a good deal of grass-roots activity.

> **NOTE** *See, for instance the news story at*
> http://news.com.com/2009-1017-966099.html, *Tim O'Reilly's thoughts on*
> http://www.oreillynet.com/cs/user/view/wlg/2342, *and Appnel's column at*
> http://www.oreillynet.com/pub/wlg/2360.

Suddenly, there was something for developers to do, namely, write clients that would use the exposed Amazon and Google functionality in interesting and innovative ways. Developers discovered that they could build on top of the deep functionality offered by those sites to create new and innovative user interfaces to existing data. This is rapidly becoming an important segment of Web Services activity. Much of this book is about writing Web Service clients, and specifically clients for the Web Services of Google or Amazon or both. In a later chapter, you will develop a Web service of your own, based on an open-source information store, and show you how it can be integrated with Google and Amazon.

Our first example of a Web Service client uses the service offered by Google. The client itself is written in cross-browser JavaScript. As you may know, JavaScript consists of several distinct subsets.

- The standard ECMAScript subset, including use of arrays and objects (the Object)

- Mozilla/Netscape-specific objects

- IE/Windows-specific ActiveX objects

- The Document Object Model (DOM) for referring to objects within the Web browser. DOM itself consists of a standard subset shared by IE and Mozilla/Netscape, and browser-specific extensions.

To clarify our terminology, we use "JavaScript" generically to refer to the whole assortment of dialects; we also say JavaScript (as opposed to JScript) to refer to the Mozilla/Netscape version of the language when comparing it to the Microsoft version. For brevity, we say "Mozilla" when referring to the common features of Mozilla and Netscape browsers.

> **NOTE** *Unless explicitly stated otherwise, all the JavaScript code in this book has been tested in both IE6 and Mozilla1.x, the two browsers that had XML support unavailable in earlier versions. If you have a Windows PC or a Macintosh, you probably have IE6 already (and if not, you should consider upgrading.) If you want Mozilla for any platform, you can download it from the Mozilla site,* `http://www.mozilla.org`. *When using browser-specific features, we always include a test for the browser, IE vs. Mozilla. The test is* `document.all == null` *; if true, the browser is Mozilla; if not true, the browser is IE.*

## Google MindShare

For the first example, we'll ask Google to do something simple. We'll give it the name of a person (Who) and the subject matter (What), and we'll get the number of hits for two queries: What, and Who+What. For instance, if Who is Einstein and What is Relativity, we run two queries: "Relativity" and "Einstein Relativity." Then we calculate the ratio (in percentage points) of Who+What hits to the What hits. If Who and What always occur together, the ratio will be 100 percent; if Who and What never occur together, the ratio will be 0 percent. In most cases, the ratio will be somewhere in between and will indicate, in a very imprecise way, the person's mindshare within the subject matter. This "GoogleShare" idea was created by Steven Berlin Johnson.

> **NOTE** *Some of our over-educated friends and family members scoffed at the gross imprecision of this measurement until we told them that we ran the application with their names and the subject matter in which they fancy themselves experts. Their dismissive irony was immediately replaced by acute interest in the results.*

The entry point to the GoogleShare application is `wsbk/googleShare_1/frameTop.html`. Like all other examples, it is accessible from the top-level `wsbk/index.html` file. Its output is shown in Figure 1-3.

*Figure 1-3. The MindShare application*

The top frame in this figure shows the form to enter the query data and view the results. The bottom two frames, initially empty, get filled with SOAP messages, a SOAP request on the left and a SOAP response on the right. The `<q>` (query) element in the request says

```
<q xsi:type='xs:string'>einstein relativity</q>
```

In other words, the frames show the request and response messages for the Who+What query.

## Outline and Application-Specific Code

SOAP messages are, of course, XML documents, and we will cover their contents in the next section. The important thing now is that the SOAP response contains the number of hits for the query.

```
<estimatedTotalResultsCount xsi:type='xsd:int'> 375000
</estimatedTotalResultsCount>
```

The code has to perform the following tasks for both queries:

1.  Given the query text, construct the SOAP request message that encodes a Google search. (Instead of "message," the term "SOAP envelope" is often used because of the way SOAP messages are structured.)

2.  Invoke the service by sending it the SOAP request.

3.  Extract the number of hits from the SOAP response.

4.  Calculate the mindshare percentage.

Except the last item on this list, these are common tasks, so the code for them should go into separate files that can be included in many applications. We put the first two into the `xmlhttp.js` file, and the third into the `getDOMdata.js` file, and all three in the `utils` directory. The code for the application consists of a frameset page and the source page for the top frame. The frameset page is Listing 1.1.

*Listing 1-1. The GoogleShare Application Frameset Page*

```
<html><head><title>frameTop.html</title></head>
<frameset rows="30%,70%">
  <frame name="ctlFrame" src="mindShare.html"/>
```

```
  <frameset cols="50%,50%">
    <frame name="callFrame" src="about:blank"/>
    <frame name="responseFrame" src="about:blank"/>
  </frameset>
</frameset></html>
```

The code of mindShare.html can be divided into three sections

- Declarations and included files

- Application-specific JavaScript code

- The body of the HTML page

These are shown in Listings 1-2 to 1-4.

*Listing 1-2. mindShare.html, Part 1*

```
<!DOCTYPE HTML PUBLIC "-//W3C//DTD HTML 4.01//EN"
        "http://www.w3.org/TR/html4/strict.dtd">
<html><head>
<meta http-equiv="Content-Type" content="text/html; charset=iso-8859-1">
<title>Google Calculations</title>
<link rel="stylesheet" type="text/css" href="google.css">
<script src="../utils/key.js"> </script>
<script src="../utils/xmlhttp.js"> </script>
<script src="../utils/getDOMdata.js"> </script>
```

The first of the included files, key.js, contains an authentication key that you have to obtain from Google (see Appendix A, "Installation") in order to start using its Web Service. The key is included in every request, as you will see in a moment. The other two included files, as explained, hold generic code that can be reused for other Google client applications.

*Listing 1-3. mindShare.html, Part 2, Application-Specific Code*

```
<script type="text/javascript">
function findMindShare(who,what){
  var whatCount=gsGetCount(what);
  var whoWhatCount=gsGetCount(who+" "+what);
  return makePercent(whoWhatCount / whatCount);
}
function makePercent(num){ // e.g., .0010 becomes .10;
```

```
 var S= ""+(num*100);
 var decPoint=S.indexOf(".");
 if(decPoint<0)return S;
 return S.substring(0,4+decPoint); // truncated, not rounded.
}
</script>
</head>
```

The function gsGetCount() performs a Google search and extracts the hit count from the SOAP response. The function findMindShare() calls gsGetCount() twice, obtains two counts, and calls the other local function, makePercent(), to calculate the result. If the result contains a decimal point, makePercent() truncates it so it doesn't look too ungainly. Therefore, we will perform two SOAP calls each time the search button is pushed.

Finally, the body of the page (shown in Listing 1-4) contains a form with a button to trigger the computation. It also contains a link to the Google APIs page, in case you, the reader, feel inspired to connect to it immediately, register, get yourself a key, and start programming.

*Listing 1-4. mindShare.html, Part 3, The Body of the Page*

```
<body>
<p><code>mindShare = WhoWhatCount/whatCount</code></p>
<p>100% if "what" is always associated
with "who", 0% if it never is.</p>
<div style="float: right">
  <a href="http://www.google.com/apis/" target="_top">Google  API
</a></div>
<form name="theForm" action="javascript:void">
Who: <input type="text" name="who" value="einstein">
What: <input type="text" name="what" value="relativity">
mindshare: <input type="text" name="mindshare"/>
<input type="button"
  onclick=
    "with(this.form) {
      mindshare.value=findMindShare(who.value,what.value);
    }"
  value="findMindShare">
</form>
</body></html>
```

This is the entire application-specific code for this application. The rest of the code, in the util directory, performs the following generic tasks:

- Given the query text, construct a SOAP request message that encodes a Google search

- Invoke the service by sending it the SOAP request

- Extract the number of hits from the SOAP response

The code uses several technologies that we will need to become familiar with before we can plunge into the code. The next section briefly describes the technologies involved, how they relate to the tasks, and which functions depend on which technologies.

## Web Services Technologies, Tasks, and Functions

In quick summary, we use the following:

- Two XML technologies: the SOAP specification and the Document Object Model (DOM) APIs

- A low-level xmlhttp API for sending XML data as the body of an HTTP message (using the POST command)

- The Google API that exposes three Web service methods: search, check spelling, and get a cached page

Matching technologies to tasks, SOAP specifies the format of the messages, the Google API determines the content of the messages, xmlhttp is a (cross-browser) way of getting the message across, and DOM provides the tools for parsing the message, extracting data from it, and converting the message from XML to XHTML for display in the browser.

Our top-level code of MindShare.html connects to the underlying technologies via the gsGetCount() function, defined in getDOMdata.js and invoked from findMindShare() of Listing 1-3. gsGetCount() uses the doSearch() method of the Google API but ignores its results except for the hit count. The search is done by the doGoogleSearch() method that is invoked from gsGetCount() and itself invokes doGoogleSearchEnvelope() to construct the SOAP request message. Once the message is constructed, doGoogleSearch() invokes doGoogle() to do the actual SOAP exchange and process the result. The dependencies between functions, files, and technologies are summarized in Table 1-1, in the depth-first, top-down order of invocation:

*Table 1-1. Functions, Files, and Technologies*

| Function | Invoked from | Defined in | Uses |
|---|---|---|---|
| findMindShare() | top-level | MindShare.html | |
| gsGetCount() | findMindShare | getDOMdata.js | JavaScript objects |
| doGoogleSearch() | gsGetCount() | xmlhttp.js | Google API |
| doGoogle() | doGoogleSearch() | xmlhttp.js | xmlhttp, DOM |
| xml2HtmlPage() | doGoogle() | xmlhttp.js | DOM |
| doGoogleSearchEnvelope() | doGoogleSearch() | xmlhttp.js | SOAP, Google API |
| getMessageData() | gsGetCount() | getDOMdata.js | DOM |

In the remainder of this chapter, we will review two APIs (xmlhttp API and the Google Web Services API) and our JavaScript functions that use them (gsGetCount(), doGoogleSearch(), and doGoogle()).

The xmlhttp API is relatively small; its centerpiece is the send() method that sends an XML payload over HTTP. The Google API exposes three methods to perform the following actions: do a search, get a cached page, and check spelling. The MindShare application shows the first method in action. We will provide examples of the other two within the same overall framework. In addition, because Google returns cached pages in base64 encoding, we explain base64 and provide a tool for viewing base64-encoded text.

In the code, each Google API method is implemented in two functions, such as doGoogleSearch() and doGoogleSearchEnvelope(). The first function is a two-line wrapper whose purpose is to hide SOAP detail from the reader. The second function constructs the appropriate SOAP request as an XML string. In addition to the two functions for the search method, we have doGetCachedPage(), doGetCachedPageEnvelope(), doSpellingSuggestion(), and doSpellingSuggestionEnvelope(). All three wrapper functions call the corresponding "envelope" function to obtain the SOAP message, and then call doGoogle() with two arguments: the name of the method to invoke and the SOAP message to send to it. doGoogle() does the actual service invocation and returns the SOAP response. We will go through doGoogle() in complete detail shortly.

The XML heavyweights, DOM and SOAP, will be presented in the next chapter. XML DOM will be illustrated by the code of getMessageData() and xm2HtmlPage(). SOAP will be illustrated by doGoogleSearchEnvelope() and examples that accompany the rest of the Google API, including doGetCachedPageEnvelope() and doSpellingSuggestion().

## The JavaScript Code and the Google API

We start witht the code for gsGetCount() and doGoogleSearch(). The code for gsGetCount() is in Listing 1-5. It consists of five parts.

- Setting up a local cache for already executed searches

- Performing the search

- Extracting the hit count from the result

- Storing the hit count in the cache

- Returning the hit count

*Listing 1-5.* gsGetCount()

```
function gsGetCount(q){ // q is the query string
// set up a local cache - a JavaScript object - for query results
  if(!gsGetCount.countCache)
    gsGetCount.countCache=new Object();
  var countCache=gsGetCount.countCache;
// check cache for result of current query, using asociative array syntax
// if found, return it as integer
  var cStr=countCache[q];
  if(cStr)return parseInt(cStr);
// if not found, do search.
// Note the four parameters of search, explained shortly.
  var msg=doGoogleSearch(key,q,0,1);
// extract the count from the query result, store in cache, return as integer
  try{
    var hitCount=getMessageData(msg,"estimatedTotalResultsCount");
    countCache[q]=hitCount;
    return parseInt(hitCount);
  }catch(ex){alert (ex+"\n"+toXML(msg));}
  return 0;
}
```

As you can see, gsGetCount() is basically a wrapper for a Google API call, doGoogleSearch(). The call takes four parameters, as follows:

- **key**: The Google key assigned to each user at registration and used for authenticating and logging (See Appendix A; you MUST register if you intend to use this book's code.)

- **q**: The query string

- **start**: The zero-based index of the first desired result

- **maxResults**: The number of results per query

The key is required for every interaction with the service. Each user is limited to 1,000 queries per day. The maximum allowed value of maxResults is 10. If you want more than 10 results, you have to write a loop that sends a number of queries incrementing the start index by maxResults each time. (In other words, you are limited not just to 1,000 queries but also to 10,000 query results.) In this program, we are not interested in query results at all, only in the count, so we set the maxResults() to 1. Alas, the current implementation of the API won't let us set it to 0.

The Google call itself is in the function doGoogleSearch(), defined in xmlhttp.js (shown in Listing 1-6).

*Listing 1-6.* gsGetCount()

```
function doGoogleSearch(key,q,start,maxResults){
  return doGoogle("doGoogleSearch",
                              doGoogleSearchEnvelope(key,q,start,maxResults));
}
```

This function does two things. First, it calls doGooogleSearchEnvelope() and passes all four parameters required by the Google API. doGoogleSearchEnvelope() constructs a SOAP request that contains the parameters and their values. The name of the Google API method to use and the SOAP request are given to doGoogle()which then uses xmlhttp to conduct SOAP exchanges.

## Code Part 2 and xmlhttp API

doGoogle() is, in effect, a manager for all three possible Google API actions. It takes the name of an action and a SOAP request and returns whatever response is returned by the Web Service. It uses a generic API, xmlhttp, for sending XML payloads over an HTTP connection. It is important to keep in mind that xmlhttp is completely ignorant of the intended meaning of XML data entrusted to it; in particular, it knows nothing about SOAP. All it does is send and receive XML data.

The xmlhttp API is encapsulated into an xmlhttp object that is available both in IE and Mozilla. The objects are implemented differently in Mozilla's JavaScript and Microsoft's JScript, but once they are created, the interfaces are identical. This is the basis of the cross-browser examples.

## Code that Uses the xmlhttp API to Connect to Google

We illustrate the xmlhttp API with the doGoogle() method. The method, shown in Listing 1-7, takes two string arguments: the name of a Google API method and an XML string that is a SOAP request message. It returns the SOAP response as a parsed XML string (that is, as a DOM object). In outline, doGoogle() proceeds as follows:

- Creates an xmlhttp object

- Uses the object to connect to the Google Web Service, sends a SOAP message, and then gets a response

- Displays the request and response messages in the Web page

*Listing 1-7.* doGoogle() *with xmlhttp*

```
function doGoogle(method,env){
  try{
// Part 1: create an xmlhttp object, set its properties
    var xmlhttp=null;
    if(inIE)
      xmlhttp=new ActiveXObject('MSXML2.XMLHTTP'); // Microsoft way
    else xmlhttp=new XMLHttpRequest();              // Mozilla way
    if(!xmlhttp)
      return alert("doGoogle("+method+"): can't initialize xmlhttp object");
    if(!inIE) // Mozilla-specific code, to set security level
```

```
        netscape.security.PrivilegeManager.
          enablePrivilege("UniversalBrowserRead");
// Part 2: use xmlhttp methods: open, setRequestHeader, send
    xmlhttp.open('POST',"http://api.google.com/search/beta2",false);
    xmlhttp.setRequestHeader("SOAPAction", method)
    xmlhttp.setRequestHeader("Content-Type", "text/xml; charset=utf-8")
    xmlhttp.send(env);

    var result=xmlhttp.responseXML; // result is a DOM object
    var xmlDoc=parseXML(env);  //creates a DOMobject
// Part 3: display SOAP request and response in frames
    displayXml(xmlDoc,parent.callFrame);
    displayXml(result,parent.responseFrame);

    return xmlhttp.responseXML;
  }catch(ex){alert("doGoogle("+method+") error: "+ex);}
    return null;
}
```

The displayXML() function (shown in Listing 1-8) takes two arguments, XML data to display, and a target frame to display it in. The XML data must be in the DOM object format.

*Listing 1-8.* displayXML()

```
function displayXML(doc,targetFrame) {
  with(targetFrame) {
    document.write(xml2Html(doc));
    document.close();
  }
}
```

The SOAP response, as returned by xmlhttp, is already in the DOM tree format, but the SOAP request (the env variable) is an XML string and needs to be parsed into a DOM tree before given to displayXML(). The parsing is done by a DOM parser object within the parseXML() function (shown in Listing 1-9). Just as with the xmlhttp object, the syntax for creating a parser object is different in JavaScript and JScript, and we have to use an if-clause to make the code cross-browser compatible. However, once a DOM parser is created, its input and output conform to rigorous and strictly enforced standards. This is the beauty of XML and one of its main advantages over HTML.

*Listing 1-9.* parseXML()

```
function parseXML(str){
  if(inIE){
    var doc=new ActiveXObject("Microsoft.XMLDOM");
    doc.loadXML(str);
    return doc; // .documentElement;
  }
  return (new DOMParser()).parseFromString(str, "text/xml");
}
```

Both the output of parseXML() and the xmlhttp.responseXML object returned after xmlhttp.send() are standard XML DOM trees. They are used by displayXML() to show the SOAP request and response messages in the frames of a Web page. In order to be displayable, XML DOM objects are made linear (converted from the DOM object in to a string) as XHTML pages by the xml2Html() method. That method is heavily dependent on XML DOM and will be discussed in the next chapter.

## Summary of xmlhttp

In doGoogle(), you can see the following xmlhttp methods: open(), setRequestHeader(), and send(). After send() is executed, the server response is stored in the xmlhttp.response object, as an XML DOM tree.

The added value of xmlhttp is that it hides all the low-level details needed to send XML payloads over HTTP. In particular, it does all the necessary character encodings to send the angle brackets and it parses the server response into a DOM object.

The methods, their parameters, and the return values are summarized in Table 1-2. For more details on the APIs, see http://msdn.microsoft.com/library/default.asp?url=/library/en-us/xmlsdk30/htm/xmobjxmlhttprequest.asp and http://www.mozilla.org/xmlextras/. For background on the HTTP protocol, see Appendix C.

*Table 1-2. Summary of xmlhttp*

| Method or Field | Parameters |
| --- | --- |
| open | **command**: an HTTP command such as POST |
| | **URI**: the URI of the server |
| | **asynchronousLoadingAllowed**: a Boolean parameter to indicate whether it's okay to load asynchronously. Synchronous loading is easier to use because the call to send does not return until the XML file has loaded. The downside is that the browser does not respond during this time. |
| setRequestHeader | **name**: header name |
| | **value**: value to assign to the header |
| send | **payload**: XML payload to send. This must be a well-formed XML document. |
| response | Server response parsed into a DOM object |

There are implementations of xmlhttp for several languages, including JavaScript and JScript.

## Google API with Examples of Use

The Google Web Services API has both a general description and a javadoc API documentation, so we will provide only a brief summary with examples in JavaScript. The API supports three actions, which correspond to the doGoogleSearch(), doCheckSpelling(), and doGetCachedPage(). You have already seen doGoogleSearch() in action and the parameters it requires. Unlike doGoogleSearch(), doCheckSpelling() and doGetCachedPage() have very simple signatures, which in Java look like this

```
String doSpellingSuggestion(String phrase) throws GoogleSearchFault
public byte[] doGetCachedPage(String url) throws GoogleSearchFault
```

The input parameter to doSpellingSuggestion() is a string to be checked, and the input parameter to doGetCachedPage() is the URL to retrieve from the Google cache. The returned value of doGetCachedPage() is the HTML source of the page, in base64 encoding.

doGoogleSearch() can have up to ten parameters. You have seen four of them passed around by doGoogleSearch() and doGoogleSearchEnvelope(). The rest are shown in Table 1-3.

*Table 1-3. Input Parameters to Google Search*

| Name | Explanation |
| --- | --- |
| filter | Activates or deactivates automatic results filtering, which hides similar results and results that all come from the same Web host. Filtering improves the end user experience on Google, but you may prefer to turn it off. (See the "Automatic Filtering" section for more details.) |
| restrict | Restricts the search to a subset of the Google Web index, such as a country like Ukraine or a topic like Linux. (See the "Restricts" section for more details.) |
| safeSearch | A Boolean value that enables filtering of adult content in the search results. (See the "SafeSearch" section for more details.) |
| lr | (Language Restrict) Restricts the search to documents in one or more languages. |
| ie | (Input Encoding) This parameter has been deprecated and is ignored. All requests to the APIs should be made with UTF-8 encoding. (See the "Input and Output Encodings" section for details.) |
| oe | (Output Encoding) This parameter has been deprecated and is ignored. All requests to the APIs should be made with UTF-8 encoding. (See the "Input and Output Encodings" for details.) |

These parameters can be set to appropriate defaults by the code. You will see all of them in the SOAP request message in the next chapter. doGoogleSearch() returns a structured object (a DOM tree) containing several pieces of information, including, as you saw in the MindShare application, an estimated number of hits.

In the rest of this section, we provide simple examples of the Google API, implemented in the same xmlhttp framework. In addition, because Google returns cached pages in base64 encoding, we explain base64 and provide a tool for viewing base64-encoded text. As before, the central piece of each example is a xxxEnvelope() function that builds the appropriate SOAP request. These functions will be shown in the next chapter.

## Google API Examples in JavaScript with xmlhttp

We provide a single entry page from which all three methods can be tested at TOMCAT_HOME/wsbk/xmlhttp/xmlhttpFrameTop.html. Figure 1-4 shows the result of the spell checker.

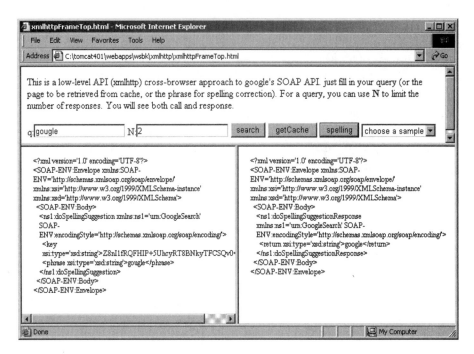

*Figure 1-4. xmlhttpGoogleApi*

As you can see, the page has three frames, two of them display SOAP messages, and the third includes a control frame with input boxes for the query string and the maxResult parameter, and buttons to invoke the methods. The control frame also contains all the JavaScript code that is needed to run Google APIs via xmlhttp. Much of this code is the same as the code in the utils directory used by the MindShare application, but for ease of reference and review we brought it all together in xmlhttpFrameCtl.html. It consists of the following functions:

- doGoogle()

- Three pairs of doXxx()-doXxxEnvelope() functions, where Xxx stands for the three Google methods

- XML-processing functions: parseXML(), displayXML(), xml2Html(), and xmlAttrs2Html(), all of which use DOM

This JavaScript code is invoked from the HTML form in the body of the page. The form is shown in Listing 1-10.

*Listing 1-10. The Form in* xmlhttpFrameCtl

```html
<form name="theForm" action="javascript:void">
  q:<input type="text" name="q" value="gougle"/>
  N:<input type="text" name="N" value="2"/>
  <input type="button" value="search"
    onclick="with(this.form){
      doGoogleSearch(key,q.value,0,N.value); // Google API call
    }"/>
  <input type="button" value="getCache"
    onclick="with(this.form){
      doGetCachedPage(key,q.value);  // Google API call
    }"/>
  <input type="button" value="spelling"
    onclick="with(this.form){
      doSpellingSuggestion(key,q.value);  // Google API call
    }"/>
  <select size="1" onchange="this.form.q.value=this.value">
    <option selected="1" value="">choose a sample</option>
    <option value="xml javascript">search</option>
    <option value="www.mozilla.org">cache</option>
    <option value="javascrap">spelling</option>
  </select></form>
```

Of the three Google API calls, you have already seen doGoogleSearch(). The other two, shown in Listing 1-11, are very similar.

*Listing 1-11. Google API calls in JavaScript*

```javascript
function doGetCachedPage(key,url){
  return doGoogle("doGetCachedPage",
                  doGetCachedPageEnvelope(key,url));
}
function doSpellingSuggestion(key,phrase){
  return doGoogle("doSpellingSuggestion",
                  doSpellingSuggestionEnvelope(key,phrase));
}
```

The rest of the code is heavily DOM and SOAP and will be reviewed in the next chapter. In anticipation, let's look at the simplest of the three Envelope methods, doSpellingSuggestionEnvelope(), in Listing 1-12.

*Listing 1-12.* doSpellingSuggestionEnvelope()

```
function doSpellingSuggestionEnvelope(key,phrase){
  var S="<?xml version='1.0' encoding='UTF-8'?>\n";
  S+='<SOAP-ENV:Envelope';
  S+=' xmlns:SOAP-ENV="http://schemas.xmlsoap.org/soap/envelope/"';
  S+=' xmlns:xsi="http://www.w3.org/1999/XMLSchema-instance"';
  S+=' xmlns:xsd="http://www.w3.org/1999/XMLSchema">';
  S+=' <SOAP-ENV:Body>';
  S+='  <ns1:doSpellingSuggestion xmlns:ns1="urn:GoogleSearch"';
  S+='   SOAP-ENV:encodingStyle="http://schemas.xmlsoap.org/soap/encoding/">';
  S+='   <key xsi:type="xsd:string">' +key+ '</key>';
  S+='   <phrase xsi:type="xsd:string">' +phrase+ '</phrase>';
  S+='  </ns1:doSpellingSuggestion>';
  S+=' </SOAP-ENV:Body>';
  S+='</SOAP-ENV:Envelope>';
  return S;
}
```

This function methodically constructs the XML document—a SOAP message—you saw in the left frame of Figure 1-4. The root element of the document is `<SOAP-ENV:Envelope>`. As explained in Appendix B, element names that have a colon-separated prefix must be in the scope of a **namespace declaration** in which the prefix is associated with a unique URI. The declaration is, syntactically, an XML attribute whose name has the form xmlns:[*prefix*] and whose value is the URI associated with the prefix. Usually, such declarations are placed in the root element, and indeed, the root element of the SOAP message has three of them, declaring three different namespaces. These namespaces are common to all SOAP messages, and we will explain them in the next chapter. In addition, within the `<SOAP-ENV:Body>` element, we have yet another namespace declaration; this one is specific to the Google Web Service. The prefix it declares, ns1, is used to qualify the name of the XML element that is the name of the Google method to be invoked by the SOAP message. In this case, the method name is doSpellingSuggestion.

The element whose name is the name of the method has children elements that contain parameters to the method. (This is a common SOAP convention for doing Remote Procedure Calls. We'll go into more detail about this in the next chapter.) The names of the parameters are specified in the Web Service API (and also in the WSDL description of the service). In this example, the names of arguments are key and phrase, both of the xsi:string type. With the method and method parameters specified, the SOAP message is complete.

For `doGetCachedPageEnvelope()`, we only have to replace the method element in the middle. Instead of the following:

```
S+='  <ns1:doSpellingSuggestion xmlns:ns1="urn:GoogleSearch"';
S+='  SOAP-ENV:encodingStyle="http://schemas.xmlsoap.org/soap/encoding/">';
S+='  <key xsi:type="xsd:string">' +key+ '</key>';
S+='  <phrase xsi:type="xsd:string">' +phrase+ '</phrase>';
S+='  </ns1:doSpellingSuggestion>';
```

We have the following:

```
S+='  <ns1:doGetCachedPage xmlns:ns1="urn:GoogleSearch" ';
S+='  SOAP-ENV:encodingStyle="http://schemas.xmlsoap.org/soap/encoding/">';
S+='  <key xsi:type="xsd:string">' +key+ '</key>';
S+='  <url xsi:type="xsd:string">' +url+ '</url>';
S+='  </ns1:doGetCachedPage>';
```

The remaining `doGetSearchEnvelope()` function has more lines in it because the corresponding Google method has more parameters and we have to set their values.

```
env+='  <a0:doGoogleSearch xmlns:a0="urn:GoogleSearch">';
env+='  <key xsi:type="xs:string">'+key+'</key>';
env+='  <q xsi:type="xs:string">'+q+'</q>';
env+='  <start xsi:type="xs:int">'+start+'</start>';
env+='  <maxResults xsi:type="xs:int">'+maxResults+'</maxResults>';
env+='  <filter xsi:type="xs:boolean">1</filter>';
env+='  <restrict xsi:type="xs:string"/>';
env+='  <safeSearch xsi:type="xs:boolean">0</safeSearch>';
env+='  <lr xsi:type="xs:string"/>';
env+='  <ie xsi:type="xs:string">utf8</ie>';
env+='  <oe xsi:type="xs:string">utf8</oe>';
env+='  </a0:doGoogleSearch>';
```

## Conclusion

In this chapter, you saw your first Web Service client, as well as three minimal clients that simply run a method and return the result without doing anything with it. All methods are written in cross-browser JavaScript. We hope that will make it easy to reuse them when you create your own clients. To reiterate the component structure of MindShare and how to reuse it: The application-specific function, `findMindShare()`, has supporting utilities. At a more general level, `gsGetCount()` returns a hit count for a given query string. It uses a Google API method and DOM utilities to process the response. Finally, the `doXxx()` and `doXxxEnvelope()` methods are general and reuseable in a variety of applications.

Now that you are more familiar with the Google API and xmlhttp, the basis for cross-browser JavaScript code, you can investigate DOM and SOAP in greater detail.

# CHAPTER 2

# The Plumbing:
# DOM and SOAP

**IN THIS CHAPTER**, we will go over the two APIs that regulate the critical junctures in a Web Service implemented on top of the HTTP protocol. (This is the dominant implementation model, and the one used throughout this book.) To see what the junctures are, consider Figure 2-1.

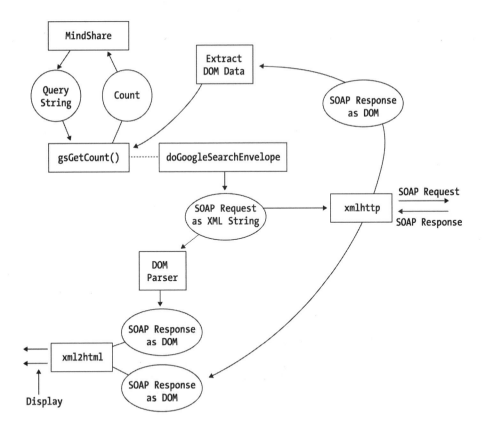

*Figure 2-1. Components of the MindShare application*

As this diagram shows, a Web Service has an inner core in which the components of a distributed application exchange SOAP messages, and an outer shell, usually structured as a client-server application, that builds an initial SOAP request and interprets the resulting SOAP response. To understand the workings of the core, you need to know SOAP; to understand the workings of the shell, you need to understand processing of XML data, which usually means the XML Document Object Model (DOM). DOM provides standard APIs (application programming interfaces) for working with XML data. Both XML DOM and HTML DOM are defined in W3C recommendations. The XML DOM recommendation says nothing about how the data structures are implemented, but the APIs clearly show that the data structures form a tree of nodes. There are functions to retrieve the parent and the children of a given node.

There are other tools for working with XML data, notably SAX (Simple API for XML) and XSLT (eXtensible Stylesheet Language for Transformations). We will use XSLT extensively in Chapters 7 and 8, but we will leave out SAX because it is less familiar and less intuitive than DOM. XML DOM is conceptually similar to HTML DOM, which has a large community of users. We use SAX because it has very modest memory requirements, whereas DOM trees for bigger documents can be prohibitively large. This consideration does not apply to SOAP messages, which tend to be quite small.

This chapter covers the following:

- DOM overview, with examples from Chapter 1 applications

- SOAP basics, with examples from Chapter 1 applications

- SOAP encoding

- XML Schema data types

We'll begin with a discussion of XML DOM.

## Using XML DOM

SOAP messages are XML documents. Two common tasks that need to be performed with them are processing the XML data (if only to retrieve specific components) and displaying the data in a Web browser. DOM can be used for both of these tasks. XML DOM processors can be implemented in a number of languages, including Javascript.

If you are familiar with the HTML DOM in Javascript, you will find the code easy to get used to. If this is your first encounter with any kind of DOM, the main thing you need to know is that XML data has two main types of representation: XML as text with markup and XML as a binary data structure. The process of converting XML text to XML data structure is called parsing. Converting XML data structure to XML text is called serializing. Usually, the same object or software library, called an XML parser, performs both operations, serving as an intermediary between a linear XML text (that is easy to send over the wire) and an XML data structure that conforms to a standard API and can be processed by portable code (a shown in Figure 2-2).

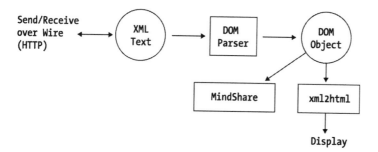

*Figure 2-2. XML document, a parser and an application*

The great thing about XML is that XML parsers are high quality, ubiquitous, and free, and their output conforms to the standard APIs, developed and published by W3C. (The current version is DOM 2, http://www.w3.org/TR/DOM-Level-2-Core/.) The data structure that implements the API is called a **DOM tree** or a **DOM document object**, and the parser that produces it is called a **DOM parser**. A DOM application frequently starts by obtaining an instance of a DOM parser and creating a DOM tree.

## DOM Basics

Components of an XML document are represented in the DOM as a **tree of nodes**, with **parent, child,** and **sibling** relations defined on them. Every node is a certain type, corresponding to the kinds of components found in XML documents: elements, attributes, PIs (processing instructions), and comments. In addition, the text content of an element is wrapped in a Text node. There is a standard integer constant associated with each node type; for example, 1 for Element, 2 for Attribute, 3 for Text, 7 for PI, and so on.

**NOTE** *See* `http://www.w3.org/TR/2000/REC-DOM-Level-2-Core-20001113/` `java-binding.html` *for a complete list.*

A common pattern of DOM programming is to traverse the DOM tree visiting each node and process each node according to its type. This is frequently done in a recursive fashion, as follows:

- Set the current node to the root node (also known as the Document object)

- If the current node is null, return

- If the current node isn't null, visit and process the current node

- Set the current node to each child and continue at the first step

You will see examples of this usage later in this chapter, but first Listing 2-1 shows a very simple document and the corresponding DOM tree.

*Listing 2-1. Simple XML Example*

```
<?xml version='1.0' encoding='UTF-8'?>
<!-- Our first example (and this is a comment) -->
<encounter>
  <greeting>Hello, XML!</greeting>
  <response>Hello, what can I do for you?</response>
</encounter>
```

Figure 2-3 shows a simple DOM tree.

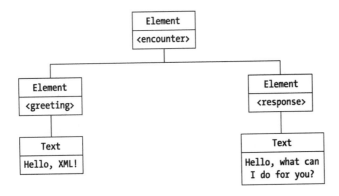

*Figure 2-3. Simple DOM tree*

With this background in place, we can look at the examples.

## DOM Code for Data Access

Our first example of how to use DOM is the function getMessageData(). This function extracts the hit count from the response to a SOAP Google query. It is called from gsGetCount() as follows:

```
var hitCount=getMessageData(msg,"estimatedTotalResultsCount");
```

The method takes two arguments: a DOM tree and an element's name. The DOM tree can be any XML, not necessarily a SOAP message. The element is assumed to contain text rather than child elements.

A slightly simplified version of getMessageData() is in Listing 2-2.

*Listing 2-2. The* getMessageData() *Function*

```
function getMessageData(msg, name){ // simplified
  try{
    var node=msg.getElementsByTagName(name)[0];
    var txtNode = node.firstChild;
    return txtNode.data;
  }catch(ex){alert("no field "+name+" in "+toXML(msg)+"\n"+ex);}
  return "";
}
```

Let's look again at the following line:

```
var node = msg.getElementsByTagName(name)[0];
```

This line uses getElementsByTagName() to obtain an array of all nodes in the tree that have the given tag name. In our case, the SOAP response contains a single element named estimatedTotalResultsCount, and that's the element we want, so we take the first (index [0]) element of the returned array. The text content of that element is in its first and only Text child, which we access as node.firstChild. (We could also have said node.childNodes[0].)

The text content of a single element can be spread over several child Text nodes, so Listing 2-3 shows a loop over the element's siblings to collect it all.

*Listing 2-3. The Complete* getMessageData() *Function*

```
function getMessageData(msg, name){  try{
    var res="";
    var node=msg.getElementsByTagName(name)[0].firstChild;
    while(node){
      res+=node.data;
      node=node.nextSibling;
    }
    return res;
  }catch(ex){alert("no field "+name+" in "+toXML(msg)+"\n"+ex);}
  return "";
}
```

## DOM Code for Data Transformation

Next consider a group of functions that transform XML into HTML for display in the browser. The central piece is a recursive function that outputs an XML element as an appropriately indented HTML <div> element and recursively calls itself on the XML element's children. It has supporting functions for Document nodes (the top-level node), Processing Instruction nodes, and Text nodes. Listing 2-4 shows the top-level xml2HtmlPage() that outputs the skeleton of an HTML page and calls the recursive function xml2Html().

*Listing 2-4.* xml2HtmlPage()

```
function xml2HtmlPage(node){ // top-level page output for an xml node
  var S="<html><head><title>Generated Page</title></head><body>";
  S+=xml2Html(node);
  S+="</body></h"+"tml>";
  return S;
}
```

The xml2Html() function, shown in Listing 2-5, takes a node as its argument and goes through the usual routine: if the node calls for immediate action, the function carries out that action by calling the appropriate supporting function; otherwise it recursively calls itself on the children of the argument node. In building HTML <div> elements, the function uses three global string constants, also shown in Listing 2-5. The constants build the opening DIV tag, and include a style attribute that sets the font size and indents the element with respect to its parent element.

*Listing 2-5.* xml2Html()

```
var fontSize=(if(inIE) 12 else 8);
var xml2HtmlStyle="margin-left:5; font-size:"+fontSize;
var xml2HtmlStyleDiv="<div style='" + xml2HtmlStyle + "'>";

function xml2Html(node){
// check these possibilities: the node is
// null, a text node, a PI, the top-level Document node
  if(null==node) return "";
  if(node.nodeType == 3)  // a text node
    return node.nodeValue;

  var name=node.nodeName;
  var S=xml2HtmlStyleDiv;

  if(node.nodeType == 7) // a processing instruction
    return S+xmlPInode2Html(node)+"</div>";

  if(node.nodeType == 9) // top-level Document node
    return S+xml2HtmlNodeChildren(node)+"</div>";

  S+="&lt;"+node.nodeName+xmlAttrs2Html(node.attributes)+"&gt;";
  S+=xml2HtmlNodeChildren(node);  // recursive call
  S+="&lt;/"+node.nodeName+"&gt;</div>";
  return S;
}
```

All the brief and self-explanatory supporting functions are shown is Listing 2-6. The only tricky detail to watch for is how to output quotes. You must put single quotes inside double quotes or the other way around.

*Listing 2-6. Friends of* xml2Html()

```
function xml2HtmlNodeChildren(node){
  var S="";
  for(var C=node.firstChild;null!=C;C=C.nextSibling)
    S+=xml2Html(C);
  return S;
}

function xmlPInode2Html(node){ // node.nodeType==7, PI node
  var S="&lt;?"+node.nodeName+xmlAttrs2Html(node.attributes)+"?&gt;";
```

```
    return S;
}

function xmlAttrs2Html(atts){
  var S="";
  if(atts!=null)
    for(var i=0;i<atts.length;i++)
      S+=" "+atts[i].name+"='"+atts[i].value+"'";
  return S;
}
```

The last function shows how XML attributes become an array of structured objects in DOM, with each object holding an attribute's name and value.

## From XML Text to DOM Tree and Back

The preceding two sections show examples of working with DOM trees, but how do you obtain a DOM tree from XML text? This process is called **parsing**, and it usually consists of two steps: first obtain a parser object and then call its parse method (which may be called "parse") to convert a marked-up string into a DOM data structure. This whole process is not standardized yet (it may be in DOM 3), and the code is different in IE and Mozilla (shown in Listing 2-7).

*Listing 2-7. Parse an XML String into a DOM Object*

```
function parseXML(str){
  var doc=null;
  if(inIE){ // IE version
    doc=new ActiveXObject("Microsoft.XMLDOM");
    doc.loadXML(str); // does the parsing
  }
  else { // Mozilla/Netscape
    var domParser=new DOMParser();
    doc=domParser.parseFromString(str, "text/xml");
  }
  return doc; // .documentElement;
}
```

Listing 2-8 shows the reverse process of converting a DOM object into a marked-up document. This process is called **serialization**.

*Listing 2-8. Serializing a DOM Object as XML Text*

```
function toXML(x){
  if(inIE)return x.xml;
  if(!toXML.serializer)
    toXML.serializer=new XMLSerializer();
  return toXML.serializer.serializeToString(x);
}
```

This concludes our discussion of DOM. You will see more examples of its use throughout the book. Our next subject is the SOAP specification, which is at the core of Web Services technology.

## The Anatomy of a SOAP message

In Chapter 1, you saw Javascript code that generates SOAP messages, and the messages themselves in the screenshot of the MindShare application. In this chapter, you will look at the messages in detail and use them as examples to illustrate the SOAP specification. We give brief explanations as we go through the examples, and we will elaborate on them later in the chapter.

For the first example, we will look at the messages that are sent and received by a doSpellingSuggestion() function call. We chose this because the function signature is the simplest: a character string is sent out and a character string is received. In the case of doGoogleSearch() and doGetCachedPage(), the structure of the response is more complex, and we will investigate it after an overview of SOAP.

Listing 2-9 shows the request message as it is submitted to xmlhttp.send().

*Listing 2-9. A SOAP Request*

```
<?xml version='1.0' encoding='UTF-8'?>
<SOAP-ENV:Envelope
  xmlns:SOAP-ENV ='http://schemas.xmlsoap.org/soap/envelope/'
  SOAP-ENV:encodingStyle='http://schemas.xmlsoap.org/soap/encoding/'
  xmlns:xsd='http://www.w3.org/1999/XMLSchema'
  xmlns:xsi='http://www.w3.org/1999/XMLSchema-instance'
>
<SOAP-ENV:Body>
<ns1:doSpellingSuggestion
  xmlns:ns1='urn:GoogleSearch'
>
  <key xsi:type='xsd:string'>Z8nI1fRQFHIP+5UhcyRT8BNkyTFCSQvO</key>
  <phrase xsi:type='xsd:string'>gougle</phrase>
```

```
    </ns1:doSpellingSuggestion>
  </SOAP-ENV:Body>
</env:Envelope>
```

The root of a SOAP message (viewed as an XML document) is an Envelope element that has a single child, a Body element. Both Envelope and Body are in the soap envelope namespace, http://schemas.xmlsoap.org/soap/envelope/. Another SOAP-related namespace, encoding style, specifies how programming language constructs (such as arrays) are encoded in XML.

The other two declared namespaces are for XML Schema and XML Schema Instance. They are used to declare data types, as in

```
<phrase xsi:type='xsd:string'>gougle</phrase>
```

This says that the data type of this element is "string," as defined in the XML Schema Part 2 specification (http://www.w3.org/TR/xmlschema-2/). That specification defines an elaborate system of data types that is used by many XML-based specifications, including SOAP. The shared system of language-independent primitive data types is one of the foundations on which SOAP interoperability is based. Another such foundation is a shared system for encoding compound data types (arrays and objects) in XML—the XML encoding.

The contents of the Body element are a remote procedure call located in a namespace of its own, urn:GoogleSearch. (The same namespace is used for all three Google API procedures.) The convention for passing a procedure call in a SOAP message is that the name of the procedure is the tag name of a child element of the Body element, and the arguments are children of that element. In our example, the name of the remote procedure is doGoogleSearch, and the arguments are key and phrase.

When the remote procedure call is automatically generated from a WSDL description of the service (as discussed in Chapter 9), the parameters (and the XML elements that encode them) are named arg0, arg1, and so on. In our hand-crafted SOAP message, we have given them application-specific names. The content of an argument element is the value of the corresponding parameter of the procedure call, and each argument element can have an xsi:type attribute to indicate its data type.

> **NOTE** *Another more structured method of attaching types to elements is to place the contents of the body in a namespace and associate that namespace with an XSchema that defines the data types of elements. We will have more to say about XML Schemas later in the book.*

Let's look at the response (shown in Listing 2-10) and see if it conforms to the same pattern.

*Listing 2-10. SOAP Response as It Comes Back From* xmlhttp.send()

```
<?xml version='1.0' encoding='UTF-8'?>
<SOAP-ENV:Envelope
  xmlns:SOAP-ENV='http://schemas.xmlsoap.org/soap/envelope/'
  SOAP-ENV:encodingStyle='http://schemas.xmlsoap.org/soap/encoding/'
  xmlns:xsi='http://www.w3.org/1999/XMLSchema-instance'
  xmlns:xsd='http://www.w3.org/1999/XMLSchema'
>
<SOAP-ENV:Body>
<ns1:doSpellingSuggestionResponse
  xmlns:ns1='urn:GoogleSearch'
>
  <return xsi:type='xsd:string'>google</return>
</ns1:doSpellingSuggestionResponse>
</SOAP-ENV:Body>
</SOAP-ENV:Envelope>
```

The structure of the response mirrors the structure of the request because in this case, both the input and the output of the remote procedure are strings.

In the case of doGoogleSearch(), the structure of the response is much more complex and the use of SOAP encoding more elaborate. Otherwise, both request and response use the same namespaces and rely on XML Schema Part 2 and SOAP encoding in exactly the same way to render programmatic contents in XML.

The SOAP messages in Listings 2-9 and 2-10 completely define the operation of the Web Service. Any SOAP client that sends the HTTP request in Listing 2-9 receives the response in Listing 2-10. (If the Google SOAP server were set up to work over SMTP instead of HTTP, any SOAP client capable of sending an e-mail with the message in Listing 2-9 would receive an e-mail with the message in Listing 2-10. We are not going to use SMTP (neither the Google nor Amazon Web Service offers this option) but we will illustrate the point by writing (in the next chapter) an alternative client in a different language that communicates with the same server using the same SOAP messages.

## Overview of SOAP 1.2

Now that we have seen several examples of SOAP messages, we can take a general look at the specification that defines them. It consists of three parts: the main Part 1; Part 0, "Primer"; and Part 2, "Adjuncts". All three can be found at http://www.w3.org/TR/).

Part 1 consists of the following sections (listed in order of size and significance):

- The XML structure of the SOAP envelope, which is by far the longest and most important.

- SOAP Message Exchange Model, which describes several alternative message patterns. In this book, we use only the Remote Procedure Call (RPC) pattern. This is by far the most common pattern of SOAP use.

- SOAP Protocol Binding Framework. We cover general principles only; a specific proposal is in Part 2.

- Two very brief supporting sections on SOAP's relationship to XML (it *is* an XML language) and the important role of URIs in SOAP.

Part 1 is very general and abstract, leaving a number of options to implementers, such as SOAP encoding and SOAP binding to the underlying HTTP protocol. Part 2, "Adjuncts," provides specific suggestions that are, theoretically, not part of the standard but do, in fact, represent dominant practices.

**NOTE** *In SOAP 1.0 and 1.1, the material of Part 2 is included in the main specification. As of this writing (January 2003), most installations implement SOAP 1.1.*

Part 2 has three major sections.

- SOAP encoding, that is, a set of specific rules for encoding data types in XML.

- Using SOAP for RPC, that is, a set of conventions for encoding a procedure call in a SOAP Envelope structure.

- Default SOAP HTTP binding.

As we mentioned earlier, the first two sections have been made into adjuncts to give more flexibility to individual developers and applications. The status of the third section is as follows: You can use any protocol, but most likely you will use HTTP. If you use HTTP, you can embed SOAP envelopes into HTTP exchanges in any way you like, but there (in the third section) is a default binding that will most likely be understood without any additional arrangements. So far, most Web Services have been using the default HTTP binding, but there is active experimentation with SMTP and instant messaging as alternatives.

In this section, we will discuss the Message Exchange Model and the XML structure of the SOAP envelope. In the next section, we will discuss SOAP Encoding and SOAP RPC conventions in the context of an RPC example that returns structured data (an array of objects) rather than a simple type, as shown in Listings 2-10 and 2-11.

> **NOTE** *In the remainder of this chapter, we will use SOAP1.2-1 to mean "SOAP 1.2 Candidate Recommendation Part 1," and likewise for SOAP1.2-2 and SOAP1.2-0.*

## SOAP Message Exchange Model

A SOAP message is a one-way transmission from a SOAP sender to a SOAP receiver. However, SOAP messages can be combined to implement various Message Exchange Patterns (MEPs) such as request/response or multicast. MEPs describe the lifecycle of an exchange conforming to the pattern within a specific transport protocol; the temporal and causal relationships of the messages within the pattern; and the terminating conditions of the pattern, both normal and abnormal. SOAP1.2-2 gives a general definition of MEPs and a specific definition of just one of them, the Single-Request-Response MEP. This is similar to the way that a web browser and a web server work: the browser sends a request, the server sends back a response, and the connection is shut down.

SOAP messages can travel from the message originator to their final destination via intermediaries that can simply pass the message on or process it and emit a modified message or a fault condition. **SOAP node** is the general name for the initial SOAP sender, the ultimate SOAP receiver, or a SOAP intermediary (which is both a SOAP sender and a SOAP receiver). Ultimately, a Web Service is a collection of SOAP nodes.

A SOAP message consists of two parts, the optional Header and the mandatory Body. Both Header and Body consist of blocks, which are XML elements. The content of the Body, sometimes called the payload, will be processed by the message's final destination. The content of the Header is intended for intermediate nodes, with each Header block targeted individually. The entire machinery of Header blocks and intermediate nodes is intended for automatic collaboration among multiple SOAP processors. For instance, a purchase order from a SOAP client to a SOAP server may travel via an intermediate node (specified in a Header block) that authenticates the digital signature of the originator of the purchase order, and another intermediate node that initiates just-in-time delivery of the ordered items. As we said, this functionality will be more relevant for future applications than anything you are likely to write today. (See the "Web Services Vision" section of Chapter 1.)

## The XML Structure of a SOAP Message

This section explains how the abstract structure of a SOAP message is expressed as an XML document. The root element of the document is `Envelope`. A SOAP envelope consists of two parts, Header and Body. The Header carries meta information about the service and its delivery path. The Body carries the data; in the case of a remote procedure call, the Body carries the procedure name and arguments one way and the result of the procedure call another way. If an error condition arises, the Body contains one or several SOAP `Fault` elements.

### The Root Element

SOAP1.2-1 and SOAP1.2-2 use the somewhat verbose terminology of the Infoset specification, `http://www.w3.org/TR/xml-infoset/`. For instance, a SOAP message is defined in SOAP1.2-1 Section 4 as follows: "A SOAP message has an XML Infoset that consists of a document information item with exactly one child, which is an element information item...." We will use the looser (but less verbose) terminology of **document**, **element**, and **attribute**. So we recast the official definition as follows:

"A SOAP message is an XML document. Its root element's name is `Envelope`, within the `http://www.w3.org/2001/12/soap-envelope` namespace. (In our discussion, we will call it the `Envelope` namespace and assume that it is mapped to the env prefix.) The `env:Envelope` element has two children in the same namespace, the optional `env:Header` and the required `env:Body`. It may also have other children as long as they come from other namespaces."

In our examples so far, the optional Header element has been absent, and we are not going to see much of it in this book because header content is mostly metadata that orchestrates collaboration between multiple SOAP nodes, and in this book, we do simple client-server exchanges between two nodes. However, we do present an example to show what a Header element looks like.

## The Header Element

According to the Message Exchange Model, both Header and Body elements consist of **blocks** that can be targeted at different SOAP nodes. Header blocks, in particular, can be independently targeted at intermediate SOAP nodes that do additional processing along the way from the source of the SOAP message to its ultimate destination. In XML terms, both env:Header and env:Body can have any number of child elements in their own namespace(s) with no constraints on their internal structure. Each such element will be processed by a SOAP node that is its target processor. To express targeting information in XML, SOAP1.2-1 defines three attributes in the Envelope namespace: actor, mustUnderstand and encodingStyle.

The value of actor can be any URI. SOAP nodes have a property called role, whose value is also a URI. If the value of actor on a header block matches the value of role, the block is targeted at that node. SOAP1.2-1 does not say how a node specifies its role, but it does say in Section 2.2: "Each SOAP node *MUST* act in the role of the special SOAP actor named http://www.w3.org/2001/12/soap-envelope/actor/next."

> **NOTE** *If the value of* actor *is not specified, the block is targeted at the ultimate receiver of the message.*

If the node's role matches a header block's actor attribute, and the value of mustUnderstand on that header block is 1 or true, the node *MUST* either process the block or emit an error message.

The encodingStyle attribute, which you have seen in our examples, specifies the XML encoding of data items. Its value is a URI. For the encoding defined in SOAP1.2-2, that URI is http://schemas.xmlsoap.org/soap/encoding/ but it can be any URI that serves as an identifier for an application-specific encoding. Listing 2-11 is an example from SOAP1.2-0 that illustrates this usage, as well the actor and mustUnderstand attributes.

*Listing 2-11. A Header Example*

```
<env:Header>
  <m:reservation xmlns:m="http://travelcompany.example.org/reservation"
        env:actor="http://www.w3.org/2001/12/soap-envelope/actor/next"
        env:mustUnderstand="true">
  <m:reference>uuid:093a2da1-q345-739r-ba5d-pqff98fe8j7d</reference>
  <m:dateAndTime>2001-11-29T13:36:50.000-05:00</m:dateAndTime>
  </m:reservation>
  <t:transaction
        xmlns:t="http://thirdparty.example.org/transaction"
        env:encodingStyle="http://example.com/encoding"
        env:mustUnderstand="true" >
            5
  </t:transaction>
</env:Header>
```

There are two header blocks in this example. The first header block must be processed by the first SOAP node it encounters. The second header block is targeted at the ultimate receiver. The content of the node is a piece of data to be processed by the targeted node in accordance with the encoding identified by http://example.com/encoding.

We have not yet seen or read about a working example that actually uses header blocks in this way.

## The Body and Fault Elements

The env:Body element never carries an env:actor attribute because it is targeted at the ultimate receiver of the message. It can have any number of two different kinds children. Under normal conditions, children of env:Body must be elements from namespaces other than the Envelope namespace. (The requirement that children of env:Body must be in *some* namespace is new in 1.2 and still under discussion.) If a SOAP error occurs, env:Body may have any number of env:Fault elements. These are SOAP-level error messages that diagnose specifically SOAP-level problems, as distinct from problems reported by the underlying protocols.

The env:Fault element has two mandatory children and two optional ones. The mandatory children are faultcode and faultstring, both in no namespace. The optional children are faultfactor and detail, also in no namespace. Their use is as follows:

- `faultcode` elements are used by software. Their value is a qualified name in the `Envelope` namespace. SOAP1.2-1 Section 4.4.5 defines half a dozen `faultcode` values, such as `env:VersionMismatch` and `env:DataEncodingUnknown`.

- `faultstring` provides a human-readable description of the fault.

- `faultfactor` is a URI, typically one used as a value for an `actor` attribute. It provides information about which SOAP node on the SOAP message path caused the fault. In a multi-node situation, intermediate nodes generating an error *MUST* emit a `faultfactor` element; the ultimate receiver may emit a `faultfactor` element, but doesn't have to because of the next element.

- `detail` is intended for error information related to `env:Body`. If the contents of the SOAP Body could not be processed successfully, `detail` *MUST* be present within `env:Fault`.

This concludes our discussion of SOAP1.2-1. By the time you read this, some details of this discussion may be out of date, but we have tried to concentrate on those aspects of the specification that seem most stable and useful in practical programming. We move on to SOAP1.2-2, and specifically to encoding and RPC conventions.

## XML Encoding and RPC Conventions

In this section, we will talk specifically about using SOAP and Web Services for Remote Procedure Call (RPC) mechanisms, but the principles of XML encoding apply to other scenarios as well.

All our previous examples have shown RPCs of the simplest possible kind, in which both the argument of the procedure call and the returned value are of a primitive type. In other words, both the SOAP request and the SOAP response only have to encode a single primitive value, whose data type, specified by an `xsi:type` attribute, is defined in XML Schema Part 2.

Usually, both the argument and the returned value are complex structures with subparts and references to them.

> **NOTE** *One argument is enough: if there are more, we can always wrap them in a structure of which they are subparts.*

Therefore, we need a set of general conventions for serializing a complex structure with references to its subparts as an XML structure within a SOAP message. That's what XML encoding is about.

## An Example: Google Search Response

In Google API, all requests are primitive types or collections of primitive types. However, the response to a doGoogleSearch() request is a very complex type, indeed. In addition to a number of primitive type components, it contains two arrays, an array of search results, and a (usually shorter) array of directory categories to which those results belong. We will illustrate XML encoding of SOAP messages that carry complex data by analyzing a response to the doGoogleSearch request shown in Figure 2-4.

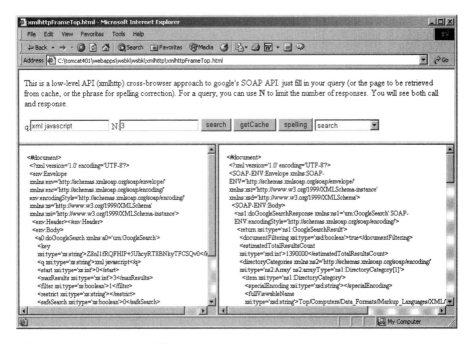

*Figure 2-4.* doGoogleSearch()

The top level of the response is familiar: the root element is Envelope in the Envelope namespace, and it contains a single child element, Body, in the same namespace. The Body element also contains a single child, doGoogleSearchResponse, in the urn:GoogleSearch namespace. This is the namespace in which the XML elements that encode the components of the returned data structure are defined.

These elements are all wrapped into a single element (the single child of doGoogleSearchResponse) called return, in no namespace whatsoever. Because return and its children are local to doGoogleSearchResponse, they don't need namespace qualifications. (This is common practice in XML documents whose structure is defined by an XML Schema. Like much else having to do with XML Schema, this practice is a subject of intense controversy among people who care about these things.) However, the names of the *data types* of return and all its descendants are indeed defined in specific namespaces.

- XML Schema namespace (http://www.w3.org/1999/XMLSchema, mapped to xsd) for primitive data types.

- GoogleSearch namespace (urn:GoogleSearch, mapped to ns1) for the type of the return element and the types of array items (ResultElement and DirectoryCategory)

- SOAP Encoding namespace (http://schemas.xmlsoap.org/soap/encoding/, mapped to ns2 and ns3) for the arrayType. Note that the same namespace can be mapped to different prefixes within the same document.

The return element and its children are listed in the Table 2-1 with their data types and namespaces in which those data types are defined.

*Table 2-1. The Children of* return *and Their Data Types*

| Element name | Data type name | Location of definition | Prefix |
|---|---|---|---|
| return | GoogleSearchResult | urn:GoogleSearch | ns1 |
| documentFiltering | boolean | http://www.w3.org/1999/XMLSchema | xsd |
| estimatedTotal ResultsCount | int | http://www.w3.org/1999/XMLSchema | xsd |
| directoryCategories (array type, length 1) | DirectoryCategory[1] | http://schemas.xmlsoap.org/ soap/encoding/ | ns2 ns3 |
| searchTime | double | http://www.w3.org/1999/XMLSchema | xsd |
| resultElements (array type, length 3) | ResultElement[3] | | |
| startIndex | int | http://www.w3.org/1999/XMLSchema | xsd |
| endIndex | int | http://www.w3.org/1999/XMLSchema | xsd |
| searchTips | string | http://www.w3.org/1999/XMLSchema | xsd |
| searchComments | string | http://www.w3.org/1999/XMLSchema | xsd |
| estimateIsExact | boolean | http://www.w3.org/1999/XMLSchema | xsd |

With these preliminary explanations in place, we can look at the actual XML code, broken into three listings. Listing 2-12 shows the top-level elements and namespace declarations. Listings 2-13 to 2-15 show the return element and its children. The children are not in the same order as in Table 2-1 because the Google service returns them that way. As we show later in the chapter, the XML Schema that specifies the structure of the return element allows its children to be in any order. Finally, grandchildren of return, that is, the items within its array children, are shown in Listings 2-14 and 2-15.

*Listing 2-12. Top-Level Elements of Google Search Response*

```
<?xml version='1.0' encoding='UTF-8'?>
<SOAP-ENV:Envelope
  xmlns:SOAP-ENV='http://schemas.xmlsoap.org/soap/envelope/'
  xmlns:xsi='http://www.w3.org/1999/XMLSchema-instance'
  xmlns:xsd='http://www.w3.org/1999/XMLSchema'
>
<SOAP-ENV:Body>
<ns1:doGoogleSearchResponse
  xmlns:ns1='urn:GoogleSearch'
  SOAP-ENV:encodingStyle='http://schemas.xmlsoap.org/soap/encoding/'
>
  <return xsi:type='ns1:GoogleSearchResult'>
<!-- see Listing 2-13 for the contents of return -->
  </return>
</ns1:doGoogleSearchResponse>
</SOAP-ENV:Body>
</SOAP-ENV:Envelope>
```

*Listing 2-13. The return Element and its Children*

```
  <return xsi:type='ns1:GoogleSearchResult'>
    <documentFiltering xsi:type='xsd:boolean'>true</documentFiltering>
    <estimatedTotalResultsCount xsi:type='xsd:int'>1390000
    </estimatedTotalResultsCount>
    <directoryCategories
      xmlns:ns2='http://schemas.xmlsoap.org/soap/encoding/'
      xsi:type='ns2:Array'
      ns2:arrayType='ns1:DirectoryCategory[1]'
    >
      <!-- array element (one in this case) goes here -->
```

```
      </directoryCategories>
      <searchTime xsi:type='xsd:double'>0.105118</searchTime>
      <resultElements
        xmlns:ns3='http://schemas.xmlsoap.org/soap/encoding/'
        xsi:type='ns3:Array'
        ns3:arrayType='ns1:ResultElement[3]'
      >
        <!-- array elements (three in this case) go here -->
      </resultElements>
      <endIndex xsi:type='xsd:int'>3</endIndex>
      <searchTips xsi:type='xsd:string'></searchTips>
      <searchComments xsi:type='xsd:string'></searchComments>
      <startIndex xsi:type='xsd:int'>1</startIndex>
      <estimateIsExact xsi:type='xsd:boolean'>false</estimateIsExact>
      <searchQuery xsi:type='xsd:string'>xml javascript</searchQuery>
  </return>
```

Listing 2-14 shows the array item of the DirectoryCategories array.

*Listing 2-14.* DirectoryCategory *Item*

```
    <item xsi:type='ns1:DirectoryCategory'>
      <specialEncoding xsi:type='xsd:string'></specialEncoding>
      <fullViewableName xsi:type='xsd:string'>
        Top/Computers/Data_Formats/Markup_Languages/XML/Tools/Parsers
      </fullViewableName>
    </item>
```

Finally, Listing 2-15 shows the fairly complex structure of an array item from the results array. We have broken many long lines to bring out its structure more clearly.

*Listing 2-15.* DirectoryCategory *Item*

```
    <item xsi:type='ns1:ResultElement'>
      <cachedSize xsi:type='xsd:string'>12k</cachedSize>
      <hostName xsi:type='xsd:string'></hostName>
      <snippet xsi:type='xsd:string'>
        HTML,CSS,JavaScript,DHTML,XML,XHTML,ASP,
        ADO and VBScript tutorial from W3Schools. ...
      </snippet>
      <directoryCategory xsi:type='ns1:DirectoryCategory'>
        <specialEncoding xsi:type='xsd:string'></specialEncoding>
```

```
    <fullViewableName xsi:type='xsd:string'>
      Top/Computers/Internet/Web_Design_and_Development/Authoring/Tutorials
    </fullViewableName>
  </directoryCategory>
  <relatedInformationPresent xsi:type='xsd:boolean'>
    true
  </relatedInformationPresent>
  <directoryTitle xsi:type='xsd:string'>
    W3Schools Web Tutorials
  </directoryTitle>
  <summary xsi:type='xsd:string'>
    Large collection of tutorials. HTML, XHTML, and Javascript.
    [Beginner to Advanced]
  </summary>
  <URL xsi:type='xsd:string'>http://www.w3schools.com/</URL>
  <title xsi:type='xsd:string'>
    W3Schools Online Web Tutorials
  </title>
</item>
```

Now that you have worked through a fairly complex example in considerable detail, we can summarize the main points of the XML encoding as defined in SOAP1.2-2.

## SOAP Encoding and the Data Model

SOAP Encoding is, in effect, a specialized XML language that is clearly based on the notions traditionally used in programming languages: struct and array. This language is described in Section 4 of SOAP1.2-2. We emphasize that the encoding of SOAP1.2-2 is "encouraged but not mandatory." However, it is a de-facto standard, used by most currently deployed Web Services, including those of Google and Amazon.

The encoding rules of SOAP1.2-2, Section 4 are described in the following sections.

### Values, Types, and Encoding

XML encoding deals with very familiar programming concepts. First, we distinguish between **values** and **types**. Within values, we distinguish between **simple values**, which don't have subparts, and **compound values**, which have subparts.

There are two kinds of compound values: **structs**, whose subparts are referenced and accessed by name, and **arrays**, whose subparts are referenced by a numerical index from a continuous range starting at 0. Within types, we also distinguish between **simple types** (classes of simple values) and **compound types** (classes of compound values).

Section 4 uses the generic term **accessor** to refer to struct accessors (names) and array accessors (numerical indices). It distinguishes between **single-reference** values that can be accessed by only one accessor and **multi-reference** values that can be accessed by more than one accessor.

The encoding rules are fairly straightforward. We will summarize the main points here; for more details, see SOAP1.2-2. In the following summary, the enc: prefix is assumed to be mapped to the namespace URI of the encoding, http://www.w3.org/2001/12/soap-encoding.

- All values are represented by element content.

- The type of a value must be represented, either using the xsi:type attribute or within an agreed-upon schema.

- Within an array representation where all array components are represented as children of the element representing the array, the type of components can be represented just once as the value of the enc:arrayType attribute on the parent element.

- A simple value must have a type specified in XS2, or a type derived from an XS2 type.

- A struct compound value is encoded as a sequence of elements and each accessor is represented by an embedded element whose name corresponds to the name of the accessor. A special appendix defines the mapping from Application Defined Names to XML Names.

- SOAP arrays are defined as having a type of enc:Array or a type derived from it. SOAP arrays *MUST* contain a enc:arrayType attribute whose value specifies the type of elements it contains and the dimension(s) of the array. (Both arrays in our example are one-dimensional but this is not always the case.)

We have not yet discussed the role of a schema language in SOAP, which is usually XML Schema as defined in http://www.w3.org/TR/xmlschema-[1,2]/. We will discuss it now, at least partially, in the next and final section of the chapter. Before we do that, though, we will quickly summarize the RPC conventions of SOAP.

## Representation of RPC in SOAP1.2-2

To represent an RPC, make an element whose name is the name of the remote procedure, and create children that represent the arguments. Each parameter child must have its type specified using some XML encoding, for instance, the encoding of SOAP1.2-2. To represent the graph structure of references, a system of id and href attributes is used. Each object has an id attribute of type ID (as in XML 1.0 DTD), and href attributes have the values of those id attributes.

## XML Schema and Its Role in SOAP

We mentioned several times that SOAP messages use data types defined in an XML Schema. There are three aspects to interaction between SOAP and XML Schemas.

- The primitive data types used in SOAP are defined in XML Schema Part 2, or they are derived from those types by rules defined in XML Schema Part 2.

- The complex data types used in SOAP (such as the type of the return element) are defined according to the rules of XML Schema Part 1.

- The types, both primitive and complex, are specified using xsi:type attributes, but if all the participating SOAP nodes have access to the defining schema and know how to interpret it, you can dispense with xsi:type attributes and simply rely on the schema. (This would make the service much easier to maintain because only the schema document would need to be updated.)

In this section, we will give an overview of XSchema Part 2 and examples of XML Schema Part 1 related to our Google examples.

> **NOTE** *To avoid clutter, we will abbreviate "XML Schema Part 1" as XS1, and "XML Schema Part 2" as XS2.*

# XML Schema Part 2

XS2 defines a great number of **built-in simple types**, some of them **primitive**, others **derived**. For instance, the primitive type, `decimal`, represents arbitrary precision decimal numbers; the built-in type `integer` is derived from `decimal` by setting the number of fraction digits to 0. From integer, a number of other integer types are derived, such as `long`, `int`, `short` and `byte`.

> **NOTE** *A complete diagram of built-in data types (with primitive and derived types color-coded and different kinds of derivation shown with different kinds of lines) can be found at* `http://www.w3.org/TR/xmlschema-2/#built-in-datatypes`.

In addition to built-in types, XS2 defines ways for users to define their own types by deriving them from built-in types. Most such derivations are by **restriction**. (For instance, you can restrict your data type to be a range of integers.) You can also derive new types by **forming a list** of simple types. The next sections provide details and examples.

## XML Schema Part 2, User-Defined Types

The notion of a data type is quite precisely defined in XML Schema. It is a triple consisting of a set of **values**, a set of **literals** to represent those values, and a set of **facets**. The set of values is called the **value space**, and the set of literals the **lexical space**. Within the lexical space, there may be multiple representations for the same values, in which case a subset of the lexical space is designated as the canonical representation. For instance, the value space "Boolean" consists of two values {true, false}, its lexical space consists of legal literals is {true, false, 1, 0}, and its canonical representation is the set of literals {true, false}. Booleans do not have interesting facets so we will introduce a more elaborate example that will also give us interesting facets to talk about.

## Data Types and Facets

The value space of the `double` data type is the set of values of the form $m \times 2^e$, where m is an integer whose absolute value is less than $2^{53}$, and e is an integer between –1075 and 970, inclusive. In addition, the value space contains positive and negative 0 (literals 0 and –0), positive and negative infinity (literals `inf` and `-inf`) and a special not-a-number value (literal `NaN`). This value space is known as "the IEEE double-precision 64-bit floating point type [IEEE 754-1985]," familiar from Java and Javascript; it is also the one used by XSLT.

The lexical representations of doubles are decimal numbers or decimal numbers in the scientific notation, with a mantissa followed (optionally) by "e" or "E," followed by an exponent that must be an integer; if there is no exponent, 0 is assumed. The canonical representation has a mantissa with a single digit before the decimal point and at least one digit after the decimal point; the exponent is required.

## Facets

Facets are properties. There are **fundamental facets** and **constraining facets**. Fundamental facets are the same for all data types. There are five of them: equal, ordered, bounded, cardinality, numeric. They describe the value space. For example, Is equality defined on it? (The answer is yes for all of them.) Is it ordered? Is it numeric? Is it bounded? Is it finite or infinite? For instance, **boolean** is not ordered, not bounded (because it's not ordered), not numeric, and finite; **double** is totally ordered, bounded, numeric and finite. There isn't much to say about fundamental facets, they are just there.

> **NOTE** *A complete table of XML Schema built-in data types and the values of their fundamental facets can be found at* `http://www.w3.org/TR/xmlschema-2/` `#section-Datatypes-and-Facets`.

Constraining facets are used with deriving data types. For instance, the constraining facets of **double** are

- pattern

- enumeration

- whitespace

- maxInclusive

- maxExclusive

- minInclusive

- minExclusive

The whitespace facet is something of an anomaly in this list; instead of constraining the set of values, it controls the whitespace handling. Its possible values are **preserve**, **replace**, and **collapse**. Preserve means "leave as is;" replace means "replace every whitespace character with #x20;" collapse means "collapse runs of #x20 characters into a single such character." The rest of the facets are discussed and illustrated as follows.

## Examples of XML Schema Type Definitions

Listing 2-16 shows examples of simple type definitions in the XML Schema language.

*Listing 2-16. Examples of XML Schema Simple Type Definitions*

```
<simpleType name="doubleRangeType">
  <restriction base="double">
   <maxInclusive value="5" />
   <minInclusive value="2" />
  </restriction>
</simpleType>

<simpleType name="doubleEnumType">
  <restriction base="double">
    <enumeration value="3.1"/>
    <enumeration value="4.7"/>
    <enumeration value="5.3"/>
  </restriction>
</simpleType>

<simpleType name="doubleListType">
  <list itemType="double"/>
</simpleType>
```

## How Are Types Used?

Ultimately, XML Schema documents serve to define the structure of XML data, including the tag name of the root element, the other elements present and how are they structured and related to each other, the attributes they have, and so on. The way Schema documents themselves are structured is defined in XS1, and that is easily the longest and most complex of XML specifications. We will give a brief overview and examples in the next section. For now, just note that with types defined as in Listing 2-17, an XML Schema document can define elements as follows.

*Listing 2-17. Examples of Element Definitions in a Schema Document*

```
<element name="doubleInRange" type="doubleRangeType"/>
<!-- 2.0, 3.7, 4.99, 5.0 are legal values; 1.5, 5.001 are not -->
<element name="doubleEnumValue" type="doubleEnumType"/>
<!-- 3.1, 4.7, 5.3 are the only legal values -->
<element name="doubleList" type="doubleListType"/>
<!-- legal values are whitespace separated lists of doubles -->
```

With element structure as in Listing 2-17, elements in instance documents (XML data) will be checked for type conformance by a Schema validator, which might be built into a SOAP processor. Depending on your environment, this may or may not be automatic. For instance, if your XML document (perhaps a SOAP message) contains an element like the following:

```
<doubleEnumValue xsi:type="doubleRangeType">4.75</doubleEnumValue>
```

The Schema validator will flag this as an error in data type. This is so the application programs will not have to do type checking themselves.

## Anonymous Types

Instead of defining a named type and using its name in defining an element, you can define an anonymous type within the element definition, as shown in Listing 2-18.

*Listing 2-18. Element Definition With an Internal Type Definition*

```
<element name="doubleList">
  <simpleType>
    <list itemType="double"/>
  </simpleType>
</element>
```

If you give a type a name, you can reuse it by reference in other element definitions.


## Non-Atomic Simple Types

List types are simple types that are not **atomic**. Another kind of **non-atomic simple type** is the union type. Suppose you want to specify a font size either as an integer in the range 8 to 72 or as one of three string tokens, small, medium and large. Listing 2-19 shows how you can define the corresponding type and an element of that type.

*Listing 2-19. Union Type*

```
<simpleType name="FontSizeType">
  <union>
   <simpleType>
     <restriction base="positiveInteger">
        <minInclusive value="8"/>
        <maxInclusive value="72"/>
     </restriction>
   </simpleType>
   <simpleType>
     <restriction base="NMTOKEN">
       <enumeration value="small"/>
       <enumeration value="medium"/>
       <enumeration value="large"/>
     </restriction>
   </simpleType>
  </union>
</simpleType>
<element name="FontSize" type="FontSizeType" />
```

### XML Schema Summary

In summary, simple XML Schema data types fall into these categories.

- primitive or derived

- built-in (primitive or derived) or user-defined (derived). The only way to create a new primitive type is by revising the Recommendation.

- atomic or non-atomic (list, union). There are built-in list types (NMTOKENS), but not union types.

Learning the simple type system is not hard because most types are familiar either from programming languages or from XML 1.0. If you want to create your own types in addition to built-in types, you need to know about facets. Here is the complete list of constraining facets, divided into groups with similar meaning.

- length, minLength, maxLength

- minInclusive, minExclusive, maxInclusive, maxExclusive

- pattern (regular expressions)

- enumeration

- duration, period (for time-based types)

- encoding (hex or base64)

- scale (number of digits in fractional part)

- precision (number of significant digits)

- whitespace (one of: preserve, replace, collapse)

## The Pattern Facet and Regular Expressions

The most important facet by far is the **pattern facet.** This facet allows you to specify a Regular Expression to constrain the values of the type. Regular Expressions, in case you have not used them before, specify sets of characters and strings of characters. They are used in the context of pattern matching: A Regular Expression forms a pattern against which strings are matched. Here are a few examples.

- Most individual characters match themselves: the character "-" matches itself.

- The pattern "\d" matches any digit. The pattern "\d{3}" matches any sequence of three digits.

- The pattern "315-\d{3}-\d{4}" matches any telephone number in the 315 area code of the U.S., in the 315-123-4567 format.

- The pattern "\(\d{3}\)\d{3}-\d{4}" matches any telephone number in the U.S., in the (315)228-7719 format. (You have to escape the parentheses characters because they have a special meaning in the Regular Expression language.)

- The pattern "(\(\d{3}\)|\d{3}-)\d{3}-\d{4}" matches any telephone number in the U.S. in either of the two formats. (The unescaped parentheses characters are used for grouping and the "|" character means "or.")

Regular Expressions are a big topic—there are whole books written on them. The entire Perl programming language is built around Regular Expressions. Regular Expressions are also an important part of Javascript, in addition to being an important part of XS2, which has a large appendix on Regular Expressions. The new feature of Regular Expressions as used in XML Schema is that they include expressions for classes of Unicode characters. (Until recently, Regular Expressions covered only ASCII.) It is a measure of XML Schema's size and ambition that it includes, as a brief aside, a 15-page specification for Unicode Regular Expressions.

## Using Regular Expressions to Define Simple Types

To define a simple type for U.S. telephone numbers in the (315) 123-4567 format, use the pattern facet.

```
<simpleType name="USPhoneType">
  <restriction base="string">
   <pattern value="\(\d{3}\)\d{3}-\d{4}"/>
  </restriction>
</simpleType>
```

The pattern facet can be used with almost any base type, including numeric types. You could define a range of integers from 23 to 76 by saying the following:

```
<simpleType name="intRange">
  <restriction base="integer">
   <pattern value="2[3-9]|[3-6][0-9]|7[0-6]"/>
  </restriction>
</simpleType>
```

The pattern reads

- 2 followed by digit in the range 3-9 **OR**

- digit in the range 3-6 followed by digit in the range 0-9 (that is, any digit; we could have used "\d" as well) **OR**

- 7 followed by digit in the range 0-6

> **NOTE** *There is a tool that automatically generates such patterns from integer and decimal ranges,* http://www.xfront.com/WebServicesTimeline.html. *It is a Java program (created by Roger Costello) that can be run from the Windows command line.*

# XML Schema Part 1: Structures

In this section, we give a very brief overview of XS1. We will start with a simple pedagogical example, continue with a summary of basic features, and conclude with a schema that defines `GoogleSearchResult` and other element types in SOAP response to the Google search method in Google API.

## A Simple Document and its Schema

Consider a simple document (shown in Listing 2-20) with mnemonic element names: r stands for "root," c stands for "child," and gc stands for "grandchild." Every grandchild is of a specific type: string, sting pattern, real number, and integer (year). A c element can be thought of as an inventory item that contains a part name, the part's stock number, its current price, and the year it was added to the product line.

*Listing 2-20. Simple Schematic Document,* `xs/xsEx1.xml`.

```
<?xml version="1.0"?>
<r>
  <c>
    <gcStr>Ingenious Widget (or any other string)</gcStr>
    <gcStrPat>22-abc-z12</gcStrPat><!-- a string pattern -->
    <gcNum>123.45</gcNum><!-- a real number -->
    <gcYear>1999</gcYear><!-- a year -->
  </c>
  <!-- many more children -->
</r>
```

We want to write a schema that defines and constrains documents of this type. The schema would specify the following constraints:

- The root element's tag name is r.

- The root element can have any number of children c elements, including zero.

- A c element must have four children named gcStr, gcStrPat, gcNum, and gcYear, in that order.

- The types of gc elements are as shown in Listing 2-20.

A schema for such a document type is shown in Listings 2-21 and 2-22. Listing 2-21 shows most of the code, leaving a gap for the declaration of the type of c element, shown in Listing 2-22. The schema (xsEx1nns.xsd) assumes that the document is in no namespace. (That's what nns stands for.) For documents with namespaces, additional markup would be required as part of the mechanism by which the schema and the document find each other.

*Listing 2-21. The First XS1 Schema,* xsEx1nns.xsd.

```
<?xml version="1.0"?>
<xs:schema xmlns:xs="http://www.w3.org/2001/XMLSchema">
<!-- An XS schema is an XML document in the XS namespace,
     mapped to the xsd prefix -->
  <xs:element name="r"><!-- start definition of r -->
    <xs:complexType><!-- start definition of r type -->
    <xs:sequence>
    <!-- the complex type of r is "zero or more repetitions of c" -->
      <xs:element name="c" minOccurs="0" maxOccurs="unbounded">
        <xs:complexType>
          <!-- see Listing 2-21 for what goes here -->
        </xs:complexType>
      </xs:element><!-- end of definition of c element -->
    </xs:complexType><!-- end definition of r type -->
  </xs:element><!-- end definition of r -->
</xs:schema>
```

The type definition of c is shown in Listing 2-22. Note that we do not specify minOccurs and maxOccurs values for children of c because both have the default value of 1. (XS1 allows attribute defaults both in instance documents and in schemas themselves.)

*Listing 2-22. Type Definition of Element* c

```
<xs:sequence>
    <xs:element name="gcStr" type="xs:string" />
    <!-- minOccurs="1" maxOccurs="1" are defaults -->
    <xs:element name="gcStrPat">
      <xs:simpleType>
        <xs:restriction base="xs:string">
          <xs:pattern value="\d{2}-[A-Za-z]{3}-\w\d{2}"/>
        </xs:restriction>
      </xs:simpleType>
    </xs:element>
    <xs:element name="gcNum" type="xs:decimal" />
```

```
<!-- XS2 defines built-in type 'year' but many schema processors
     do not support it, so we use 'positiveInteger instead -->
         <xs:element name="gcYear" type="xs:positiveInteger" />
      </xs:sequence>
```

With a document and a schema in place, we can validate the document against the schema. Before we do that, we have to specify what schema it wants to be validated against.

### Schema-Related Markup in the Document

A reference to the schema appears as an attribute of the document's root element. The attribute is in the same Schema Instance namespace as the type attribute in SOAP messages, as shown in Listing 2-23.

*Listing 2-23. Schema-Related Markup in a No-Namespace Document*

```
<?xml version="1.0"?>
<r
   xmlns:xsi="http://www.w3.org/2001/XMLSchema-instance"
   xsi:noNamespaceSchemaLocation="xsEx1nns.xsd"
>
  <!-- the rest as in Listing 2-21 -->
</r>
```

Obviously, you may frequently want to validate an instance document against a schema of your own. (For example, when you don't trust the document.) For this reason, xsi:noNamespaceSchemaLocation and xsi:schemaLocation are, according to XS1, only hints that the processors don't have to support and applications don't have to follow. In practice, all processors so far support them, but they also allow you to turn off automatic schema validation and program your own validation.

### What If the Document Is in a Namespace

What if the simple document of Listing 2-20 had a markup vocabulary in a namespace? You would need to make changes in both the document and in the schema.

In the document, obviously, we would have to declare the namespace. In addition, we would change the schema-instance attribute that references the schema. Instead of using noNamespaceSchemaLocation, we would use schemaLocation. The value of schemaLocation, a quoted string, has internal structure that has to consist of two tokens, the first of which is the document's namespace, and the second is the location of the schema (see Listing 2-24).

*Listing 2-24. Schema-Related Markup in a Namespaced Document,* `xsEx1ns.xml`

```
<?xml version="1.0"?>
<r xmlns="http://www.n-topus.com/schemas/"
   xmlns:xsi="http://www.w3.org/2001/XMLSchema-instance"
   xsi:schemaLocation ="http://www.n-topus.com/schemas/
                                  xsEx1a.xsd"
>
  <!-- the rest as in Listing 2-20 -->
</r>
```

We repeat the document's schema in the schema-instance attribute because we want to provide for the possibility that a single document contains vocabularies from several namespaces, each of which can be validated by a schema of its own. In other words, **a schema validates a certain namespace**. The value of `schemaLocation` can consist of any number of pairs that establish a connection between a namespace and a schema document that validates it. (There is no assumption that such a document has to be unique: the same namespace may be subject to validation by several schemas.)

In the schema itself, the namespace it is supposed to validate is specified as the `targetNamespace` attribute, as shown in Listing 2-25.

*Listing 2-25. Namespace-Related Markup in a Schema Document,* `xsEx1ns.xsd`

```
<?xml version="1.0"?>
<xs:schema
  xmlns:xs="http://www.w3.org/2001/XMLSchema"
  targetNamespace="http://www.n-topus.com/schemas/1ns/"
>
<!-- the rest copied unchanged from Listing 2-20 -->
  <xs:element name="r"><!-- start definition of r -->
    <xs:complexType><!-- start definition of r type -->
     <xs:sequence>
     <!-- the complex type of r is "zero or more repetitions of c" -->
      <xs:element name="c" minOccurs="0" maxOccurs="unbounded">
        <xs:complexType>
          <!-- see Listing 2-22 for what goes here -->
        </xs:complexType>
      </xs:element><!-- end of definition of c element -->
    </xs:complexType><!-- end of definition of r type -->
  </xs:element><!-- end definition of r -->
</xs:schema>
```

Our next and final example shows XML Schema type definitions for elements in the urn:GoogleSearch namespace: GoogleSearchResult, ResultElementArray, ResultElement, DirectoryCategoryArray, and DirectoryCategory.

## Type Definitions for Google API

Type definitions for Google API are contained in a schema document that is contained in the definitions section of a WSDL document for the Google Web Service. The overall structure is shown in Listing 2-26.

*Listing 2-26. Overall Structure of the Google Web Service Definitions*

```
<?xml version="1.0"?>
<!-- lots of WSDL stuff ... -->
<definitions name="urn:GoogleSearch"
            targetNamespace="urn:GoogleSearch"
            xmlns:typens="urn:GoogleSearch"
            xmlns:xsd="http://www.w3.org/2001/XMLSchema"
            xmlns:soap="http://schemas.xmlsoap.org/wsdl/soap/"
            xmlns:soapenc="http://schemas.xmlsoap.org/soap/encoding/"
            xmlns:wsdl="http://schemas.xmlsoap.org/wsdl/"
            xmlns="http://schemas.xmlsoap.org/wsdl/">
  <types>
    <xsd:schema xmlns="http://www.w3.org/2001/XMLSchema"
                targetNamespace="urn:GoogleSearch">
    <!-- definitions of types go here, Listings 2-26 and 2-27 -->
    </xsd:schema>
  </types>

  <!-- definitions of Google messages go here -->

</definitions>
```

Notice that the start tag of the definitions element declares a number of namespaces, including

- The target namespace for the type definitions, urn:GoogleSearch

- The SOAP Encoding namespace, in which the base Array type is defined

- The WSDL namespace that contains the names specific to this Web Service

We divide the definitions in two listings, array types are shown in Listing 2-27 and complex types that are not arrays are shown in Listing 2-28.

*Listing 2-27. Definitions of Array Types*

```
<xsd:complexType name="ResultElementArray">
  <xsd:complexContent>
    <xsd:restriction base="soapenc:Array">
      <xsd:attribute
          ref="soapenc:arrayType"
          wsdl:arrayType="typens:ResultElement[]"/>
    </xsd:restriction>
  </xsd:complexContent>
</xsd:complexType>

<xsd:complexType name="DirectoryCategoryArray">
  <xsd:complexContent>
    <xsd:restriction base="soapenc:Array">
      <xsd:attribute
          ref="soapenc:arrayType"
          wsdl:arrayType="typens:DirectoryCategory[]"/>
    </xsd:restriction>
  </xsd:complexContent>
</xsd:complexType>
```

It is not our intention to explain all the complexities of these definitions. The general picture should be reasonably clear: the array types defined here are derived, by restriction, from the array type that is defined in the SOAP Encoding namespace. The derived type overrides the value of the arrayType attribute to give it the value defined in this WSDL. The value is the name of the type defined in the same XML Schema (see Listing 2-28) followed by [], a common convention for array type names.

The remaining definitions are quite similar to the definitions of Listings 2-20 to 2-24. The new feature is the xsd:all element, which indicates that the children of the element being defined can be in any order. As we saw earlier, the children of GoogleSearchResult appear in the SOAP response message in an order that is different from the definition.

*Listing 2-28. Definitions of Other Types in the* GoogleSearch *Namespace*

```
<xsd:complexType name="GoogleSearchResult">
  <xsd:all>
    <xsd:element name="documentFiltering"            type="xsd:boolean"/>
    <xsd:element name="searchComments"               type="xsd:string"/>
    <xsd:element name="estimatedTotalResultsCount"   type="xsd:int"/>
    <xsd:element name="estimateIsExact"              type="xsd:boolean"/>
    <xsd:element name="resultElements"
                 type="typens:ResultElementArray"/>
    <xsd:element name="searchQuery"                  type="xsd:string"/>
    <xsd:element name="startIndex"                   type="xsd:int"/>
    <xsd:element name="endIndex"                     type="xsd:int"/>
    <xsd:element name="searchTips"                   type="xsd:string"/>
    <xsd:element name="directoryCategories"
                 type="typens:DirectoryCategoryArray"/>
    <xsd:element name="searchTime"                   type="xsd:double"/>
  </xsd:all>
</xsd:complexType>

<xsd:complexType name="ResultElement">
  <xsd:all>
    <xsd:element name="summary" type="xsd:string"/>
    <xsd:element name="URL" type="xsd:string"/>
    <xsd:element name="snippet" type="xsd:string"/>
    <xsd:element name="title" type="xsd:string"/>
    <xsd:element name="cachedSize" type="xsd:string"/>
    <xsd:element name="relatedInformationPresent" type="xsd:boolean"/>
    <xsd:element name="hostName" type="xsd:string"/>
    <xsd:element name="directoryCategory"
                 type="typens:DirectoryCategory"/>
    <xsd:element name="directoryTitle" type="xsd:string"/>
  </xsd:all>
</xsd:complexType>

<xsd:complexType name="DirectoryCategory">
  <xsd:all>
    <xsd:element name="fullViewableName" type="xsd:string"/>
    <xsd:element name="specialEncoding" type="xsd:string"/>
  </xsd:all>
</xsd:complexType>
</xsd:schema>
```

Although definitions of RPC messages are outside the XML Schema part of WSDL, they follow the same conventions and are quite easy to read. Listing 2-29 shows the definitions for the most complex method, doGoogleSearch().

*Listing 2-29. Definitions of SOAP Messages*

```
<message name="doGoogleSearch">
    <part name="key"         type="xsd:string"/>
    <part name="q"           type="xsd:string"/>
    <part name="start"       type="xsd:int"/>
    <part name="maxResults"  type="xsd:int"/>
    <part name="filter"      type="xsd:boolean"/>
    <part name="restrict"    type="xsd:string"/>
    <part name="safeSearch"  type="xsd:boolean"/>
    <part name="lr"          type="xsd:string"/>
    <part name="ie"          type="xsd:string"/>
    <part name="oe"          type="xsd:string"/>
</message>

<message name="doGoogleSearchResponse">
    <part name="return"      type="typens:GoogleSearchResult"/>
</message>
```

This concludes our discussion of XML Schema and its role in SOAP. You may never have to write XML Schema documents yourself (certainly not while working through the material of this book) but it is useful to develop a reading knowledge of WSDL, including a reading knowledge of XML Schema. We will return to the larger picture of WSDL and how it is used in Web Services in a later chapter.

## Conclusion

In this chapter, we presented the XML foundations on which the interoperability of Web Services is based. (We assumed the HTTP mechanisms for carrying the XML. We'll expand on these as we get into Java code where we can present them explicitly.) Ultimately, it rests on open standards, primarily XML standards, including XML DOM and XML Schema, and the SOAP specification, including SOAP encoding and the shared RPC conventions. You will see multiple examples of these technologies throughout the remainder of the book.

There is another foundation called REST (REpresentational State Transfer), which is described at `http://internet.conveyor.com/RESTwiki/moin.cgi` and at many other places on the Web. It is supported as an alternative to SOAP by Amazon, Google (although not as part of the free service), and others. Instead of having SoapActions as an extensible set of verbs, REST simply uses the HTTP operations GET, PUT, DELETE, and POST as verbs, with URIs as nouns representing the XML data values. REST provides a very clean world view in which interoperability is often completely trivial and security can be enhanced. You don't end up fooling your firewall with operations hidden inside XML payloads. On the other hand, SOAP directly represents whatever API you want to create. Discussions of the relative merits of SOAP vs. REST sometimes turn into a religious war, but we don't think they have to be mutually exclusive. (One view of combining them is described by Sam Ruby at `http://www.intertwingly.net/stories/2002/07/20/restSoap.html`.) We'll bring in REST solutions, or parts of REST solutions as needed when we set up our own Web Service.

Next we move on from Javascript to other languages and from the Google API to other Web Services. In the next chapter, we will develop a Java applet that communicates with the Amazon Web Service.

# CHAPTER 3

# More Services: Java Applet

ENOUGH GOOGLE FOR NOW. In this chapter, we introduce two new Web Services: the weather report service from `http://live.capescience.com/ccx/GlobalWeather` and the Amazon Web Services from `www.amazon.com/webservices`. Initially, we approach them using the xmlhttp framework from Chapter 1. However, within that framework, we generalize `doGoogle()` as `doSoapCall()`. This function can invoke several different Web Services, including Google, the Cape Science weather service, and Amazon. In fact, you can use `doSoapCall()` to develop a Javascript client for any SOAP service for which you have sample SOAP requests to work from.

After we have generalized the Javascript client, we switch to Java and write a Java command-line application to invoke those services. The reason we start with an application rather than an applet is that the applet has an additional layer of complexity having to do with permissions to connect to a URI that is not the same as the one it originates from. After developing the application, we develop the applet and move on to the security issues.

This chapter covers the following:

- The weather service and an Amazon Web Service example in the generalized xmlhttp Javascript framework

- The Amazon Web Services API

- A Java application for a Web Service client

- A Java applet for a Web Service client

We'll start with our weather example.

## Service-Independent Javascript

In this section, we present a generic `doSoapCall()` function that can invoke any Web Service.

### *How's the Weather?*

Figure 3-1 is a weather report for Syracuse NY, the closest big city to where we live.

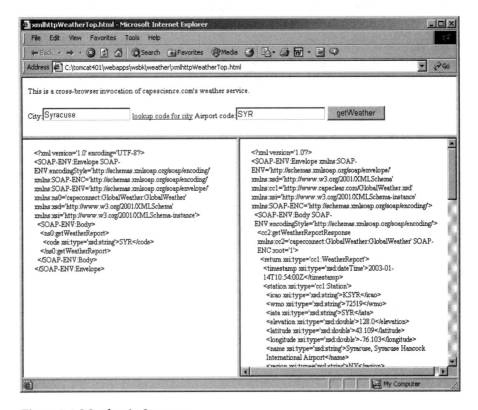

*Figure 3-1. Weather in Syracuse*

The source code for the top frame, which contains all Javascript code, is shown in Listing 3-1. It contains a supporting function that looks up the airport code(s) for a given city. Its main action is in the `onclick` event handler that invokes the service.

*Listing 3-1. Web Page for the Weather Report*

```
<html><head><title>xmlhttpWeatherCtl.html</title></head><body>
<script src="../utils/xmlhttp.js"></script>
<script>
  function airportCode(){
    var ur='http://www.ar-group.com/Airport-Locator.asp?RequestCity=';
    return ur+document.theForm.cityName.value;
  }
</script>
This is a cross-browser invocation of capescience.com's weather service.
<form name="theForm" action="javascript:void">
  City:<input type="text" name="cityName" value="Syracuse"/>
  <a href="javascript:parent.location=airportCode()">
    lookup code for city
  </a>,
  Airport code:<input type="text" name="airportCode" value="SYR"/>
<input type="button" value="getWeather"
  onclick="with(this.form){doGetWeatherReport(airportCode.value);}"/>
</form></body></html>
```

The punchline is the function call that invokes the service. The code of the function and all its supporting machinery is in `utils/xmlhttp.js`.

Next let's look at the code for `doGetWeatherReport()`, shown in Listing 3-2. It invokes the service by calling `doSoapCall()`:

*Listing 3-2. Cross-Browser Web Service Invocation Using* `doSoapCall()`

```
function doGetWeatherReport(airportCode){
  return doSoapCall(
    "http://live.capescience.com/ccx/GlobalWeather",
    "capeconnect:GlobalWeather:GlobalWeather#getWeatherReport",
    doGetWeatherReportEnvelope(airportCode));
}
```

As you can see, invoking a specific service calls a service-independent
doSoapCall() and passes it three parameters. The first and the third are easy to
recognize. The first is the URI of the service and the third is the SOAP request,
constructed, as before, by a doXxxEnvelope() function. The second argument is the
value of the SOAPAction header that some services insist should be present among
the HTTP headers of the HTTP POST message that delivers the SOAP envelope as
its payload. (If required, it will be part of the Web Service's description, however
that is given. If it is not needed, an empty value may be indicated with a pair of
quotation marks.)

The code of doSoapCall() is shown in Listing 3-3. It is a straightforward gener-
alization of doGoogle() (seen in Listing 1-7). You may want to review the discussion
of that function in Chapter 1 before reading the code of doSoapCall(). Just like
doGoogle(), it uses parseXML() to get a DOM tree for a SOAP envelope and
xml2HtmlPage() to display XML in a text area.

*Listing 3-3.* doSoapCall()

```
// the variables showCallRequest and showCallResponse are
// initialized to true
function doSoapCall(uri,soapAction,env){
  try{
    var xmlDoc=parseXML(env); // get DOM tree for SOAP request
    if(showCallRequest)
      with(parent.callFrame) {
        document.write(xml2HtmlPage(xmlDoc));
        document.close();
      }
    var xmlhttp=null; var doc=null;
    if(inIE) xmlhttp=new ActiveXObject('MSXML2.XMLHTTP');
    else xmlhttp=new XMLHttpRequest();
    if(!xmlhttp)
      return
alert("doSoapCall("+soapAction+"): can't initialize xmlhttp object");
    if(!inIE) // Netscape/Mozilla require a PrivilegeManager
      netscape.security.PrivilegeManager.
        enablePrivilege("UniversalBrowserRead");
    xmlhttp.open('POST',uri,false);
    xmlhttp.setRequestHeader("SOAPAction", soapAction)
    xmlhttp.setRequestHeader("Content-Type", "text/xml; charset=utf-8")
    xmlhttp.send(env);
    var result=xmlhttp.responseXML;
    if(showCallResponse)
      with(parent.responseFrame) {
```

```
        document.write(xml2HtmlPage(result));
        document.close();
      }
    return xmlhttp.responseXML;
  }catch(ex){ alert("doSoapCall("+soapAction+") error: "+ex); }
  return null;
}
```

It would be easy to rewrite our Google calls using doSoapCall(). We are not going to do that—like we said, enough Google for now. Instead, we will use it to explore the Amazon Web Services.

## Amazon Keyword Search

Just like Google, Amazon opened some of its databases for Web Services access. Unlike Google, though, Amazon offers both SOAP and REST (pure XML) APIs in the freely available interface. In this section, we explore only the SOAP version, but we will use REST later (as most Amazon developers do).

Figure 3-2 shows a Web Service call that uses Amazon's keyword search and returns an array of ten responses. There are ten because the Amazon Web Service, like Google's, returns query results in batches of ten. In code that generates the SOAP request envelope, there is a line that says

```
S+='    <page>1</page>';
```

This hard-codes a request for the first batch (or "page"). We could generalize the function to take a page parameter, and then this line would be

```
S+='    <page>'+page+'</page>';
```

In general, any tag name within the SOAP envelope can be made a parameter in this way.

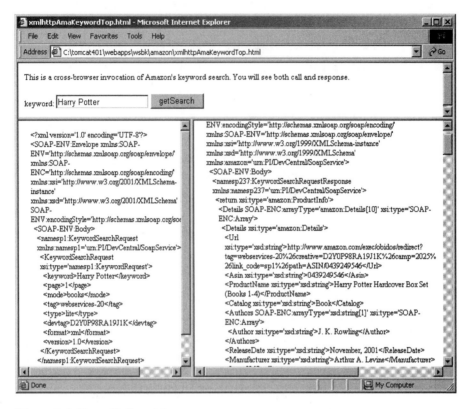

*Figure 3-2. Harry Potter at Amazon*

The Web Service is invoked from a web page with a form that is the source of the top frame in Figure 3-2, file amazon/xmlhttpAmaKeywordCtl.html. The form action is javascript:void, which does nothing, but the form contains an onclick event handler that calls doAmazonKeywordSearch() (shown in Listing 3-4).

*Listing 3-4. Control Frame for Amazon Web Service Invocation*

```
<html><head><title> xmlhttpAmaKeywordCtl.html</title>
<script src="../utils/xmlhttp.js"></script>
<script src="../utils/key.js"></script>
</head><body>
This is a cross-browser invocation of Amazon's keyword search.
<form name="theForm" action="javascript:void">
  keyword:
  <input type="text" name="keyword" value="Harry Potter"/>
  <input type="button" value="getSearch"
    onclick="with(this.form){
```

```
    doAmazonKeywordSearch(amazonToken,keyword.value);
  }"/>
</form></body></html>
```

The doAmazonKeywordSearch arguments are similar to the arguments used in a Google search: the user-identifying "key" (which Amazon calls the "developer token") and the keyword(s) to search for. As with the weather example of Listing 3-2, doAmazonKeywordSearch(), shown in Listing 3-5, calls doAmazonKeywordSearchEnvelope() to construct the SOAP request, and doSoapCall() to do the rest.

*Listing 3-5. Cross-Browser Amazon Web Service Invocation*

```
function doAmazonKeywordSearch(token,keyword){
  return doSoapCall(
      "http://soap.amazon.com/onca/soap",
      "KeywordSearchRequest",
      doAmazonKeywordSearchEnvelope(token,keyword));
}
<!-- the envelope function, for comparison with the Java version,
     Listing 3-16
-->
function doAmazonKeywordSearchEnvelope(token,keyword){
  var S='<?xml version="1.0" encoding="UTF-8"?>\n';
  S+='<SOAP-ENV:Envelope';
  S+='  xmlns:SOAP-ENV="http://schemas.xmlsoap.org/soap/envelope/"';
  S+='  xmlns:SOAP-ENC="http://schemas.xmlsoap.org/soap/encoding/"';
  S+='  xmlns:xsi="http://www.w3.org/2001/XMLSchema-instance"';
  S+='  xmlns:xsd="http://www.w3.org/2001/XMLSchema"';
  S+='  SOAP-ENV:encodingStyle="http://schemas.xmlsoap.org/soap/encoding/">';
  S+='  <SOAP-ENV:Body>';
  S+='    <namesp1:KeywordSearchRequest';
  S+=' xmlns:namesp1="urn:PI/DevCentral/SoapService">';
  S+='      <KeywordSearchRequest xsi:type="namesp1:KeywordRequest">';
  S+='        <keyword >'+keyword+'</keyword>';
  S+='        <page >1</page>';
  S+='        <mode >books</mode>';
  S+='        <tag >webservices-20</tag>';
  S+='        <type >lite</type>';
  S+='        <devtag >'+token+'</devtag>';
  S+='        <format >xml</format>';
  S+='        <version >1.0</version>';
  S+='      </KeywordSearchRequest>';
```

```
S+='    </namesp1:KeywordSearchRequest>';
S+='   </SOAP-ENV:Body>';
S+='</SOAP-ENV:Envelope>';
return S;
}
```

As an example of the information returned by Amazon, Listing 3-6 shows the beginning of the return element in the SOAP response. It contains an array of ten items. Each item is an XML Details element of the amazon:Details type. They have the following children (familiar to every user of Amazon):

- **Url**: The complete URL of the item, including the query string

- **Asin**: The Amazon standard identification number; for books, this is the same as an ISBN.

- **ProductName**: The title; used for books and music.

- **Catalog**: The catalog category (books, electronics, video, DVD, and so on).

- **Authors**: An array of authors, each represented by a string. In the first item of Listing 3-5, the Authors array has just one element, J.K. Rowling, but the second item, whose title is *Ultimate Unofficial Guide to the Mysteries of Harry Potter*, has two authors.

- **ReleaseDate** and **Manufacturer**: The publication date and publisher for books.

- **ImageUrl**: The book cover in three sizes: small, medium, and large

- **Prices**: The three prices, ListPrice, OurPrice, and UsedPrice.

Note that this is a "lite" request. You can request even more information by changing the line

```
S+='      <type >lite</type>';
```

To

```
S+='      <type >heavy</type>';
```

*Listing 3-6. The Return Element of the SOAP Response, Reformatted to Break
Long Lines*

```
<return xsi:type='amazon:ProductInfo'>
<Details SOAP-ENC:arrayType='amazon:Details[10]' xsi:type='SOAP-ENC:Array'>
<!-- begin first element of the array, ->
<!-- an XML element with these children:
  URL: the
-->
<Details xsi:type='amazon:Details'>
<Url xsi:type= 'xsd:string'>http://www.amazon.com/exec/obidos/redirect?
           tag=webservices-20%26creative=D2YOP98RA19J1K%26camp=2025
           %26link_code=sp1%26path=ASIN/0439249546

</Url>
<Asin xsi:type='xsd:string'>0439249546</Asin>
<ProductName xsi:type='xsd:string'>
Harry Potter Hardcover Box Set (Books 1-4)
</ProductName>
<Catalog xsi:type='xsd:string'>Book</Catalog>
<Authors SOAP-ENC:arrayType='xsd:string[1]' xsi:type='SOAP-ENC:Array'>
  <Author xsi:type='xsd:string'>J. K. Rowling</Author>
</Authors>
<ReleaseDate xsi:type='xsd:string'>November, 2001</ReleaseDate>
<Manufacturer xsi:type='xsd:string'>Arthur A. Levine</Manufacturer>
<ImageUrlSmall xsi:type='xsd:string'>
  http://images.amazon.com/images/P/0439249546.01.THUMBZZZ.jpg
</ImageUrlSmall>
<ImageUrlMedium xsi:type='xsd:string'>
  http://images.amazon.com/images/P/0439249546.01.MZZZZZZZ.jpg
</ImageUrlMedium>
<ImageUrlLarge xsi:type='xsd:string'>
http://images.amazon.com/images/P/0439249546.01.LZZZZZZZ.jpg
</ImageUrlLarge>
<ListPrice xsi:type='xsd:string'>$85.80</ListPrice>
<OurPrice xsi:type='xsd:string'>$60.06</OurPrice>
<UsedPrice xsi:type='xsd:string'>$51.25</UsedPrice>
</Details>
<!-- end of first returned item, start second one -->
<Details xsi:type='amazon:Details'>
<Url
xsi:type='xsd:string'>
http://www.amazon.com/exec/obidos/redirect?tag=webservices-20%26
creative=D2YOP98RA19J1K%26camp=2025%26link_code=sp1%26path=ASIN/0972393609
```

```
    </Url>
    <Asin xsi:type='xsd:string'>0972393609</Asin>
    <ProductName xsi:type='xsd:string'>
      Ultimate Unofficial Guide to the Mysteries of Harry Potter
    </ProductName>
    <Catalog xsi:type='xsd:string'>Book</Catalog>
    <Authors SOAP-ENC:arrayType='xsd:string[2]' xsi:type='SOAP-ENC:Array'>
    <Author xsi:type='xsd:string'>Galadriel Waters</Author>
    <Author xsi:type='xsd:string'>Astre Mithrandir</Author>
    </Authors>
    <ReleaseDate xsi:type='xsd:string'>15 September, 2002</ReleaseDate>
    <Manufacturer xsi:type='xsd:string'>
      Wizarding World Press
    </Manufacturer>
    ...
    </Details>
    <!-- eight more array items of type amazon:Details -->
    </Details>
    </return>
```

You may wonder why we display all this information in raw XML code rather than in a nicely formatted XML or HTML page. In fact, once we have our XML parsed into a DOM, it is relatively straightforward to display it any way we like, using either DOM interfaces or XSLT. (Most XSLT processors can take a DOM object as input.) XSLT is a separate topic that we will address in a later chapter. Also, note that the REST interface to the Amazon Web Services includes a server-side XSLT processor. In this chapter, we will use the familiar Javascript DOM methods.

## *SOAP Response in an HTML Table*

Figure 3-3 shows an HTML page that displays an Amazon query result in a table. A better page would have a `target="_top"` attribute so the target of a link is not buried in a frame, but we wanted to show both the control frame from which queries are run and a query result. (We provide such a page in `xmlhttpAmaKeyBetterTableCtl.html`.)

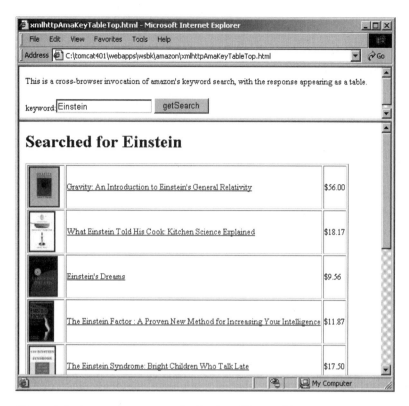

*Figure 3-3. Amazon query result displayed in a table*

The Javascript code for this example is in `amazon/xmlhttpAmaKeyTableCtl.html`. It shows how the simple `getElementsByTagName()` DOM method extracts all that we need from a SOAP response as returned by our Javascript `doSoapCall()`.

### Top-Level Function and SOAP Fault

A SOAP response, as you know, will be either a query result within a `return` element, or a SOAP fault message containing the elements `faultcode`, `faultstring`, and `detail`. The top function we invoke from the HTML `getSearch` button in Figure 3-3 is shown in Listing 3-7.

*Listing 3-7. The Return Element of SOAP Response, Reformatted*

```
function showAmazonResultTable(keyword){
  var resultOb=doAmazonKeywordSearch(amazonToken,keyword);
  var returnOb=resultOb.getElementsByTagName("return");
  if(!returnOb || returnOb.length == 0)
    return showError(keyword,resultOb,parent.dataFrame);
  showResultTable(keyword,returnOb[0],parent.dataFrame);
}
```

The showError() method (shown in Listing 3-8) simply looks for each SOAP fault element and displays it.

*Listing 3-8. Find and Display SOAP Fault Elements*

```
function showError(key,resOb,win){
  var S="<html><head><title>Error from "+key+"</title></head>\n";
  S+="<body><h1>ERROR in search for:"+key+"</h1><table>";
  S+="<tr><td>faultCode=</td><td>"+
      getMessageData(resOb,"faultcode")+
      "</td></tr>\n";
  S+="<tr><td>faultString=</td><td>"+
      getMessageData(resOb,"faultstring")+
      "</td></tr>\n";
  S+="</table><p>"+getMessageData(resOb,"detail")+"</p>\n";
  S+="</body></html>";
  win.document.write(S);
  win.document.close();
}
```

We will show an example of a faultcode in the next section, but if you want to see it right away, run a search for, say "xxxxxxxxxx," and you will get the faultcode "SOAP-ENV:Client," the faultstring will be "Bad Request," and the detail will tell you "There were no exact matches for the search."

## Displaying Results of a Successful Search

A successful search, as you saw in Listing 3-6, produces a much more complex result, with a Details array element that contains a series of Details data elements. Our code (shown in Listing 3-9) loops through the series and generates one row of a table from each.

*Listing 3-9. Loop Through the Details Array*

```
function showResultTable(key,retOb,win){
  var S="<html><head><title>Search Result for "+key+"</title></head>\n";
  S+="<body><h1>Searched for "+key+"</h1><table border='1'>\n";
  var topDetails=retOb.getElementsByTagName("Details");
  if(topDetails && topDetails.length > 0) {
    var details=topDetails[0].getElementsByTagName("Details");
    for(var i=0;i<details.length;i++)
      S+=showDetailsAsRow(details[i]);
  }
  S+="</table></body></html>";
  win.document.write(S);
  win.document.close();
}
```

Each iteration of the loop calls the showDetailsAsRow() function to make a table row out of the XML output. The exact form of that function depends on what you want to display and how you want to display it. In Figure 3-3, we made a table containing the cover page images as thumbnails in column 1, the titles in column 2, and the Amazon price in column 3. In addition, each thumbnail is a link to the corresponding full-sized image, and each title is a link to the corresponding Amazon detail page. The code is shown in Listing 3-10; the only tricky part is outputting quotes within quotes.

*Listing 3-10. Display Each Result in a Row*

```
function showDetailsAsRow(details){
  var smallImageUrl=getMessageDataDefault(details, 'ImageUrlSmall','');
  var largeImageUrl=getMessageDataDefault(details, 'ImageUrlLarge','');
  var bookUrl=getMessageData(details, 'Url');
  var productName=getMessageData(details,"ProductName");
  var price=getMessageDataDefault(details,"OurPrice",'');
  var S="<tr>";
  S+="<td><a href='"+largeImageUrl+
     "'><img src='"+smallImageUrl+
     "'/></a></td>";
  S+="<td><a href='"+bookUrl+"'>"+productName+"</a></td>";
  S+="<td>"+price+"</td>";
  S+="</tr>\n";
  return S;
}
```

## Extracting Data Fields

We extract individual data fields from the returned Amazon records with getMessageData() and getMessageDataDefault(). The first of these functions is familiar (seen in Listing 2-2, repeated in Listing 3-11), but the second one (shown in Listing 3-12) is not. We add it because sometimes a data field is missing. If you search for "Henry Cabot Lodge," for example, you'll find some books with neither images nor prices. The getMessageData() function complains about that, whereas getMessageDataDefault() tries to supply an appropriate default instead. Both functions are in utils/getDOMdata.js.

*Listing 3-11.* getMessageData()

```
function getMessageData(msg, name){ // simplified
  try{
    var node=msg.getElementsByTagName(name)[0];
    var txtNode = node.firstChild;
    return txtNode.data;
  }catch(ex){alert("no field "+name+" in "+toXML(msg)+"\n"+ex);}
  return "";
}
```

The getMessageDataDefault() function is prepared for three arguments, but it can be called with two. It uses getMessageDataDefault.arguments.length to see if a default has been provided, as shown in Listing 3-12.

*Listing 3-12.* getMessageDataDefault()

```
function getMessageDataDefault(msg,name,deflt){
  try{
    var res="";
    var node=msg.getElementsByTagName(name)[0].firstChild;
    while(node){
      res+=node.data;
      node=node.nextSibling;
      }
    return res;
  }catch(ex){
    if(getMessageDataDefault.arguments.length >= 3)
      return deflt;
    alert("no field "+name+" in "+toXML(msg)+"\n"+ex);
    return "";
  }
}
```

> **NOTE** *Many variations on data display are, of course, possible. As you display query results in increasingly sophisticated and tastefully formatted HTML pages, the underlying XML is no longer visible, but it may be useful for debugging purposes. Consider adding a debugging flag or switch to your application so that you can view the underlying XML on demand.*

This may be the right place to mention a tool that can make XML visible without cluttering your page or otherwise getting in your way. It is called TCPMonitor, and the Google API FAQ recommends it. The tool is not specific to SOAP or to Web Services (it can be used to monitor any TCP/IP exchanges) but it is included with the Apache Axis Web Services toolkit that we used in *XML Programming* (Apress 2002). We will use it later in this book, both with a local server and for automated client construction from WSDL descriptions.

In the meantime, we are going to take a closer look at Amazon's Web Services offerings. The keyword query shown in Listing 3-6 is one of many offered by the Amazon Web Services API. The next section presents an overview and a multi-query example.

## Amazon Web Services API

Amazon's Web Services API is very well documented. When you sign up (at `http:// /www.amazon.com/webservices`), /), you download a developer's kit that includes a good deal of documentation. Its centerpiece, `Amazon Web Services API and Integration Guide.htm`, contains a detailed description of all the search methods (in "Accessing Amazon.com Data via SOAP") and transactions (in "Enabling Transactions with Amazon.com"). Better yet, the documentation contains a directory called SoapRequestSamples that is full of exactly that, SOAP request samples. These are very useful as starting points for your own experiments.

Just as with Google, in order to use Amazon Web Services, you have to register and obtain a key (called a "developer token" by Amazon). Also like Google, Amazon imposes restrictions on how much information you can get, including a constraint that you can run only one request per second.

Within those constraints, you can run 16 different kinds of queries, described in the guide in the "Accessing Amazon.com Data" section. We are not going to list them all here (read the guide!), but we will show an example that runs nine of them and explain how they are put together.

## Amazon Multi-Query Example

Figure 3-4 shows the available queries. To run a query, select the appropriate mode and click the button for the query. If there is a mismatch between the mode and the query, you will get a SOAP fault message back saying that there were no matches. In the example, we ask for Actor="Bogart" but the mode is "Books" so we get a SOAP fault.

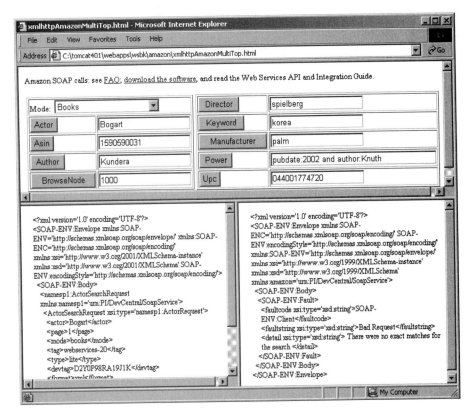

*Figure 3-4. Multiquery example with a SOAP fault*

The searches are largely self-explanatory, but some do require comment. For instance, you may wonder what a "browsenode" is and how is one selected. For answers, go to the Concepts Used in This Document section of the Amazon Web Services API and Integration Guide. The concepts are not in alphabetical order, but there aren't that many of them, so a quick perusal will yield this information:

*A browse node (or browse ID) is a number that corresponds to a general subject area of Amazon.com. Browse IDs can generally be found in the URL string when visiting a specific browse section at the Amazon.com Web site. Please see Appendix A for more information on how to find browse nodes.*

Furthermore, if you go to subsection 8.5 that deals with browse node searches via SOAP, you will learn that "The BrowseNodeSearch request returns a ProductInfo node. The ProductInfo node contains an array of Detail nodes." If you run the BrowseNode query from our multi-query example, you will discover that node 1000 corresponds to the first Harry Potter query result from Figure 3-2.

We will give brief explanations of what the queries do, as well how the functions work, as we go through the code.

## The Multi-Query Code

All the queries are invoked from the control (top) frame of xmlhttpAmazonMultiTop.html whose source is xmlhttpAmazonMultiCtl.html. The control frame consists of a table that contains two tables, each with five rows, making ten rows altogether. One of the rows contains the selection element for modes, and the remaining nine rows are for queries. Each query row has two cells, one for a button to invoke the query and the other for an input element with a value in it. For instance, the query row for the BrowseNode search request looks like as shown in Listing 3-13.

*Listing 3-13. Amazon Search Invocation*

```
<tr><td>
<input
  type="button"
  value="BrowseNode"
  onclick="with(this.form){
    doAmazonBrowseNodeSearch(token,browsenode.value,mode.value)
  }"
/>
</td><td>
<input type="text" name="browsenode" value="1000"/>
</td></tr>
```

The function that runs the query, doAmazonBrowseNodeSearch(), is in utils/AmazonEnvelopes.js with the rest of Amazon-related utilities. It is shown in Listing 3-14.

*Listing 3-14. Running an Amazon Query*

```
function doAmazonBrowseNodeSearch(token,browsenode,mode){
  return doSoapCall(
    "http://soap.amazon.com/onca/soap",
    "BrowseNodeSearchRequest",
    AmazonBrowseNodeSearchRequestEnvelope(token,browsenode,mode));
}
```

The envelope function, as before, constructs the SOAP envelope that is passed as a parameter to the general doSoapCall(). To construct an envelope, the envelope function needs two general parameters (the user's token and the mode of the search), and the search-specific value—the browse node number in this case.

This completes our discussion of the multi-query Amazon search and the entire Javascript section of this chapter. Our next challenge is to do it all in Java, from an applet in the browser window.

# A Java Version of a SOAP Client

All our Web Services so far rely on the xmlhttp object, which is implemented in both Javascript and JScript. Ultimately, the job is done by the object's open(), setRequestHeader(), and send() methods (see Table 1-2).

Suppose we want to write a SOAP client in a language where the xmlhttp object is not available. What should we do? We can we use HTTP to send XML ourselves. We show how to do that in Java, but the same algorithm applies to Perl, PHP, C#, or any other language. The underpinnings are language-independent because XML and HTTP are language-independent.

We proceed as follows:

1. Open a socket to the server.

2. Set the usual HTTP headers and one unusual one, called "SoapAction."

3. Skip a line between headers and body, and send the SOAP envelope as the body of the HTTP message.

The response is also an HTTP message. Its headers may be of interest (for instance, indicating cookies or the session ID), but for a preliminary system we will ignore the headers and look for the empty line after them and then pick up the SOAP response.

In our Java version, we will preserve the same overall framework that we used in Javascript. By "the same overall framework" we mean that in order to do an Amazon keyword search, for instance, we call a function like the one shown in Listing 3-15.

*Listing 3-15.* doXxx() *in classes/soapUtil/XmlHttp.java*

```
public static String doAmazonKeywordSearch(String code,String keyword)
    throws IOException{
  return sendSoap("http://soap.amazon.com/onca/soap",
             "KeywordSearchRequest",
             doAmazonKeywordSearchEnvelope(code,keyword));
}
```

Here, doAmazonKeywordSearch() and doAmazonKeywordSearchEnvelope() are Java equivalents of identically-named Javascript functions, and sendSoap() is the equivalent of doSoapCall().

As you can see, recasting Javascript code in Java is quite easy—it generally requires only that you introduce explicit data types and fix quotation marks because Java does not accept an apostrophe as a string-delimiter.

Listing 3-16 shows the Java version of doAmazonKeywordSearchEnvelope().

*Listing 3-16.* doXxxEnvelope() *in classes/soapUtil/XmlHttp.java*

```
public static String doAmazonKeywordSearchEnvelope(String code,String keyword){
  String S="<?xml version='1.0' encoding='UTF-8'?>\n";
// the rest is identical to the Javascript function, Listing 3-5
// including the next two lines, repeated for clarity
  return S;
}
```

What about sendSoap()? This time, we don't have a Javascript function to recast, but the code is still manageable thanks to the facilities provided by the java.net.URL and java.net.Socket classes. Read on for further explanation.

## XML over HTTP in Java

The sendSoap() method (in the same classes/soapUtil/XmlHttp.java) receives three arguments: the URI to connect to, the SOAP action to perform, and the XML payload to deliver. Following the language-independent outline that we described earlier, it goes through the following steps:

1. Open the connection and associated streams

2. Construct the HTTP header

3. Send header and payload over the connection

4. Receive and return the result

Before any of this happens, you must import the required libraries. We show the imports in Listing 3-17, the connection and streams are opened in Listing 3-18, the header is constructed in Listing 3-18, and the rest is in Listing 3-19.

The imports are all from the java.net and java.io packages. As you may know, all IO in Java is done via the same streams library whether the data is coming from a local file or over a network. The java.net.Socket object that encapsulates network protocols has getInputStream() and getOutputStream() methods that layer stream APIs over the protocols.

*Listing 3-17. Imported Classes for java.net and java.io*

```
import java.net.URL;
import java.net.Socket;
import java.io.OutputStream;
import java.io.InputStream;
import java.io.BufferedOutputStream;
import java.io.BufferedInputStream;
import java.io.StringWriter;
import java.io.InputStreamReader;
import java.io.IOException;
```

With imports in place, we proceed to the code that establishes a connection to the given URL and creates the associated streams. In a typical Java pattern, the Socket object provides associated byte streams. To process characters, we wrap the streams in buffered character streams (Readers), specifying UTF-8 as the character encoding.

*Listing 3-18. URL, Socket and Streams*

```
public static String sendSoap(
      String urlString,
      String soapAction,
      String payload) throws IOException{
  URL url=new URL(urlString);
  int timeout=20000;
  int port= url.getPort();
  if(port<0) port=80; // port 80 is default for HTTP

  Socket s = new Socket(url.getHost(),port);
  s.setSoTimeout(timeout);

  OutputStream outStream = s.getOutputStream ();
  BufferedOutputStream bOutStream = new BufferedOutputStream(outStream);

  InputStream inStream = s.getInputStream ();
  BufferedInputStream bInStream = new BufferedInputStream(inStream);
  InputStreamReader reader=new InputStreamReader(bInStream,"utf-8");
```

Next, we construct HTTP headers (including SOAPAction), deliver the HTTP message, and close up (see Listing 3-19).

*Listing 3-19. HTTP Headers*

```
  /* Construct headers */
  StringBuffer headerbuf = new StringBuffer();
  headerbuf.append("POST ")
            .append(url.getFile()).append(" HTTP/1.0\r\n")
          .append("Host: ")
            .append(url.getHost()).append(':')
              .append(port).append("\r\n")
          .append("Content-Type: text/xml; charset=utf-8\r\n")
          .append("Content-Length: ")
            .append(payload.length()).append("\r\n")
          .append("SOAPAction: \"")
```

```
                .append(soapAction).append("\"\r\n")
            .append("\r\n");

  /* Send header and payload. */
        bOutStream.write(headerbuf.toString().getBytes("utf-8"));
        bOutStream.write(payload.getBytes("utf-8"));
        bOutStream.flush();
        outStream.flush();

     StringWriter sw=new java.io.StringWriter();
       for(int ch=reader.read();ch>=0;ch=reader.read())
         sw.write((char)ch);
       String resString=sw.toString();
       int endHeaderPos=resString.indexOf("\r\n\r\n");
       if(endHeaderPos>=0)
         resString=resString.substring(endHeaderPos+4);
  /* close all streams and the socket */
        bOutStream.close(); outStream.close();
        bInStream.close();  inStream.close();
        s.close();
        return resString;
  }
```

This completes sendSoap(). Its only SOAP-specific feature is the insertion of the SOAP-Action header in the HTTP message head. Otherwise, it is a completely general mechanism for sending XML payloads over HTTP, just as xmlhttp is in the Javascript world. It would be a trivial exercise to rewrite all our Javascript functions for invoking specific services in Java.

How can we use those Java functions? To invoke, for instance, Amazon keyword search, we can write the trivial command-line application shown in Listing 3-20. We include it in the same file, classes/soapUtil/XmlHttp.java, as a way of testing the operation of XmlHttp.

*Listing 3-20. The* main() *Method for Amazon Keyword Search*

```
public static void main(String[]args)
throws IOException{
  if(args.length==0){
    System.out.println("usage: java XmlHttp aKeyword");
    return;
  }
  String token="**********"; // insert your token here
  System.out.println(doAmazonKeywordSearch(token,args[0]));
}
```

To compile and test the client, run the `testXmlHttp.bat` file in the same directory. This will return the raw XML of SOAP response that is not going to be very useable. We could redirect the response to an XML file that we would then view in a browser, but it would be much better if the response arrived in the browser window to begin with so that the browser could handle it. One way to achieve this is to call `sendSoap()` from an applet, which is in turn invoked from Javascript. However, this poses problems of its own: `sendSoap()` has to open a socket to a Web Service URL, and unsigned applets are not allowed to do that for obvious security reasons. We are going to tackle this and other problems in the next section.

## Applet with Privileged Access

The Java 2 platform provides an elaborate security model in which access to resources by either local or remote code is controlled by a security policy that can be configured by the user or the system administrator. The initial Java notion of a sandbox to which untrusted code is confined is still present but there is more flexibility in constructing sandboxes of various shapes and sizes. The notion of trust is also graduated to allow degrees and specific areas of access. For a detailed discussion see `http://java.sun.com/docs/books/tutorial/security1.2/overview/index.html`. Here is a quick summary:

- The security policy defines the set of permissions available for code from various signers or locations and can be configured by a user or a system administrator. Each permission specifies a permitted access to a particular resource, such as read and write access to a specified file or directory, and connect access to a given host and port.

- The runtime system organizes code into individual domains, each of which encloses a set of classes whose instances are granted the same set of permissions. Applets by default run in an equivalent to the sandbox but can be configured to have more access depending on signature, originating domain, and so on. Applications run unrestricted by default but can be subject to a security policy. The default security policy is formulated in the security policy file, which is `JAVA_HOME/lib/security/java.policy`, with slash direction modified as appropriate for the operating system. Security policy for individual users can be formulated in user.home/.java.policy, where user.home is the user's home directory.

- There is a security-policy shortcut within the java.policy file that grants all and every permission to "extension code," that is, code that is placed in JAVA_HOME/jre/lib/ext directory. Presumably, whoever has the permissions to place code in that directory can be trusted to put only safe code there. If you have code you think you can trust (for instance, some people trust their own code) you can simply put it in the lib/ext directory (or two such directories in Windows), and it will be treated as privileged code.

Because we want our applet to run our own sendSoap() code, we are precisely in the situation where the shortcut can be used, provided we put the code in the right place. Specifically, we create a soapUtil package, compile and jar it, and put the resulting jar file into JAVA_HOME/jre/lib/ext. (On Windows, we put the jar both in JAVA_HOME/jre/lib/ext and in Program Files/Java/*JreDir*/lib/ext, where JreDir is JDK-version-specifc.) At this point, we are ready to give the code privileged access to restricted resources, such as network connections.

## SOAP Applet with Privileges

As described in http://java.sun.com/docs/books/tutorial/ext/security/policy.html, giving privileged access to extension code involves two steps.

- Place the code that performs security-sensitive operations within the run() method of an object of type java.security.PrivilegedAction.

- Use that PrivilegedAction object as the argument in a call to the doPrivileged() method of java.security.AccessController.

Listing 3-21, AmazonApplet_1.java, shows how these two steps work for an applet that runs an Amazon keyword search.

*Listing 3-21. Amazon Keyword Search from an Applet, Version 1*

```
package soapUtil;
import java.security.*;
class AmazonKeywordSearch implements PrivilegedAction {
  private String token;
  private String keyword;
  public AmazonKeywordSearch(String t,String k){token=c; keyword=k;}
  public Object run(){
    try{return XmlHttp.doAmazonKeywordSearch(token,keyword);
    } catch(Exception e) {e.printStackTrace(); return ""+e; }
```

```
    }
  }
public class AmazonApplet_1 extends java.applet.Applet{
  public String doAmazonKeywordSearch(String token,String keyword){
    PrivilegedAction pA=new AmazonKeywordSearch(token,keyword);
    return (String) AccessController.doPrivileged(pA);
  }
} // end of AmazonApplet_1
```

As a minor variation, we can implement the PrivilegedAction class as an anonymous inner class within the Applet class, as seen in Listing 3-22. The code, AmazonApplet_2.java, is a rewrite of Listing 3-21, except the arguments to the SOAP call are now declared final because inner classes have access only to final variables.

*Listing 3-22. Applet with Inner Class that Implements* PrivilegedAction

```
package soapUtil;
import java.security.*;
public class AmazonApplet_2 extends java.applet.Applet{
  public String doAmazonKeywordSearch(final String token,final String keyword){
    PrivilegedAction pA= new PrivilegedAction(){
      public Object run() {
        try{return XmlHttp.doAmazonKeywordSearch(token,keyword);
        } catch(Exception e) {e.printStackTrace(); return ""+e; }
      }
    };
    return (String)AccessController.doPrivileged(pA);
  }
} // end of AmazonApplet_2
```

Either version, when run from the page shown in Listing 3-23 (within a frameset) produces the output of Figure 3-5.

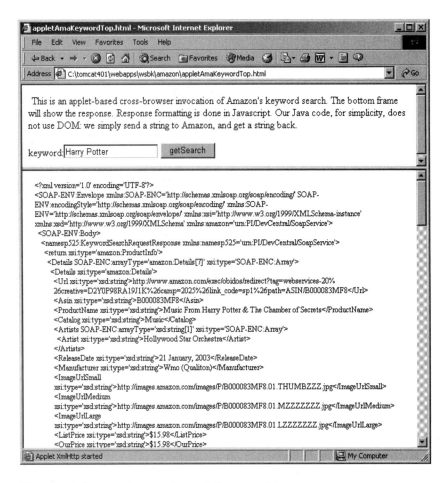

*Figure 3-5. Amazon keyword search from applet*

*Listing 3-23. Page with Applet, Source for the Top Frame of Figure 3-5*

```
<html><head><title>appletAmaKeyword1Ctl.html</title>
<applet name="XmlHttp"
  height="2"
  width="2"
  code="soapUtil/AmazonApplet_1.class"
>
</applet></head><body>
<script src="../utils/key.js"></script><!-- contains token -->
<script src="../utils/xmlhttp.js"></script>
<script>
function doAmazonKeywordSearch(token,keyword){
```

```
    var res=document.XmlHttp.doAmazonKeywordSearch(token,keyword);
    var ob=parseXML(res);
    res=xml2HtmlPage(ob);
    with(parent.dataFrame)
      {document.write(res);document.close();}
}
</script>
This is an applet-based cross-browser invocation of Amazon's
keyword search...
<form name="theForm" action="javascript:void">
  keyword:<input type="text" name="keyword" value="Harry Potter"/>
<input type="button" value="getSearch"
  onclick="doAmazonKeywordSearch(amazonToken,this.form.keyword.value);"/>
</form>
</body></html>
```

We use the same Javascript functions, parseXml() and xml2HtmlPage() to pretty-print the incoming XML code.

## Applet Generalized

Our next step is to rewrite the applet using the service-independent sendSoap() that we used in the command-line application. The idea is to put the code of the Soaper class and sendSoap() into a SoapApplet that will be completely ignorant of any specific Web Services. To create a client for a service, we will extend SoapApplet and call its sendSoap() method.

The code of SoapApplet.java is in Listing 3-24.

*Listing 3-24. Web-Service-Independent SoapApplet*

```
package soapUtil;
import java.security.*;

public class SoapApplet extends java.applet.Applet{
  class Soaper implements PrivilegedAction {
    String urlString;String soapAction;String payload;
    public Soaper(String u,String a,String p){
      urlString=u;soapAction=a;payload=p;
    }
    public Object run(){
      try{return XmlHttp.sendSoap(urlString,soapAction,payload);
      } catch(Exception e) {e.printStackTrace(); return ""+e; }
```

```
      }
      public String sendSoap(){
        return (String)AccessController.doPrivileged(this);
      }
    }
    public String sendSoap(String url,String act,String env){
      return new Soaper(url,act,env).sendSoap();
    }
  }
```

With SoapApplet taking care of security arrangements, the Amazon applet can be reduced to bare essentials, as in AmazonApplet_3.java, shown in Listing 3-25. If run from the page of Listing 3-23, it will produce exactly the same result as in Figure 3-5.

*Listing 3-25. Amazon Keyword Search Using SoapApplet*

```
package soapUtil;
  // we do NOT need to import the security classes here.

public class AmazonApplet_3 extends SoapApplet{
  public String doAmazonKeywordSearch(String token,String keyword){
    return sendSoap(
        "http://soap.amazon.com/onca/soap",
        "KeywordSearchRequest",
        XmlHttp.doAmazonKeywordSearchEnvelope(token,keyword)
                  );
  }
}
```

## Multi-Service Applet

The code in Listings 3-24 and 3-25 completely separates the security arrangements for using an applet to send SOAP messages from the specifics of creating a SOAP message for a given service. This makes it possible to design a page that, in effect, offers a menu of services to connect to, and uses the same SoapApplet to connect to them all. Such a page, with forms for three services, is shown in Figure 3-6.

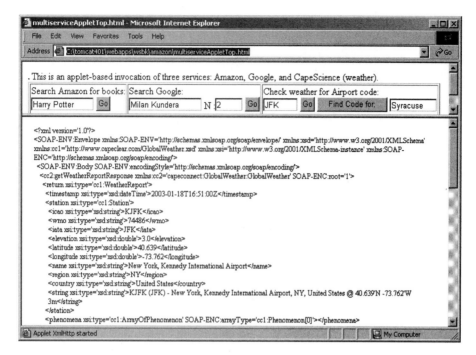

*Figure 3-6. Multi-service applet*

The code for the top frame, file `multiserviceAppletCtl.html`, is shown in Listings 3-26 and 3-27. Listing 3-26 shows the top elements of the page and Javascript code.

*Listing 3-26. Multiple Services from* `multiServiceAppletCtl.html`

```
<html><head><title>multiserviceAppletCtl.html</title>
<applet
  name="XmlHttp"
  height="2" width="2"
  code="soapUtil/SoapApplet.class" >
</applet>
</head><body>
<script src="../utils/key.js">
  /* included for amazonToken and google "key" */
</script>
<script src="../utils/xmlhttp.js">
  /* included for parseXML, xml2Html, and Envelope functions */
</script>
<script>
```

```
function showRes(res){
  displayXML(parseXML(res),parent.dataFrame);
}
function doAmazonKeywordSearch(token,keyword){
  if(!confirm("amazonSearch("+token+","+keyword+")"))
    return false;
  showRes(document.XmlHttp.sendSoap(
      "http://soap.amazon.com/onca/soap",
      "KeywordSearchRequest",
      doAmazonKeywordSearchEnvelope(token,keyword)));
  return false;
}
// two more such functions for Google and weathre services
</script>
```

Listing 3-27 shows the rest of the page, with omissions.

*Listing 3-27. The Rest of* multiServiceAppletCtl.html, *with a Sample Form*

```
This is an applet-based invocation of three services: Amazon, Google, and
CapeScience (weather).
<table border="1"><tr><td>
<form name="AmaKey"
  action="javascript:void"
  onSubmit=
    "return doAmazonKeywordSearch(amazonToken,document.AmaKey.keyword.value);"
>
Search Amazon for books:<br/>
<input type="text" size="12" name="keyword" value="Harry Potter"/>
<input type="submit" value="Go" />
</form></td>
<!-- two more forms for the other two services -->
</tr></table>
</body></html>
```

The applet code is the same as before. This concludes our discussion of the multi-service applet.

# Conclusion

In this chapter, we developed two fairly general frameworks for building Web Services clients, one in Javascript using xmltttp, the other in Java using an applet that combines two ideas: privileged access, so an applet can access a Web Service URL and an XML-over-HTTP tool that simplifies sending SOAP messages from an applet. You can use either of these to write a client for any Web Service, but you have to know how to formulate the SOAP envelope for a given request.

We illustrated our generic facilities with Web Service clients for two new Web Services: a weather service and the Amazon collection of services. We will be building more interesting clients for both. In addition to building more interesting clients, there are several directions we can go from here.

First, we want to start small SOAP services of our own. We'll show you how to do this without involving a full-scale Web Server at all; instead we will expose a small database as a service that combines local and Amazon data. After developing a bare-bones version, we will elaborate on it and add user authentication. We will also use this application to introduce the distinction between SOAP and REST-based Web Services. Our application will support both, just as Amazon Web Services do. This material will be discussed in Chapters 4 and 5.

Next, we will bring in another great tool, eXtensible Stylesheet Language for Transformations (XSLT). XSLT is very good at transforming XML structures, including SOAP message, but it is easier to invoke within the REST approach. Our application, just like Amazon's Web Services, will support server-side XSLT for REST only. This material is covered in Chapter 6. In Chapter 7, we will introduce the Apache Tomcat Web server and show you how to use JavaServer Pages (JSPs) to provide REST access to a SOAP service. This will make it possible to apply XSLT scripts to SOAP messages. In Chapter 7, we will also set up a WebDAV service as an extension of the REST approach. (DAV stands for Distributed Authoring and Versioning; it is an IETF standard based on an extension of the HTTP protocol.)

In Chapter 8, we'll use Tomcat's WebDAV filter concept to set up a community repository of searchable documents. The documents are first saved as HTML from any convenient word processor and later converted into XML data by a program called Tidy. (Tidy is a W3C project by Dave Ragget that is now open-source at http://tidy.sourceforge.net/.) With Tidy as our tool, we can start mining the Web, taking data from one XML source, and using it to invoke another. This is the most ambitious application of the book, with many potential uses.

Finally, in Chapter 9 we will return to our SOAP roots, and show you how to automate the development of SOAP clients using the Web Services Description Language (WSDL). With the Apache Axis tools we use in this book or with Microsoft's .NET and other tools, you can often look at a Web Service, ask it for its WSDL description, and generate a client stub for it, greatly simplifying coding Web Service clients. Theoretically this can be done without ever reading any XML, but in an example of any complexity, things will go wrong and require post-editing. In Chapter 9, we show you both a simple case in which everything works as intended, and the kind of post-editing that is needed in more complex cases, including the WSDL description of our Chapter 5 service.

# CHAPTER 4

# DBService and
# a Book Club

Now that we have created a few SOAP clients, we are going to create a SOAP server. The server will provide a database service, accept SQL queries wrapped in SOAP messages, and return query results (or SOAP faults). We will call it DBService.

Why would such a service be useful? We can think of at least four reasons, and others may well come up in later chapters.

- Interoperability: The database can provide its service to clients written in any language and running on any platform.

- Security: As some system administrators have found over the past few years, it is a bad idea to let your database be visible to the outside world. Our DBService will expose its database only to pre-approved queries from pre-approved places, that is, only to the extent that we're willing to risk.

- Local-cache: The DBService can be used as a local cache to reduce bandwidth use. Because both Google and Amazon restrict access to their services, a local cache can be very useful.

- Flexibility: DBService can easily combine data from other services with local data from approved database users.

For instance, a book club can use the DBService to combine Amazon data with locally produced book reviews and ratings. We present such a book club application in this chapter. Its client code is Javascript based on xmlhttp.js, and the server is written in Java, but even if you have not done any programming in Java you should be able to read and understand its code.

In this chapter, we will cover the following:

- The application demonstrated

- The main components of the application

- Server initialization from an XML configuration file

- Socket management

- HTTP and SOAP processing: sending and receiving messages

- Database management from Java: the JDBC APIs

- Returning the response to the client

We don't discuss the client code at all because it has relatively few new ideas.

## The Book Club Application

The client for the book club application looks as shown in Figure 4-1.

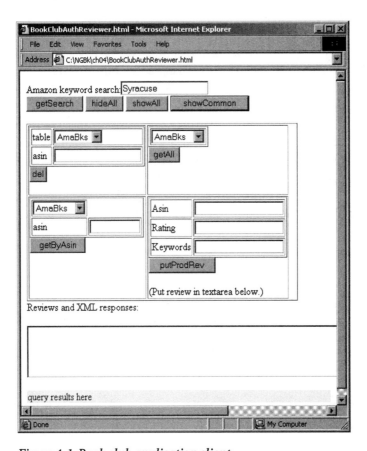

*Figure 4-1. Book club application client*

This client supports two main use cases. In one of them, a registered book club member adds a record to the book club database. In the other, a reader queries the database for information. The first use case proceeds as follows:

1. The user queries the Amazon database using keywords, as in the last application of Chapter 3.

2. The results of the query are displayed in a table similar to the one shown in Chapter 3 except that each row of the table has an additional cell with a button in it. Clicking the button copies the row's data to the Book Club database. (Only fields present in the Amazon table of the Book Club database are copied.)

3. The user adds local information to the book record copied from Amazon. Specifically, the user fills out the fields for User ID, Rating, Keywords, and a review. (The review is entered in a text area with simple formatting capabilities for a paragraph break, boldface, italics, and a hypertext link.) Clicking the Submit button sends the information to the Reviews table of the Book Club database.

To make sure the review is in the database, the user may want to go through the second use case and enter some query data into the search form and submit. The table of query results is displayed.

Although the two use cases are quite different, they are processed by the same code and follow the same path through software components and data formats. We will trace that path in the next section.

## Main Components, in Order of Appearance

The application springs into action when the client generates a SOAP envelope and sends it as the body of an HTTP message using xmlhttp, exactly as in Chapter 3. The differences begin on the other end. In Chapter 3, when an HTTP message is sent to a specific port on a specific host, the receiver is a Web Server that listens to HTTP messages on that port. More precisely, at the byte level, the software object that listens to traffic on a given port is called a socket; the socket passes the raw bytes to the Web server to interpret as an HTTP message (shown in Figure 4-2).

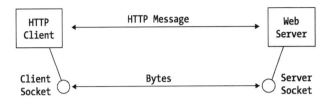

*Figure 4-2. HTTP and sockets*

The default port for HTTP communication is 80 but you can specify any port in the URL, as in `http://localhost:8080/index.jsp`. Even when a port other than 80 is used, the software listening to that port is usually a Web Server—but not in the Book Club application. In this application, we take control of the socket (which is easy to do in Java) and pass the raw bytes to our DBService directly (as shown in Figure 4-3) to interpret as a SOAP message inside an HTTP message.

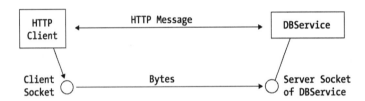

*Figure 4-3. HTTP, sockets, and DBService*

In other words, the DBService has an outer layer that functions as a very simple Web Server in that it parses the HTTP message. It separates its headers from the body and sends the body (which is a SOAP envelope) to the next layer, a SOAP service. The SOAP service parses the SOAP envelope, extracts the procedure call and parameters, and invokes the procedure. Then the action moves on to the database component of the service that handles the traffic between the SOAP service and the database. The service sends an SQL query and receives the query result, represented as a text string that is, in fact, an XHTML table element. The service integrates the query result into a SOAP message, integrates the SOAP message into an HTTP message, and sends it back to the client. This sequence of actions is shown in Figure 4-4.

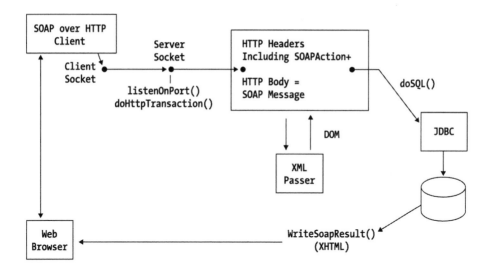

*Figure 4-4. Main components and data transformations*

Much of the rest of the chapter is a more detailed examination of the data path shown in Figure 4-4. Transitions along that path are executed by methods of the DBService class. Before data can begin to flow, we have to start the service by creating an instance of the class and telling it to listen for incoming SOAP messages. This is done by starting the application from the command line on the server.

## Service Startup

Java command-line applications start in the main() method of the class whose name is the name of the application. If your application is called MyApp, there must be a class called MyApp whose object code is in the file MyApp.class, compiled from the source file MyApp.java. The class must have a main() method with a specific signature. (The signature of a method is the data type of its return value and the data type(s) of its argument(s)). In the case of main(), there is no return value and its single argument is an array of strings.

```
public static void main(String[]args)
```

This says that the method is public and therefore visible from outside the class. It is static, which means you don't have to create an instance of the class in order to call the method. Its argument is an array of string objects that are command-line arguments to the application call. For instance, note the following example:

```
java MyApp abc 17 true
```

In this example, args[0] is "abc," arg[1] is "17," and args[2] is "true." If you run your application without any command arguments, the args array is empty and its length is 0.

In our case, the application is called DBService, and it can be invoked in one of the following three ways:

```
java DBService
java DBService someXmlConfigFile.xml
java DBService someXmlConfigFile.xml serviceArg1 serviceArg1 ...
```

If the application call has any arguments at all, the first argument (which becomes args[0]) must be the name of an XML configuration file that is used to create an instance of the DBService class. If there are no arguments, a default XML configuration file is used. If there is more than one argument, the arguments following the XML file are interpreted as arguments to a SOAP remote procedure call, and the first call to the service takes place immediately at startup.

The main() method of the DBService class is in shown in Listing 4-1.

*Listing 4-1. The* main() *Method of DBService*

```
public static void main(String[]args)throws Exception{
  String fileName="DBServiceConfig.xml"; // default XML configuration file
  if(args.length > 0) // an alternative configuration file is supplied
    fileName=args[0];
// create an instance of DBService using an XML decoder
  XMLDecoder xmlDecoder=
      new XMLDecoder(new FileInputStream(fileName));
  DBService dbService=(DBService)xmlDecoder.readObject();
// if there are additional arguments, call the service
  if(args.length > 1){
// copy command-line args to a new array
    ArrayList aL=new ArrayList();
    for(int i=1;i<args.length;i++)
      aL.add(args[i]);
// call doSQL method of the service, output result to the screen
```

```
    dbService.doSQL(aL,new PrintWriter(System.out,true));
  }
// start DBService listening to incoming SOAP requests
// on port specified in the XML configuration file
  dbService.listenOnPort();
} // end of main()
```

We will revisit this code after we work through the rest of the application, and many details will become more meaningful in the accumulated context. In the meantime, note the following:

- The method checks to see if there are any arguments; if so, an alternative XML config file is used.

- To create an instance of the class from an XML file, we use an XML decoder object, which is an instance of the XMLDecoder class. As of version 1.4, this class is part of the Standard Edition of the Java Development Kit, j2sdk1.4. We will inspect the XML encoding of Java objects in a separate section.

- If there are extra command-line arguments, they are copied to a new array and the service is invoked. To invoke the service, you call its doSLQ() method. The method takes two arguments: an array we create and a destination for the returned result. A later section of this chapter explains Java IO and streams.

Finally, the method tells the service to begin listening on a specific port. This is because our service is not invoked via a standard Web Server but through a direct socket-to-socket communication. In effect, our service *is* a web server. This is explained in the next section.

## Sockets and Ports

As explained earlier, the byte-level connection between two nodes on the Internet connects objects called sockets. There are two kinds of sockets: client sockets and server sockets. Client sockets initiate a connection by contacting a server socket. A server socket is associated with a specific host and a specific port on that host (so that hosts can carry on more than one communication at a time). Client sockets associated with HTTP clients indicate the server socket they want to contact in their destination URIs, which contain the name of the host or its IP address and the port number, for example, http://localhost:65432.

Client sockets are represented in Java by java.net.Socket class objects. Server sockets are represented java.net.ServerSocket class objects. To create a server socket on port 65432, for example, you say the following:

```
serverSocket=new ServerSocket(65432);
```

To have our server socket listen for HTTP messages on its port, we start an infinite loop that calls the socket's accept() method (shown in Listing 4-2). That method blocks (is not executed) until a client socket is detected trying to connect. At that point, the method returns a socket object representing the client. We call the badSocket() method, which checks that the client is not one we don't want to talk to (currently the method does nothing and returns false). If the client is not bad, we call doHttpTransaction() and give it the client socket as an argument.

*Listing 4-2. Server Socket Listening*

```
protected void listenOnPort()throws Exception{
  if(serverSocket==null) // socket has not been created yet
    initSocket();
  Socket clientSocket=null;
  try{
    while(true){ // infinite loop, listening
      try{
        clientSocket=serverSocket.accept();
        if (badSocket(clientSocket)){ // security checks can go here
          closeSocket(clientSocket);
          continue;}
      }catch(Exception ex){
        System.out.println("DBService failed to accept on "+
                          getPortNumber()+": "+ex);
        System.exit(1);
      }
      doHttpTransaction(clientSocket);
      }
    }catch(IOException e){e.printStackTrace();}
}
```

To understand how doHttpTransaction()works, we need to make a detour to cover Java IO and its collection of streams.

## Java IO and Streams

All Java IO is performed in a uniform way, by using APIs via objects called streams. Whether the data comes from a keyboard, a file, or an Internet connection, it arrives via an input stream that is associated with the data source. It works similarly for output. All input streams have a read() method that reads the next byte or the next character, depending on the stream. Specialized streams have methods like readLine(), which reads the next line of characters; readDouble(), which reads the next double value; or even readObject(), which reads the next (serialized) object from an object stream.

All Java streams are divided into four groups based on two characteristics: input vs. output streams, and byte vs. character streams. There are, correspondingly, four general stream classes.

- Byte stream: InputStream

- Byte stream: OutputStream

- Character stream: Reader

- Character stream: Writer

In addition to these general classes, there are a number of other streams with more specific capabilities. For instance, to read data from files, you use FileInputStream or FileReader; to read data in chunks that are accumulated in a buffer (for improved performance, among other reasons) you use BufferedReader or BufferedInputStream, and so on. To create a buffered reader that can read characters line by line from the text file textData.txt, you proceed as follows:

```
FileReader fReader = new FileReader("textData.txt");
BufferedReader bfReader = new BufferedReader(fReader);
```

You can combine these into a single line of code.

```
BufferedReader bfReader = new BufferedReader(new FileReader("textData.txt"));
```

With a buffered reader in place, you can read the first line of the file.

```
String firstLine = bfReader.readLine();
```

## Bytes and Characters

The distinction between byte and character streams deserves an explanation. Java characters are Unicode. Each Unicode character is a 16-bit number called a "code point." These 16-bit numbers can be represented in different ways called Unicode Transfer Formats or UTF for short. Two most common formats are UTF-16, in which each code point is represented by two bytes, and UTF-8, which is a variable-length format—the most frequently used characters are represented by a single byte, whereas less frequently used characters are represented by two or three bytes. The most frequently used characters are, of course, those of the ASCII table; UTF-8 represents them by a single byte and is backward compatible with ASCII.

In addition to Unicode characters, Java character streams support (more or less successfully) a variety of single byte character encodings such as ISO or ANSI standards, and proprietary (but widely used) formats from IBM, Microsoft and Apple. (These are sometimes called code pages or CP for short, such as the CP-1251 for Windows Cyrillic characters.)

Suppose you have a byte input stream `myInStream` that is carrying character data. In order to read data from the stream as characters rather than bytes, you have to convert that byte input stream into a character stream, as follows:

```
Reader myReader = new InputStreamReader(myInStream, "utf-8");
```

This tells the program to read the bytes from myInStream as characters encoded in UTF-8 standard.

## Socket Communications

Back to sockets. The Socket class hides all the complexities of Internet communication into two methods, `getInputStream()` and `getOutputStream()`. The methods return byte streams attached to client socket, and all subsequent input operations use the standard stream APIs so neither the program nor the programmer has to remember where a particular stream of data is coming from. We would, however, know that it is an HTTP connection delivering and expecting character data in UTF-8 encoding (a reasonable choice for Web interactions). So our `doHttpTransaction()` starts by creating appropriate character streams (shown in Listing 4-3).

*Listing 4-3.* doHTTPTransation() *Part 1: Create Streams for Sockets*

```
public void doHttpTransaction(Socket clientSocket)
    throws Exception{
  OutputStream os=null;
  BufferedOutputStream bos=null;
  PrintWriter pW=null;
  try{
    InputStream is=clientSocket.getInputStream();
    BufferedInputStream bis = new BufferedInputStream(is);
    InputStreamReader reader=new InputStreamReader(bis,"utf-8");
    os=clientSocket.getOutputStream();
    bos = new BufferedOutputStream(os);
    pW=new PrintWriter(new OutputStreamWriter(bos,"utf-8"),true);
```

With a buffered InputStreamReader and a PrintWriter in place, we can read in the HTTP request, process it, and send the response back to the client socket. We encapsulate these tasks into two methods, readHttpData() and doPost(), shown in Listing 4-4.

*Listing 4-4.* doHTTPTransation() *Part 2: Use Streams to Do HTTP*

```
// read HTTP data into a hashtable
    Hashtable httpData=readHttpData(reader);
    if(!authorized(httpData)) // a hook to do authorization
      throw new Exception("authorization failure:\n"+httpData);
    String cmd=(String)httpData.get("METHOD");
    if("POST".equals(cmd))
// the rest of the processing done here
      doPost(httpData, pW);
    else // other commands are used in the next chapter's version
      throw new Exception("unknown command ["+cmd+
                          "]; only POST supported in this version");
    reader.close(); bis.close(); is.close();
    pW.close(); pW=null; bos.close(); os.close();
  }catch(Exception ex){
    if(pW!=null){
      sendExceptionFault(ex,pW);
      pW.close();bos.close();os.close();
    }
  }
} // end of doHttpTransaction
```

If something goes wrong with processing HTTP request, we call sendExceptionFault() to construct and send back a SOAP fault message. It follows the familiar pattern: the SOAP message is constructed as a string and sent back to the client, after the command line and the headers of the HTTP response message. In Listing 4-5, we skip a few familiar lines of the SOAP header.

*Listing 4-5. SOAP Fault Message*

```
protected void sendExceptionFault(Exception ex,PrintWriter pW){
StringBuffer sB=new StringBuffer();
sB.append("<?xml version='1.0' encoding='UTF-8'?>\n")
  .append("<SOAP-ENV:Envelope \n")
...
  .append(" <SOAP-ENV:Body>\n")
  .append("   <SOAP-ENV:Fault>\n")
  .append("     <SOAP-ENV:faultcode>")
  .append(42).append("</SOAP-ENV:faultcode>\n")
  .append("     <SOAP-ENV:faultstring>internal error</SOAP-ENV:faultstring>\n")
  .append("     <SOAP-ENV:detail>\n").append(ex.toString())
  .append("</SOAP-ENV:detail>\n")
  .append("   </SOAP-ENV:Fault>\n")
  .append(" </SOAP-ENV:Body>\n")
  .append("</SOAP-ENV:Envelope>\n");
  String msg=sB.toString();
  pW.print("HTTP/1.0 500 Server Error: Malformed HTTP Request \r\n");
  pW.print("Content-Type: text/xml; charset=utf-8\r\n");
  pW.print("Content-Length: "+msg.length()+"\r\n\r\n");
  pW.print(msg);
  pW.flush();
}
```

At this point we are done with socket communications. The action moves to processing HTTP data, extracting the SOAP message from it, and acting upon it.

# Processing HTTP Request

As you recall, an HTTP request has the following structure:

- Line 1: *command uri http-version*

- Several non-blank lines: *header-name* : *header-value*

- A blank line consisting of two characters, CarriageReturn and LineFeed, ASCII 10 and 13, denoted \r and \n in Java code

- The body of the message, possibly empty, but in our case containing the SOAP payload

The readHttpData() method processes an HTTP request and stores its data in a Java hashtable object for easy retrieval. Its operation is fairly transparent, but there is one little quirk: instead of the readLine() method of Java-buffered character streams, we use our own readLine(), shown in Listing 4-6. The reason is that Java's built-in readLine() recognizes system dependent end-of-line markers that are different in different operating systems, whereas we want to recognize the HTTP-specific \r\n sequence.

*Listing 4-6.* readLine() *for HTTP Data*

```
public String readLine(Reader reader) throws Exception{
  StringBuffer sB=new StringBuffer();
  int ch;
  for(ch=reader.read();ch>=0 && ch!='\r';ch=reader.read())
    sB.append((char)ch);
  if(ch<0) // read() returns -1 on end of file
    return sB.toString();
  ch=reader.read();
  if(ch!='\n')
    throw new Exception("line ["+sB.toString()+"] lacks \\n");
  return sB.toString();
}
```

The readHttpData() method parses the first line and then parses and stores header lines until it finds the blank line separating the headers from the body. The body is stored as PAYLOAD. In this method, we don't use any headers except Content-Length to control the loop that reads in the body of the message. To make sure ContentLength has a value, we initialize it to 0, as shown in Listing 4-7.

*Listing 4-7. Read HTTP Request from Stream, Store in Hashtable*

```
public Hashtable readHttpData(Reader reader)throws Exception{
  ArrayList httpHeaderList=new ArrayList();
  Hashtable hashtable=new Hashtable();
  hashtable.put("Content-Length","0"); // default
// read and process the first line (command line)
  String cmdLine=readLine(reader);
  int firstBlank=cmdLine.indexOf(' ');
  int lastBlank=cmdLine.lastIndexOf(' ');
  if(firstBlank < 0 || firstBlank == lastBlank)
    throw new Exception("Invalid HTTP method line ["+cmdLine+"]");
  hashtable.put("METHOD",cmdLine.substring(0,firstBlank));
  hashtable.put("URL",cmdLine.substring(1+firstBlank,lastBlank));
  hashtable.put("HTTP",cmdLine.substring(1+lastBlank)); // HTTP version
// read headers, store in hashtable
  String hdr=readLine(reader);
  while(hdr.length()>0){
    String[]nameVal=hdr.split(": ",2); // split at colon, two items at most
    if(nameVal.length > 1)hashtable.put(nameVal[0],nameVal[1]);
    hdr=readLine(reader);
  }
// get Content-Length from the Hashtable
  int len=Integer.parseInt((String)hashtable.get("Content-Length"));
// read and store HTTP body in Hashtable
  String httpBody = readUpToLength(reader,len);
  hashtable.put("PAYLOAD", httpBody);
  return hashtable;
}
```

With the HTTP request parsed and packaged and an output character stream attached to the client socket, we can leave the world of HTTP behind. The hashtable and the PrintWriter are all we need for SOAP messaging and database access. They are the two arguments that are passed to doPost() (shown in Listing 4-8). doPost(), in turn, passes them on to doDBServiceCall() after checking that the HTTP message has a soapAction header.

*Listing 4-8.* doPost()

```
public void doPost(Hashtable httpData,PrintWriter pW)throws Exception{
  String soapAction=(String)httpData.get("SOAPAction");
  if("DBServerCall".equals(soapAction))
    doDBServiceCall(httpData,pW);
  else
    throw new Exception("POST with unknown SOAPAction:["+soapAction+"]");
}
```

doDBServiceCall() does all the remaining work.

## Parse SOAP, Return Query Result

The code of doDBServiceCall() can serve as an outline for the rest of the chapter.

- Extract the SOAP message from the HTTP message

- Parse the SOAP message as an XML document

- Extract the parameters of the SOAP call into an array

- Run the database query

- Write the results of the query to output

Except for the database query, we will cover each of these items in the current section, starting with doDBServiceCall() itself (shown in Listing 4-9).

*Listing 4-9.* doDBServiceCall()

```
public void doDBServiceCall(Hashtable httpData,PrintWriter pW)
    throws Exception{
// retrieve the HTTP body ("PAYLOAD") from the hashtable
  String docString=(String) httpData.get("PAYLOAD");
// parse SOAP message as XML, get DOM Document
  Document doc=readDocument(docString);
// extract parameters of SOAP call into an array
  ArrayList arrayList=getSOAPParams(doc);
// do database query, return result as an XML String
  String soapRes=doSQL(arrayList);
// Integrate the SOAP result as SOAP body into
  writeSOAPResult(soapRes,pW);
} // end doPost()
```

As you can see, each item is encapsulated into a separate procedure. We will now discuss each item in the order of its appearance, one subsection per procedure.

## XML Parsing in Java

You saw XML parsing in Mozilla Javascript and IE JScript in Chapter 2, Listing 2-8. We repeat it here for comparison with the Java version.

*Listing 2-8. Parse an XML String into a DOM Object*

```
function parseXML(str){
  var doc=null;
  if(inIE){ // IE version
    doc=new ActiveXObject("Microsoft.XMLDOM");
    doc.loadXML(str); // does the parsing
  }
  else { // Mozilla/Netscape
    var domParser=new DOMParser();
    doc=domParser.parseFromString(str, "text/xml");
  }
  return doc; // .documentElement;
}
```

As we will explain in Chapter 8, the parsing process usually consists of two steps: obtain a parser object (which may or may not be called parser) and call its parse method (which may or may not be called parse). In Java, there is one more preliminary step: you obtain a "parser factory" that can be configured to produce a parser and set its properties. When you need a parser, you ask the parser factory for it. This way, you can have more than one parser available and your code is the same no matter which parser you use. Only the system property that specifies the parser factory needs to be changed to switch from one parser to another. The parser, incidentally, is called DocumentBuilder and the parser factory is DocumentBuilderFactory, both in the javax.xml package.

In the DBService class, DocumentBuilderFactory is a class variable, declared at the top level:

```
DocumentBuilderFactory dbf;
```

We obtain an instance of DocumentBuilderFactory in the getDBF() method, using the following line of code:

```
dbf=DocumentBuilderFactory.newInstance();
```

With a parser factory in place, the readDocument() method can obtain a parser object and parse (shown in Listing 4-10). An additional Java complication is that the argument to the parse() method has to be an object of class InputSource. To obtain such an object, we first convert our XML string to a character stream (StringReader), and give that stream as an argument to the InputSource constructor.

*Listing 4-10. Parse an XML string into a DOM object using DocumentBuilder*

```
public Document readDocument(String str)throws Exception{
  try{
    DocumentBuilder db=getDBF().newDocumentBuilder();
    InputSource is=new InputSource(new StringReader(str));
    Document doc=db.parse();
    return doc;
  }catch(Throwable ex){
    System.out.println("readDocument failure:"+ex);
    return null;
  }
}
```

Now that the SOAP message is parsed into a DOM object, we can take it apart and extract what we need from it.

## SOAP Parameters

To extract the parameters of our SOAP call, we pass the DOM object to getSOAPParams(), which uses the DOM getElementsByTagName() method to extract all <dbParam> elements into a NodeList object. That object has a getLength() method to find out how many items it contains and an item() method to yield an item at the specified index. The text content of an item is not stored in the item directly but in its child Text node. We go through a loop picking out each item in turn until we get to its first (and only) child to obtain the SOAP parameter (shown in Listing 4-11).

*Listing 4-11. Extract SOAP Parameters to an Array of String*

```
public ArrayList getSOAPParams(Document doc){
  NodeList nodeList=doc.getElementsByTagName("dbParam");
  ArrayList arrayList=new ArrayList();
  for(int i=0;i<nodeList.getLength();i++){
   Node child=nodeList.item(i).getFirstChild();
    String param="";
    if(child!=null)
       child.getNodeValue();
    arrayList.add(param);
  }
  return arrayList;
}
```

The parameters of the SOAP call now travel to the database to run the query, and the result of the query is returned as a string. The string becomes part of the output produced by writeSOAPResult().

## Output the Result of SOAP Call

This is largely familiar code: construct the SOAP envelope, construct the HTTP message, and send (shown in Listing 4-12).

*Listing 4-12. Output the Result of SOAP Call*

```
public void writeSOAPResult(String soapRes,PrintWriter pW)
    throws Exception{
// construct SOAP envelope that contains soapRes
  StringBuffer sB=new StringB uffer();
  sB.append("<?xml version='1.0' encoding='UTF-8'?>\n")
    .append("<SOAP-ENV:Envelope \n")
// SOAP-ENV attributes are appended here; start SOAP body
    .append(" <SOAP-ENV:Body>\n")
// append doSQLResponse element that contains soapRes
    .append("  <doSQLResponse>\n")
    .append(soapRes)  // result of SOAP call goes here
    .append("  </doSQLResponse>\n")
// append closing tags
    .append(" </SOAP-ENV:Body>\n")
    .append("</SOAP-ENV:Envelope>\n");
  soapRes=sB.toString();
```

```
// output HTTP command line and headers
  pW.print("HTTP 1.0 200 OK\r\n");
  pW.print("Content-Type: text/xml; charset=utf-8\r\n");
  pW.print("Content-Length: "+soapRes.length()+"\r\n");
  pW.print("Date: "+rfc1123DateFormat.format(new java.util.Date())+"\r\n");
  // pW.print("Date: Sun, 10 Feb 2002 22:19:37 GMT\r\n");
// output blank line and HTTP body, i.e., SOAP message
  pW.print("Server: DBService 0.11\r\n\r\n");
  pW.print(soapRes);
  pW.flush();
}
```

This completes our travels around the middle layer of the application. It is now time to penetrate into the database core where data is stored and retrieved from the database. The interaction between the middle layer and the core is encapsulated into the doSQL() method. Before we can tackle its code, we need to go over the general framework of interaction between a Java program and a database.

# Driver, Database, Connection, and Statement

Java libraries for database access are collectively known as JDBC, Java Database Connectivity. JDBC makes it possible to connect to a database from Java code, run SQL queries and process query results. This activity is encapsulated in such classes and interfaces as Connection, Statement, and ResultSet, among others. They are all found in the java.sql package, part of the JDK Standard Edition.

## JDBC Driver

As you know, different database vendors may implement different functionality and support slightly different flavors of SQL. JDBC aims to be vendor-independent. The key to vendor independence is a **JDBC driver**, a software package produced by database or third-party vendors that encapsulate DBMS-specific features. (For instance, it switches between DBMS-specific data types and JDBC data types.) A list of over 150 JDBC drivers is available at http://industry.java.sun.com/products/jdbc/drivers; some of them are free, others are commercial products. In addition, Sun provides a JDBC-ODBC bridge as part of the standard Java distribution. This bridge makes it possible to connect to ODBC data sources using JDBC APIs. This is the driver you use to connect to an Access database or an Excel spreadsheet.

In our code, we store the name of the driver in the dbDriver variable. This variable is initially set to sun.jdbc.odbc.JdbcOdbcDriver, but this assignment is overridden by the XML configuration file. In that file, we specify a driver for the MySQLdatabase, which is what we use in the book.

JDBC drivers are usually distributed as .jar (Java archive) files. To install it, simply put the .jar file on your Java classpath. To use it, include a line like this in your code:

```
Class.forName(your--driver-name);
```

Because the name of the driver is stored in the dbDriver variable and the getDbDriver() method returns the value of that variable, in our code this line comes out (in our getDBConnection() method) as

```
Class.forName(getDbDriver());
```

Once the driver is instantiated, you can use JDBC code. A typical database access proceeds as follows:

1. Obtain a connection, typically from a connection pool.

2, Create a statement object to execute SQL statements.

3. Run a database session, execute statements, process result sets, and so on.

4. Close connection (or return it to the connection pool).

The following sections explain these steps and illustrate them with examples from our code. The first step is to obtain a connection to your database.

## Connections and Connection Pooling

The simplest way to obtain a connection is via a public static getConnection() method of the java.sql.DriverManager class. The method takes three parameters: the database URI, the username, and the password. The format of the database URI is specific to the JDBC driver in use. In the case of the JDBC-ODBC bridge, you must create a DSN (Data Source Name) using the ODBC manager and use that name as the database URI. Assuming that the DSN is "wsbkdb" and the user name and password are empty strings, you would obtain a connection by the following line of code:

```
Connection con=DriverManager.getConnection("jdbc:odbc:wsbkdb","","");
```

For the MySQL database and its driver, you specify the database URI like this (quoted from the XML configuration file):

```
jdbc:mysql://localhost:3036/wsbkdb
```

Here localhost is the host name of the computer on which the database is running, and wsbkdb is the name of the MySQL database. MySQL DBMS runs on port 3036 by default, so we could remove :3036 from the URL and it would make no difference.

Just as with the driver name, we store the database URI, the username, and the password in Java variables that we initialize from XML. Each variable has a get() and a set() public methods, as shown in Listing 4-13.

*Listing 4-13. Variables for Database Connection*

```
protected String dbURL="jdbc:odbc:wsbkdb";
  public void setDbURL(String S){dbURL=S;}
  public String getDbURL(){return dbURL;}
protected String dbUser="";
  public void setDbUser(String S){dbUser=S;}
  public String getDbUser(){return dbUser;}
protected String dbPwd="";
  public void setDbPwd(String S){dbPwd=S;}
  public String getDbPwd(){return dbPwd;}
```

With variables and access methods in place, we obtain a connection by the expression

```
DriverManager.getConnection(getDbURL(),getDbUser(),getDbPwd());
```

This expression is in our own getDBConnection() method. This method can be changed to use a more sophisticated method of managing connections called "connection pooling." Obtaining a connection is a computationally expensive operation that should be done as rarely as possible. With connection pooling, the application obtains a pool of connections in one action, typically at startup, and asks for another connection to be added to the pool only if the pool dries up. When a user asks for a connection, it is allocated from the pool, and when a user releases a connection, it is returned to the pool. In our code, releasing a connection is also encapsulated as a method, freeConnection(), that currently does nothing but can be rewritten to use connection pooling.

There are several connection pool implementations available, and the latest version of JDBC implements a standard API for managing a connection pool. To incorporate connection pooling in our application, you would only have to install the appropriate software and rewrite our getConnection() and freeConnection() methods.

## SQL Statements and Result Sets

Once you have a connection, you can obtain a statement object and run SQL statements. A typical sequence is shown in Listing 4-14.

*Listing 4-14. Statement and Query String*

```
    Statement stmt = con.createStatement();
// SQL to insert an author into record specified by Asin ID number
    String sqlStr=
"INSERT INTO AmaAuth (Asin,Author) VALUES (7346,'Jay Jones')";
    int numberUpdates=stmt.executeUpdate(sqlStr);
```

Note that character strings (but not integers) have to be quoted in the query string, so we use single quotes within double quotes. The returned integer, in this case 1, indicates the number of rows affected by the update. (If you were to delete 3 rows, the method would return 3.)

To run a SELECT query, you would use executeQuery() rather than executeUpdate(), and the returned value would be a ResultSet object that provides sequential access to the returned records. ResultSet has a next() method that returns the next record or null if you have reached the end of the record set. Within each record, individual fields are retrieved by getXX() methods, where XX stands for a data type: getInt(), getString(), and so on. The argument for all these methods is either an integer giving the number of the field in the record or the field's name in the database table.

In many situations, a better alternative to Statement is the JDBC Prepared-Statement. PreparedStatement has an SQL query imprinted on it at construction. It is more efficient than plain Statement because its SQL query is compiled once and can be reused many times with different parameters.

Consider a simple example. You have a database table that includes names and e-mail addresses and you want to retrieve the addresses by name. You created a database connection as described in the preceding section and you are ready to create a query string and a statement object. Assume that the name to search by is in the currentName variable. With plain Statement, you would create a query string like this

```
    "SELECT addr FROM addrBook WHERE name='" + currentName + "'"
```

Remember, you need single quotes within double quotes so the value of currentName comes out quoted in the resulting string. This is error-prone and may result in nasty complications: what if the name is "O'Donnell"? In addition, you have to remember to quote strings but not integers or dates unless you insert dates as strings. The PreparedStatement, is not only more efficient, it provides a simple and uniform way of filling in arbitrary parameters.

First, you create a query string with question marks as placeholders for parameters to be filled in, and you use the query string in creating your PreparedStatement.

```
String queryStr = "SELECT addr FROM addrBook WHERE name=?";
PreparedStatement prepStmt = conn.prepareStatement(queryStr);
```

Next, you fill in the value of the parameter using one of many datatype-specific procedures that are provided for that purpose: setString(), setInt(), setBlob(), setBoolean(), setDate(), or even setObject() in which we provide an arbitrary object and tell the database what standard SQL type to convert it to. In this case, we need setString().

```
// set the value of the first parameter of PreparedStatement to currentName
prepStmt.setString(1,currentName);
// run the query
ResultSet rs= prepStmt.executeQuery();
```

Note that executeQuery() does not take any arguments because the query string is already imprinted on the PreparedStatement and its parameter is already set. For UPDATE queries, you would again use executeUpdate() rather than executeQuery(). If you don't know what kind of query to expect, you can use the general execute() method that can execute both SELECT and UPDATE queries. It returns a Boolean value—true for SELECT queries and false for UPDATE ones. To extract the update count or the result set, use getUpdateCount() or getResultSet(). Let's work through an example from our code to see how it all fits together. In the course of the example, we will also take a first look at the XML encoding of Java code.

## *Prepared Statements and Our Method to Query Data*

Because each PreparedStatement is associated with a specific query, if you name a PreparedStatement, you in effect name a query. If the user can access the database only by selecting from a list of query names, you have restricted the database access to pre-approved queries that can be specified in the XML configuration file.

We develop this idea a little further by creating a hashtable of DBQueryData objects, where each object contains the following:

- The ID of a query

- The SQL text of the query

- The array of data types of the parameters of the query

For instance, recall the query of Listing 4-14:

```
"INSERT INTO AmaAuth (Asin,Author) VALUES (7346,'Jay Jones')"
```

The variables of the DBQueryData object for that query would be as shown in Listing 4-15.

*Listing 4-15. Variables of a DBQueryData Object*

```
qID: INS_AmaAuth (simply because that's what we decided to call it)
qStr: "INSERT INTO AmaAuth (Asin,Author) VALUES (?,?)"
qTypes: {INT, TEXT}
```

We create a hashtable of DBQueryData objects from an array of such objects in the method setQueryHashtable(), shown in Listing 4-16.

*Listing 4-16. Java Code to Create a Hashtable of DBQueryData Objects*

```java
public void setQueryHashtable(ArrayList SS){
    queryStrings=SS;
    queryHashtable=new Hashtable();
    if(SS==null) return;
    for(int i=0;i<queryStrings.size();i++){
        DBQueryData dbqd=(DBQueryData)(SS.get(i));
        String keyString=dbqd.getQID().toUpperCase();
        queryHashtable.put(keyString, dbqd);
    }
}
```

This is pretty straightforward, but there are two puzzling things about this method. First, where do we get an array of DBQueryData objects for our queries? Second, where is it called? If you inspect the text of DBService.java, you will see that setQueryHashtable() is defined but not invoked in that file. Both of these puzzling questions are answered if we look in the code of the XML configuration file, DBServiceConfig.xml.

# XML Encoding of Java Code

To construct the DBQueryData object of Listing 4-15, we could use the Java code of Listing 4-17.

*Listing 4-17. Java Code to Create a DBQueryData Object*

```
DBQueryData dbqd=new DBQueryData();
dbqd.setQID("INS_AmaAuth");
dbqd.setQStr("INSERT INTO AmaAuth (Asin,Author) VALUES (?,?)");
dbqd.setQTypes('INT,TEXT');
```

Note that this code uses a default no-argument constructor to create the empty shell of an object and a sequence of setXX() methods to set the object's properties. This is precisely the kind of code that XML encoding is good at. Instead of placing that code into the Java file, we include the text of Listing 4-18 into the XML configuration file.

*Listing 4-18. XML Encoding to Create a DBQueryData Object*

```
<object class="soapUtil.DBQueryData">
    <void method="setQID"><string>INS_AmaAuth</string></void>
    <void method="setQStr">
        <string>
          INSERT INTO AmaAuth (Asin,Author) VALUES (?,?)
        </string>
    </void>
    <void method="setQTypes"><string>INT,TEXT</string></void>
</object>
```

Note three simple conventions.

- To create an object of class MyClass, you include an XML element <object class="MyClass">. This invokes the default constructor of MyClass.

- To invoke a method myMethod() that returns void, you include an XML element <void method="myMethod">.

- The XML elements representing arguments to a method are contained in the element representing the method itself.

The code in Listing 4-18 creates one DBQueryData object for a single query. The setQueryHashtable() method of Listing 4-16 needs an array of such objects. We use a dynamic array class called ArrayList in Java; it has an add() method that adds elements to the array and returns void. The XML code to construct an array of DBQueryData objects has the following structure (shown in Listing 4-19).

*Listing 4-19. XML Encoding for an Array of* DBQueryData *Objects*

```
<object class="java.util.ArrayList">
   <void method="add">
     <object class="soapUtil.DBQueryData">
        <!-- code to create a single DBQueryData object goes here -->
     </object>
   </void>
   <!-- other <void method = "add"> elements go here, one for each query -->
</object> <!-- end of <object class="java.util.ArrayList"> element -->
```

The XML code that invokes setQueryHashtable() has the following structure (shown in Listing 4-20).

*Listing 4-20. XML Encoding for an Array of* DBQueryData *Objects*

```
<void method="setQueryHashtable">
  <!-- code of the preceding listing,
       representing the single argument of the method,
       goes here -->
</void>        <!-- end of void method="setQueryHashtable" element -->
```

The entire DBServiceConfig.xml file invokes the default constructor for DBService and sets the properties of the created DBService object. The overall structure of the file is best seen by looking at that file in the browser with all second-tier elements collapsed, as shown in Figure 4-5.

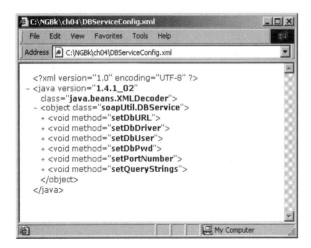

*Figure 4-5. XML configuration file in the browser*

From this screenshot, you can see the variables of the DBService class. XML encoding is described in http://java.sun.com/products/jfc/tsc/articles/ persistence3, and we will see more of it in the next chapter. For now, you can usefully compare the sample of Listing 4-18 to the Java code of Listing 4-17. We are ready to look at the code of doSql() and supporting methods.

## Database Access in DBService

The database access code in this chapter contains hooks for further improvements such as connection pooling or different access levels for different categories of users. Some of these improvements will be developed in Chapter 5; in this chapter we'll just get the basic functionality going.

We last saw doSql() method in Listing 4-9 where it was invoked from doDBServiceCall(), in the following lines of code:

```
// extract parameters of SOAP call into an array
  ArrayList arrayList=getSOAPParams(doc);
// do database query, return result as an XML String
  String soapRes=doSQL(arrayList);
```

We can now explain what parameters the SOAP client sends to the SOAP server. The first parameter is the name of the DBQueryData object for the Prepared-Statement to execute, and the rest are the parameter values to insert into that statement. Our plan is to use the name of the DBQueryData object to retrieve the object itself. From the object, we retrieve the query string and the data types array. We use these two items of information together with the parameter values supplied by the SOAP call to construct the PreparedStatement object, fill in its parameters, and run the query (shown in Listing 4-21).

*Listing 4-21.* doSql()

```
protected void doSQL(ArrayList nameParams, PrintWriter out)
    throws Exception{
  PreparedStatement pS=null;
  String qName=((String)nameParams.get(0)).toUpperCase();
  DBQueryData dbqd=(DBQueryData) queryHashtable.get(qName);
  if(dbqd==null)
    throw new Exception("ERR NO SUCH QUERY AS "+qName+"");
  String[]qTypes=dbqd.getQTypeArray();
  if(qTypes.length+1 !=nameParams.size())
    throw new Exception("Query ["+qName+"] expects "+qTypes.length+
                        " params, not "+(nameParams.size()-1));
// if we get here, we are ready to run the query
  Connection con = getDBConnection();
  try{
    pS=con.prepareStatement(dbqd.getQStr());
    for(int i=0;i<qTypes.length;i++)
      setParamStr(pS,i+1,(String)nameParams.get(i+1),qTypes[i]);
    if(pS.execute()) writeResultSet(pS.getResultSet(),out);
    else writeResultCount(pS.getUpdateCount(),out);
  } catch(Exception ex){
    throw new Exception("ERR doSQL("+qName+","+ex+")\n");
  }
  finally{
    if(pS!=null)try{pS.close();}catch(Exception ex){}
    pS=null;
    freeDBConnection(con);
  }
}
```

As you can see, setting the parameters is encapsulated into the setParamStr() method. The execution results are in a call on writeResultSet() (if a **ResultSet** has been returned) or on writeResultCount() (if the returned value is an integer showing the number of updated records). We will take these up next, in the remainder of this section.

The setParamStr() method sets the value of a query parameter in a PreparedStatement. As we mentioned, PreparedStatement has a number of setXX() methods for that purpose, each corresponding to a data type or a group of related data types. setParamStr() consists of a conditional with many branches that examine the value of the data type argument and invokes the corresponding setXX() method. Listing 4-22 shows the first three of the branches.

*Listing 4-22. Partial Listing of* setParamStr()

```
public void setParamStr(
    PreparedStatement pStmnt,
    int i,
    String pVal,
    String pType)  throws Exception{
  String t=pType;
  try{
// conditions for using setString()
    if(t==null || t.length()==0 ||"text".equalsIgnoreCase(t)
    ||"varchar".equalsIgnoreCase(t) || "string".equalsIgnoreCase(t))
      pStmnt.setString(i,pVal);
// conditions for using setObject()// allow for MS Access limitations
    else if("longtext".equalsIgnoreCase(t)||"longvarchar".equalsIgnoreCase(t))
      pStmnt.setObject(i,pVal,java.sql.Types.LONGVARCHAR);
// conditions for using setDate()
    else if(t.equalsIgnoreCase("date")){
      java.util.Date d=null;
      try{d=simpleDateFormat.parse(pVal);}
      catch(Exception ex){d=rfc1123DateFormat.parse(pVal);}
      java.sql.Date dbdate=new java.sql.Date(d.getTime());
      pStmnt.setDate(i,dbdate);
    }
// several more branches
    else pStmnt.setString(i,pVal);
  }catch(java.text.ParseException e){
    throw new
    SQLException("setParamStr failed to parse ["+pVal+"] as ["+t+":"+e);
  }catch(java.lang.NumberFormatException e){
    throw new
    SQLException("setParamStr failed to parse ["+pVal+"] as ["+t+":"+e);
  }catch(Exception e){
    throw new
```

```
                SQLException("setParamStr failed to set param "+i+
                                    ", ["+pVal+"] as ["+t+":"+e);
    }
}
```

Once the query parameters are set, we can run the query with the execute() method of PreparedStatement. As we mentioned, this method returns a Boolean value indicating whether the query returns a ResultSet (for SELECT queries) or an integer (for UPDATE queries and data definition operations such as CREATE TABLE). For an integer, we have only to say the following (in writeResultCount()):

```
out.println("<span class='updateCount'>"+count+"</span>\n");
```

For a ResultSet, however, we output a <table> (shown in Listing 4-23). In order to output a table, we need to know how many columns it will have, which is the number of fields requested by the query. We obtain this information from the ResultSetMetaData object associated with the ResultSet shown in Listing 4-23.

*Listing 4-23. The DBService* writeResultSet() *Method*

```
protected void writeResultSet(ResultSet res,PrintWriter out)throws Exception {
    try{
        out.println("<table border='1'>");
        ResultSetMetaData rsmd=res.getMetaData();
        int colCount=rsmd.getColumnCount();
        out.println("<tr>");
        for(int i=0;i<colCount;i++)
        out.println("<th>"+rsmd.getColumnName(i+1)+"</th>");
        out.println("</tr>\n");
        while(res.next()){
            out.println("<tr>");
            for(int i=0;i<colCount;i++)
                out.println("<td>"+xmlEncode(res.getString(i+1))+"</td>");
            out.println("</tr>\n");
        }
        out.println("</table>\n");
    }finally {
        if(res!=null)try{res.close();}catch(Exception ex){}
    }
}
```

This concludes our travels through the DBService. In the next chapter, we will re-implement and extend it. Before we end this chapter, we will fulfill the promise we made in the beginning of it and revisit the main() method of Listing 4-1, repeated here.

*Listing 4-1. The* main() *Method of DBService*

```
public static void main(String[]args)throws Exception{
  String fileName="DBServiceConfig.xml"; // default XML configuration file
  if(args.length > 0) // an alternative configuration file is supplied
    fileName=args[0];
// create an instance of DBService using an XML decoder
  XMLDecoder xmlDecoder=
      new XMLDecoder(new FileInputStream(fileName));
  DBService dbService=(DBService)xmlDecoder.readObject();
// if there are additional arguments, run the service
  if(args.length > 1){
// copy command-line args to a new array
    ArrayList aL=new ArrayList();
    for(int i=1;i<args.length;i++)
      aL.add(args[i]);
// call doSQL method of the service, output result to the screen
    dbService.doSQL(aL,new PrintWriter(System.out,true));
  }
// start DBService listening to incoming SOAP requests
// on port specified in the XML configuration file
  dbService.listenOnPort();
} // end of main()
```

As you can see, an instance of the service is created by running XMLDecoder on our XML configuration file. This invokes the default constructor and sets the properties of the service. If additional arguments are provided, we explicitly store them in an ArrayList and invoke doSql() with the ArrayList as the first argument. The second argument of the invocation is a PrintWriter wrapped around the System.out standard output stream that sends data to the screen. Finally, we start the normal operation of the service on its default port.

## Conclusion

In this chapter, we built a lightweight Web Service that is not specific to the kind of information it sends and receives. DBService is a fairly generic tool for integrating information from different sources. Because it was built in Java by using XML encoding, it is easy to configure in XML without changing the code. Because it is a wrapper for an all-purpose DBMS, it can do very sophisticated data retrieval and modification, including finely graduated access levels for different categories of users based on HTTP's standard password authentication. Because it is a SOAP service, it can communicate with any SOAP client.

In the next chapter, we will further pursue some of these options. We will also re-implement the service in pure HTTP without a SOAP level on top of it by using the HTTP commands GET, POST, PUT, and DELETE. This so-called REST (Representational State Transfer) approach is frequently compared and contrasted to SOAP, and we are going to look at the pros and cons of the two approaches. (Somewhat surprisingly, very few changes in code will be needed to re-implement DBService as a REST application.)

# CHAPTER 5

# Authentication and REST

IN THIS CHAPTER, we continue working with DBService and the book club application; we will use standard HTTP facilities to extend them in two ways. First, we will add authentication so different groups of users have different access privileges. We will distinguish three groups of users: *admins*, who can grant privileges and create tables; *members*, who can submit reviews and otherwise change tables; and *visitors*, who can only browse and look things up. We will show you how to use HTTP-based authentication and indicate ways to provide more robust security. The revised service is called DBAuthService, DBService with authentication.

Our second revision will be more drastic: we will re-implement DBAuthService without using the SOAP protocol. Instead of deploying a completely separate protocol on top of HTTP, we will make greater use of HTTP commands and URIs to provide the functionality of a Web Service. Although a SOAP-based Web Service uses the Web only as a convenient vehicle for SOAP messages (and could use e-mail or ftp or direct socket connections instead), in this chapter, we implement a Web Service using only the architecture of the Web.

The official name for that architecture is REST, short for Representational State Transfer. Roy Fielding introduced the name in his doctoral dissertation, found at `http://www.apache.org/~fielding/pubs/dissertation/top.htm`. REST uses the browser as an abstract machine that changes from one state to another in response to an HTTP message, subject to certain constraints. We will explain the rules of transition as we implement a RESTful Web Service. In the meantime, be aware that REST is an article of faith for some people, and SOAP is an article of faith for other people, and religious wars sometimes break out. We appreciate the Amazon position of providing support for both SOAP and REST because both have pros and cons, which we discuss later in the chapter.

In this chapter we will cover the following:

- DBAuthWalkthrough

- HTTP authentication and base64 encoding

- REST summary; SOAP vs. REST

- REST implementation of DBAuthService

- REST variations and common violations (the query string abuse)

We start by running through a simple scenario using the Book Club Reviewer application.

## BookClubReviewer in Action

Open BookClubReviewer.html, and click the showCommon button. You will see something similar to Figure 5-1.

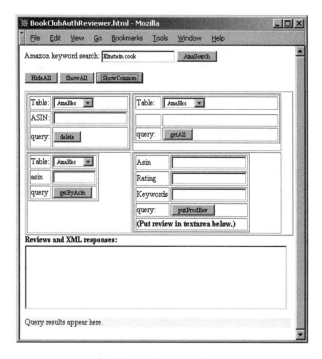

*Figure 5-1. Book club application client*

There are ten forms, including one at the top for doing Amazon keyword searches. There is a table of other forms, one for each type of Amazon query. The HideAll, ShowAll, and ShowCommon buttons control how many of these forms are visible. In Figure 5-1, with ShowCommon clicked, we see five forms that support the following actions:

- Run an Amazon query (at the top)

- Delete a record by its ASIN

- View the entire contents of a database table

- Look up a specific record or records by ASIN

- Submit a product review

Type **Einstein cook** in the input box for Amazon search and click AmaSearch. The result will be similar to Figure 5-2. The SOAP response appears in the text area and the results of the search appear below it.

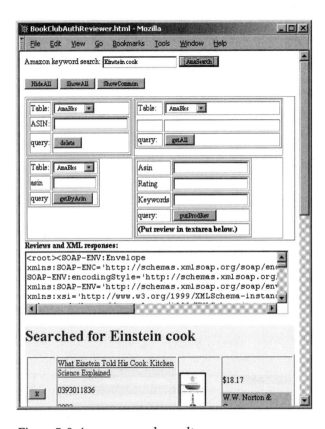

*Figure 5-2. Amazon search results*

If you click HideAll, you see much more of the search result, as shown in Figure 5-3.

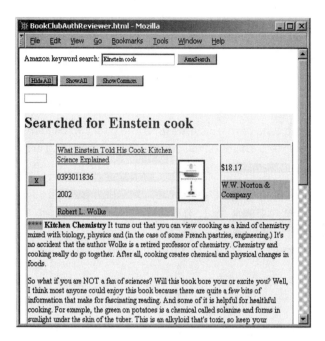

*Figure 5-3. Amazon search results with HideAll*

In this case, the result contains a single record. We formatted the output of that record as two table rows. The first row has the book's basic data, including ASIN, and the second row has readers' reviews from Amazon. (If more records had been returned, each one of them would be formatted this way.) This should be familiar material from earlier chapters. One new item is a button in the first (and every odd numbered) row. This button activates Javascript SOAP calls that put basic data about the ASIN into the tables called AmaBks (one row per ASIN) and AmaAuth (one row for each ASIN, author pair). Because this operation changes the database, a dialog box pops up to prompt the user for a username and passport. Enter **tjm** and **tjm** and submit. The query result area will show the number of records changed in the last call on DBService. (We added one record.) In addition, the program copied a few data fields into the putProdRevs form and the text of all customer reviews into the textarea (see Figure 5-4).

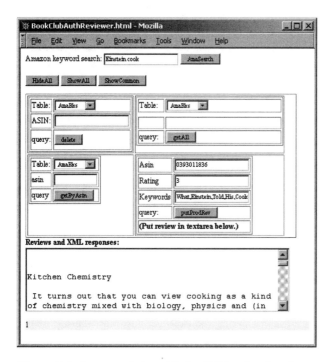

*Figure 5-4. Amazon data added to DBService database*

Now we are going to do something truly audacious and write our own review. We could reuse other people's reviews but in this case we won't. Instead, delete what's there (press Ctrl+A, and then Delete) and write a simple review: **This is a new and original review.** Change the rating to 5, and click putProdRev. Again a "1" appears at the bottom to indicate that one record has been changed. Note that this changes our local copy of the data, not the actual review on the Amazon.com server.

How can we check that our review has been added to the database? Copy the ASIN value into the form whose submit button reads getByAsin, use the drop-down list to select the ProdRevs table, and click the submit button. You will see several fields, including the time your review was submitted and the review itself, as shown in Figure 5-5.

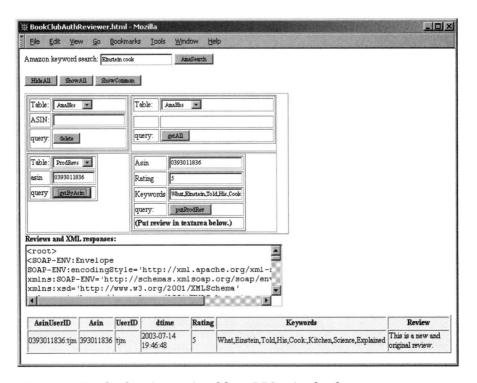

*Figure 5-5. New book review retrieved from DBService database*

If you suspect that this is all sleight of hand and wonder if there really is a database lurking somewhere in the background, keep reading, beginning with Authentication.

## HTTP User Authentication

The DBService of Chapter 4 provides security in two ways. It restricts the queries to be performed so you don't have to worry about people accessing areas of the data that you don't want to expose, and it allows you to restrict the IP addresses from which user connections arrive. However, it does not attempt to authenticate users. For a book club with reviews, that's bad—you might allow visitors to browse your database, but you want only members to be able to submit reviews. You also want to ensure that a user can't place a review in another user's name. Authentication provides this kind of security. It requires the user to enter a username and password to verify that the user is a member. Then that username is automatically inserted into a review record along with the book information and the timestamp of the review. In the version of the system shown in Chapter 4, the user inserted her ID as part of the query; in the authenticated version of this chapter, the ID is obtained by the system and plugged into the parameter specified by the config.xml file. We will go through the process of authentication before inspecting how the authentication data is stored and used.

## HTTP Transactions Revisited

Authentication is handled by the authorized() method called from doHttpTransaction() that we saw in Listing 4-4. We repeat it in Listing 5-1 with an important change: in Chapter 4, only the POST HTTP command was recognized and the rest resulted in error; this time, we also provide methods for handling GET, PUT, and DELETE. These methods will be covered in the REST section of this chapter. For now we concentrate on the authentication code.

*Listing 5-1.* doHTTPTransaction()

```
public void doHttpTransaction(Socket clientSocket) throws Exception{
  OutputStream os=null;
  BufferedOutputStream bos=null;
  PrintWriter pW=null;
  try{
// set up streams, as in Listing 4-4
    InputStream is=clientSocket.getInputStream();
    BufferedInputStream bis = new BufferedInputStream(is);
    InputStreamReader reader=new InputStreamReader(bis,"utf-8");
    os=clientSocket.getOutputStream();
    bos = new BufferedOutputStream(os);
    pW=new PrintWriter(new OutputStreamWriter(bos,"utf-8"),true);
// read HTTP data into hashtable, check authorization,
// throw an exception if authorized() returns false
    Hashtable httpData=readHttpData(reader);
    if(!authorized(httpData))
      throw new Exception("Authorization failure:\n"+httpData);
// if Authorization exception is not thrown, process HTTP data
    String cmd=(String)httpData.get("METHOD");
    if("POST".equals(cmd))doPost(httpData,pW);
    else if("GET".equals(cmd))doGet(httpData,pW);
    else if("PUT".equals(cmd))doPut(httpData,pW);
    else if("DELETE".equals(cmd))doDelete(httpData,pW);
    else
      throw new Exception("unknown command ["+cmd+
                                      "]; POST,GET,PUT,DELETE okay");
```

```
    reader.close(); bis.close();  is.close();
    pW.close(); pW=null; bos.close(); os.close();
  }catch(Exception ex){
    if(pW!=null){
      sendExceptionFault(ex,pW); // send SOAP fault based on Exception
      pW.close();bos.close();os.close();
    }
  } // end catch
}
```

If authorized() returns false, a Java exception is thrown, caught in the same method, and given as argument to sendExceptionFault(). In Chapter 4 (see Listing 4-5), that method  simply wrapped the Java exception into a SOAP fault message and sent. To handle authorization, we add a conditional in the beginning that checks to see whether the exception is caused by authorization failure, in which case sendAuthorizationException() is called (shown in Listing 5-2).

*Listing 5-2.* sendExceptionFault() *with Authorization Check*

```
protected void sendExceptionFault(Exception ex,PrintWriter pW){
// new in DBAuthService
  String message=ex.getMessage();
  if(message!=null && 0<=message.indexOf("Authorization")){
    sendAuthorizationException(ex,pW);
    return;
  }
// the rest is as in Listing 4-5
}
```

sendExceptionFault() sends an appropriate HTTP response rather than a SOAP fault. The response has the 401 Unauthorized error code and a WWW-authenticate header (shown in Listing 5-3).

*Listing 5-3.* sendAuthorizationException()

```
public void sendAuthorizationException(Exception ex,PrintWriter pW){
  StringBuffer sB=new StringBuffer();
  sB.append("<p>Security Error:"+ex+"</p>\n");
  String msg=sB.toString();
  pW.print("HTTP/1.0 401 Unauthorized\r\n");
  pW.print("WWW-Authenticate: Basic realm=\"DBAuthServer Data\"\r\n");
  pW.print("Content-Type: text/html; charset=utf-8\r\n");
  pW.print("Content-Length: "+msg.length()+"\r\n\r\n");
```

```
  pW.print(msg);
  pW.flush();
}
```

The top two lines of this output arrive at the browser as

```
HTTP/1.0 401 Unauthorized
WWW-Authenticate: Basic realm="DBAuthServer Data"
```

In response to this HTTP message, the browser displays the dialog box shown in Figure 5-6.

*Figure 5-6. HTTP-induced login dialog box*

The user fills in the username and password and clicks OK. The browser concatenates the two separated by a colon, encodes the resulting string in base64 encoding, and sends it to the server as the value of the authorization header. For instance, with username and password both "tjm," the string tjm:tjm gets sent as

```
Authorization: Basic dGptOnRqbQ==
```

On the server end, the string is decoded and submitted to the `authorized()` method again. We return to the server code after we explain how the base64 encoding works.

## Base64 Encoding and More Secure Alternatives

Base64 encoding is a standard way of encoding binary data as characters to be sent over channels that expect 7-bit ASCII character data. For instance, this is how MIME attachments are sent over email, and if you ask Google's SOAP API for a cached Web page, it is returned in base64 encoding. The idea is that 8-bit data (256 possible characters) is to be read 6 bits at a time (64 possibilities), and we choose 64 ASCII characters to represent them. The characters used as base64 digits are

```
ABCDEFGHIJKLMNOPQRSTUVWXYZ
abcdefghijklmnopqrstuvwxyz
0123456789+/
```

In this sequence, think of "A" as representing the digit "0" = "000000" in binary, "B" as "000001" and so on; "a" is digit "26;" the "/" at the end represents the digit "63" = "111111." Our collection of digits has a unique substitution for every possible sequence of 6 bits.

What if the number of bits in the string to be encoded does not divide by 6 without a remainder? For instance, if we have four bytes, that's 32 bits, and we have five 6-bit sequences and two bits left over. If we have five bytes, we'll have four bits left over. Because the numbers we divide by 6 are multiples of 8, the only possible remainders are 2 or 4, meaning that either one or two pairs of bits are missing in the end. We indicate that by adding one or two equal sign (=) characters to the encoded string. This will be clearer once we work through an example. Suppose both the username and password are the string "tjm" so that the string to be encoded is "tjm:tjm." Converting this to ASCII codes we get a string of seven bytes, 56 bits altogether.

```
01110100011010100110110100111010011101000110101001101101
```

Taking those 6 at a time, we get

```
011101,000110,101001,101101,001110,100111,010001,101010,011011,01
```

These represent the number sequence

```
29,6,41,45,14,39,17,42,27, "01"
```

The last of these can be read either as the beginning or the end of a six-bit sequence. Base64 encoding resolves the ambiguity by treating that "01" as "010000," the number 16, which corresponds to the character "Q" in the 64-digit sequence. Because two pairs of bits are missing, we add "=" twice, so that number sequence is encoded by the string dGptOnRqbQ==. The 29th digit is "d," the 6th is "G," and so on. That's really all there is to base64 encoding. As we said, the browser does it for you but if you ever use a non-browser client you'll have to do it yourself. You will find Javascript code that implements base64 encoding in DBService/tstBase64.htm.

What about decoding? This happens on the server, and we use a Java class, org.apache.catalina.util.Base64, within the authorized() method to do the work. This class is part of the standard Tomcat distribution, which you will need in any case for Axis Web Services and clients.

## Checking Authorization

Let's think through what the authorized() method needs to do.

- Store the time stamp in the httpData hashtable

- Extract the authorization string from that hashtable; if there is no such string, no authorization is required

- If the string (base64) was given, decode it and break it into username and password

- Check the username and password against the data structure in which usernames and passwords are stored

- If authorization checks out, retrieve the user group of the user from the data structure in which this information is stored. If the authorization does not check out, throw an exception that will be sent back to the client as an authentication challenge.

- Store the username, password, and user group in the hashtable

What are the data structures that hold information about users, passwords, and groups? We use Java Property class objects, which are essentially hashtables for holding text strings. You store data in them with setProperty() and retrieve it with getProperty(), as shown in Listing 5-4.

*Listing 5-4. Property Objects for Authorization Data*

```
protected Properties userPwd=new Properties();
protected Properties userGroup=new Properties();
public void addAuthorization(String userID,String pwd,String group){
  if(userID==null)return;
  userPwd.setProperty(userID,pwd);
  userGroup.setProperty(userID,group);
}
```

This method is called at startup from the XML configuration file. The XML code of Listing 5-5 creates two authorized users, an admin and a member (Joe).

*Listing 5-5. XML Configuration Data for Initializing Authorization*

```
<void method="addAuthorization">
  <string>tjm</string>
  <string>tjm</string>
  <string>admin</string>
</void>
<void method="addAuthorization">
  <string>joe</string>
  <string>joe#3_Pwd</string>
  <string>member</string>
</void>
```

We now have all the pieces in place to work through the authorized() method, as shown in Listing 5-6.

*Listing 5-6. HTTP-Based Authorization*

```
public boolean authorized(Hashtable httpData)throws Exception{
  httpData.put("Now",getRfc1123DateFormat().format(new java.util.Date()));
  httpData.put("userGroup","");
  String auth=(String)httpData.get("Authorization");
  if(auth==null || !auth.startsWith("Basic "))
//This is a GET query, no authorization needed
    return true;
//  public static byte[] decode( byte[] base64Data )
//  Use java.util.Base64 class to decode
  auth=new String(Base64.decode(auth.substring(6).getBytes()));
// separate decoded string into username and password, store in hashtable
  int colLoc=auth.indexOf(':');
  if(colLoc<0)
    throw new Exception("invalid Basic Authorization: '"+auth+"'");
  String userID=auth.substring(0,colLoc);
  String pwd=auth.substring(colLoc+1);
  // check password
  if(!pwd.equals(userPwd.getProperty(userID)))
    throw new Exception("invalid Authorization: userID/pwd='"+
                                       userID+"'/'"+pwd+"'");
  httpData.put("userID",userID);
  httpData.put("pwd",pwd);
  httpData.put("userGroup",userGroup.getProperty(userID));
  return true;
}
```

This completes our authorization system. How secure is it? Its main security feature is that it exposes only a few predefined queries so an intruder cannot do any real harm to the system. Its main weak spot is basic authentication because it sends unencrypted passwords over the Internet. (Base64 encoding cannot count as encryption because everybody can decode it, as we just did.) This is a major security breach. In addition to the emerging SOAP and Web Services security standards, there are three secure alternatives: Digest Authentication, Secure HTTP (HTTPS), and Transport Level Security (TLS).

## Digest Authentication and HTTPS

We've seen that basic authentication is not secure because it's possible for a bad guy to eavesdrop on your transmissions and copy your authentication string. Even if the authentication string were encrypted, he could still copy the string and send it whenever he wanted to sign on as you. He wouldn't know your password, perhaps not even your userID, but he could resend your encrypted `userID:pwd` string and it would be accepted. We're not going to worry about this for DBAuthService, but within HTTP, there are two standard solutions to the problem. (Because we will not add them to DBAuthService, you may prefer to skip this section on a first reading.) The solutions are to encrypt the authentication using digest authentication, or to encrypt the whole session using HTTPS.

When you use digest authentication, you don't send your password at all—after all, the server already knows your username's password. Instead, you (as client) send a number, the MD5 hash value, to prove you know your password. The server's 401 authentication challenge has header data containing a nonce, which is a string generated just for that individual 401 response and no other. You combine your username, password, and the nonce into one string and compute its MD5 hash value, a 128-bit number. You also send your username in the clear, as a separate header. Now the server receives your username; it looks up the password for that username. It remembers the nonce it just sent to you, combines them, and computes the MD5 hash value just as you did. If the MD5 numbers don't match, it will reject the authorization. An attacker is welcome to look at the nonce as it goes to you and at your username and your MD5 code as they go back, but there is no known way to take these three items and compute the password. Without the password, there's no known way for the bad guy to compute the MD5 value for your username, password, and a new nonce.

This is described at `http://frontier.userland.com/stories/storyReader$2159`, which also links to the RFCs defining the authentications. Listing 5-7 shows MD5 encryption implemented in Java.

*Listing 5-7. MD5 Encryption*

```
public static byte[] md5Digest(String x) throws Exception {
    java.security.MessageDigest d
        = java.security.MessageDigest.getInstance("MD5");
    d.reset();
    d.update(x.getBytes("utf-8"));
    return d.digest();
}
```

Given this definition of md5Digest, the value of

```
new String(Base64.encode(md5Digest("tjm:tjm")))
```

is

```
PxQSCekK7PrLpnwJQ6mgSA==
```

The MD5 result will always have 128 bits so its base64 representation will always have 22 digits followed by ==.

The second HTTP standard approach is HTTPS, which stands for "HTTP over SSL (Secure Sockets Layer);" the acronym TLS (Transaction Layer Security) is another name for the same thing. The idea is that everything is encrypted so basic authentication is not a problem. In a browser client like BookClubAuthReviewer.html, this does not require extra client-side programming: just replace the "HTTP" with "HTTPS." (The server will have to work harder, and system administrators may need to change configurations.) If you're writing a non-browser-based client, perhaps in Java, you can do the same with Java 1.4 but with earlier versions you need to download the security libraries separately.

```
http://java.sun.com/j2se/1.4.2/docs/api/javax/net/ssl/package-summary.html
```

At the server end, with a full-strength Web server like Apache or IIS (or even Apache Tomcat running standalone), you control the use of HTTPS by configuration, not by doing any special programming. In fact, the easiest way to make DBAuthService support HTTPS is to restructure it within Tomcat as an Axis Web Service and then reach it with HTTPS. We'll talk about Tomcat and Axis in the next chapter.

Security tools, both generic and specific to Web Services, are getting better all the time. For now, we suggest using digest authentication if you want only to authenticate your users, or using basic authentication within HTTPS if you want to protect all your data. The remainder of DBAuthService is unaffected by these extensions.

# Using the Authorization System

Now that we have a system to collect and check login data, let's see how it is used on the back end. Its purpose, remember, is threefold.

- Restrict certain types of queries to certain groups of users

- Record the identity of the user and the timestamp of the query in the database for each update query

- Use that record to disallow users to change or delete reviews created by other users

To implement these tasks, we need changes in three places.

- The DBQueryData class must have access to user data to be able to store it in the database

- The SQL queries must have user ID and date/time parameters (and the database tables must have the corresponding fields)

- The doSql() method must have access to query data to check the user's group and identity

We will go over these changes in the next two subsections.

## Changes in Database Invocation

Queries are run in the doSql() method (see Listing 4-21). In the Chapter 4 version, the method takes only two arguments: an array of query parameters to insert into the PreparedStatement and a PrintWriter to send the query output to. In order to use authentication information, the current version of the method (shown in Listing 5-8) needs a third argument, the httpData hashtable in which the user group information is stored. The method extracts the required authorization from the DBAuthQueryData and the actual user data from the httpData hashtable. If there is a mismatch, an authorization exception is thrown (which results in a login dialog box appearing to the user); otherwise, the user can run the query.

There are two kinds of mismatch we're looking for: the query requires admin privileges but the user is not an admin, and the query requires member privileges but the user is just a visitor (which in our system is indicated by the nonexistent or empty string for the user group).

*Listing 5-8.* doSql() *with Authorization, Part 1*

```
protected void doSQL(ArrayList nameParams,Hashtable ht,PrintWriter out)
   throws Exception{
  PreparedStatement pS=null;
  String qName=((String)nameParams.get(0)).toUpperCase();
  DBAuthQueryData dbqd=(DBAuthQueryData)queryHashtable.get(qName);
  if(dbqd==null)
    throw new Exception("ERR NO SUCH QUERY AS "+qName+"");
  String qAuth=dbqd.getQAuth();
  String userGroup=(String)ht.get("userGroup");
  if("admin".equals(qAuth) && !"admin".equals(userGroup))
    throw new Exception("Authorization: admin privileges needed for "+qName);
  if("member".equals(qAuth) &&
        (null==userGroup || userGroup.length()==0))
    throw new Exception("Authorization: member privileges needed for "+qName);
// if we get here, authorization checked out, proceed as in Chapter 4
  String[]qTypes=dbqd.getQTypeArray();
  String[]qVals=dbqd.getQValArray();
  int paramCount=dbqd.getParamCount();
  if(paramCount!=nameParams.size()-1)
    throw new Exception("Query ["+qName+"] expects "+paramCount+
                         " params, not "+(nameParams.size()-1));
  Connection con=getDBConnection();
// if we get here we're ready to run the query
```

For now, we can assume that the method continues as in Listing 4-21. In fact, doSql() has an additional block of code shown in Listing 5-12, later in this chapter. This block of code is needed to construct SQL query parameters for our Prepared-Statements. As we mentioned, a DBAuthQueryData object now needs to store information not only about its SQL query but also about the authorization required to run that query. That information is of two kinds: the user group and the user identity. We have shown how user group information is retrieved by the getQAuth() method and used in doSql(). This information is known at SQL query design time and does not change from one HTTP request to another. User ID information requires additional machinery because it only becomes known at query invocation time. The next two sections explain how this information is handled.

## Changes in DBQueryData

The user named Joe should be allowed to delete a review he entered earlier, but he shouldn't be allowed to delete Jane's review. This means that a review record in the database must have a field for the username of the review's author. How would the query object know which field it is? We could adopt a rigid convention that this is always the second field, right after the primary key, or we could adopt a more flexible approach at the cost of making the code more complicated. We present here the more flexible solution but emphasize that this is a minor sideshow, unrelated to the main subject matter of the book. We allow the Type property of a field to carry more information than just database type—it can also specify the value to be stored. Consider the DELETE_ProdRevs SQL.

```
DELETE FROM ProdRevs WHERE AsinUserID=?
```

This requires one Text parameter. In Chapter 4, this parameter came directly from the user and would use the value "123:tjm" to delete the review of product "123" by user "tjm." That's not good; we want only user "tjm," whose userID is authenticated as HTTP header information, to be able to delete his own reviews. He should supply "123" (the first and only parameter he gives) as the ASIN, and the system should append the rest, including his userID. We do that by redeclaring the TEXT parameter as

```
TEXT=$1+:+userID
```

Here $1+:+userID specifies the value to be filled in as the TEXT parameter; it's the concatenation of three values. "$1" is the first user-parameter, the ASIN; the colon (:) is just a colon; and "userID" is the authenticated value from the HTTP header. The code that prepares and runs the PreparedStatement will combine the two sources of information. We will present this code in a moment, but first here's a complete spec for a DBAuthQueryData object in the XML config file, Listing 5-9.

*Listing 5-9. XML Spec of DBAuthQueryData Object for DELETE Query*

```
<void method="add">
   <object class="soapUtil.DBAuthQueryData">
       <void method="setQAuth"><string>member</string></void>
       <void method="setQID">
         <string>DELETE_ProdRevs</string>
       </void>
       <void method="setQStr">
```

```
            <string>
             DELETE FROM ProdRevs WHERE AsinUserID=?
            </string>
           </void>
           <void method="setQTypes">
             <string>TEXT=$1+:+userID</string>
           </void>
        </object>
     </void>
```

The Java code of DBAuthQueryData (shown in Listing 5-10) separates the structured strings of XML config into an array of types qTypeArray and an array of string values qValArray. It accepts a type-string such as the following example from the INS_ProdRevs statement:

```
TEXT=$1+:+userID,INT,TEXT=userID,DATETIME=Now,INT,TEXT,TEXT
```

This is a comma-separated list of seven parameters, and from it setQTypes() constructs two String arrays.

```
["TEXT",        "INT",    "TEXT", "DATETIME", "INT", "TEXT", "TEXT"]
["$1+:+userID",  "", "userID",      "Now",    "",     "",     ""]
```

The first array is just QTypes the way it was in Chapter 4. QVals matches it and defines the first, third, and fourth parameters. The invocation, whether SOAP or REST, will supply the other four parameters. These are an ASIN, a rating, a keyword list, and a review—two Ints and two Texts. The first of them, the ASIN, will also be used as "$1" in the doSQL method that interprets the string. The setQTypes() method doesn't know anything about the values of the three non-empty strings except that they're non-empty.

The additional code within doSQL then takes these QVal strings and the four provided parameters and pieces together the seven parameters needed for database invocation. Each empty value is filled in with the corresponding provided parameter. Each non-empty value is split up with a plus sign (+) as separator and the resulting substrings are used as values. Numbers represent provided parameters, strings such as "userID" and "Now" are defined in the HttpData table, and any strings not so defined simply represent themselves.

*Listing 5-10. DBAuthQueryData Code for Parsing "Structured Types"*

```
public void setQTypes(String S){
  qTypes=S;  paramCount=0; int minParams=0;
  if(S==null||S.length()==0){qTypeArray=new String[0]; return;}
  int nc=0;for(int i=0;i<S.length();i++)if(S.charAt(i)==',')nc++;
  qTypeArray=new String[nc+1];
  qValArray=new String[nc+1];
  java.util.StringTokenizer st=new java.util.StringTokenizer(S,",");
  for(int j=0; st.hasMoreTokens(); j++){
    String typeVal=st.nextToken();
    int delimLoc=typeVal.indexOf('=');
    if(delimLoc<0){
      qTypeArray[j]=typeVal;
      qValArray[j]=""; paramCount++;
    }
    else{
      String qT=typeVal.substring(0,delimLoc);
      String qV=typeVal.substring(delimLoc+1);
      qTypeArray[j]=qT;
      qValArray[j]=qV;
      for(int nLoc=qV.indexOf('$');nLoc>=0;nLoc=qV.indexOf('$',nLoc+1)){
        int pLoc=qV.indexOf('+',nLoc); if(pLoc < 0) pLoc=qV.length();
        String nStr=qV.substring(nLoc+1,pLoc);
        try{
          int N=Integer.parseInt(nStr);
          if(N>minParams)minParams=N;
        }catch(Exception ex){
          System.out.println("Error parsing ["+nStr+"] from ["+qV+
                             "] as integer");
        }
      }
    }
  }
  if(minParams > paramCount)
    paramCount = minParams; // found ref $i otherwise unused.
}
```

The access methods for query types (shown in Listing 5-11) reconstruct the initial strings and concatenate all types together into a comma-separated string.

*Listing 5-11. Access Methods of the* DBAuthQueryData *Class*

```
// get a single type, possibly concatenated with string value
public String getQType(int i){
  String S=qValArray[i];
  if(S.length()==0)
    return qTypeArray[i];
  return qTypeArray[i]+"="+S; // catenate with value string
}
// get all types as a comma-separated string
public String getQTypes(){
  if(qTypeArray==null || qTypeArray.length==0)
    return "";
  StringBuffer sB=new StringBuffer();
  for(int i=0;i<qTypeArray.length;i++)
    sB.append(",").append(getQType(i));
  return sB.toString();
}
```

These methods are used by doSql() to fill in the parameters of the query. We are ready to look at the remainder of doSql() code.

## Processing Type and User ID Information in Database Invocation

We are now in a position to complete the code of doSql(), whose first part was shown in Listing 5-8. The last lines of that listing, repeated here, extract the information from the DBAuthDBQuery object and obtain a database connection. The method then fills in the SQL query parameters and runs the query. As you read through Listing 5-12, remember that it has to integrate information from several sources.

- ArrayList nameParams contains SOAP parameters extracted from the HTTP body

- Hashtable ht contains user data extracted from the HTTP authentication header and the user group hashtable

- ArrayList qTypes and ArrayList qVals are from the DBAuthQueryData object

The method uses all this information to fill in the SQL query parameters of the PreparedStatement and run the SQL query.

*Listing 5-12.* doSql() *with Authorization, Part 2*

```
// LAST LINES OF Listing 5-8: if we get here, authorization checked out
String[]qTypes=dbqd.getQTypeArray();
  String[]qVals=dbqd.getQValArray();
  int paramCount=dbqd.getParamCount();
  if(paramCount!=nameParams.size()-1)
    throw new Exception("Query ["+qName+"] expects "+paramCount+
                        " params, not "+(nameParams.size()-1));
  Connection con=getDBConnection();
// END OF LISTING 5-8; if we get here, we're ready to run the query
  try{
    pS=con.prepareStatement(dbqd.getQStr());
    int i=0; int j=0; // i for qVals array, j for qnameParams array
    for(;i<qTypes.length;i++){
      String val=qVals[i];
      if(val.equals("")){
        j++;
        val=(String)nameParams.get(j);
      }
      else {
      // break value into fields, extract parts from hashtable and nameParams
        java.util.StringTokenizer st=new java.util.StringTokenizer(val,"+");
        StringBuffer sB=new StringBuffer();
        for(; st.hasMoreTokens();){
          String label=st.nextToken();
          if(label.startsWith("$")){ // parameter number
            int N=Integer.parseInt(label.substring(1));
            sB.append((String)nameParams.get(N));
          }else {
            String valPart=(String) ht.get(label);
            if(valPart==null)
              sB.append(label);
            else sB.append(valPart);
          }
        }
        val=sB.toString();
      }
// finally, parameters are ready to be set by setParamStr as in Chapter 4
      setParamStr(pS,i+1,val,qTypes[i]);
    }
// run SQL query; if SELECT query, output ResultSet
// if UPDATE query, output the UpdateCount integer
```

```
    if(pS.execute()) writeResultSet(pS.getResultSet(),out);
    else writeResultCount(pS.getUpdateCount(),out);
  } catch(Exception ex){
    throw new Exception("ERR doSQL("+qName+","+ex+")\n");}
  finally{
    if(pS!=null)try{pS.close();}catch(Exception ex){}
    pS=null;
    freeDBConnection(con);
  }
}
```

The output methods `writeResultSet()` and `writeResultCount()` are unchanged from Chapter 4, Listing 4-23.

## The REST Version

In this section, we present two SOAP-less versions of DBService. Both use only HTTP commands and URIs to implement the functionality of the SOAP service. The first version uses those commands and URIs in ways that are consistent with the REST architecture. The second version violates the rules of REST in ways that are very common on the Web. We start by explaining the rules of REST.

### HTTP Commands and REST

The argument between people who favor SOAP and people who favor REST is about using the best architecture for distributed applications, that is, applications that run on many processes while presenting themselves to the user as a single unified system. We want our distributed applications to have these properties: interoperability (interop, for short), transparency, and scalability. Interop means that the participating processes can be written in any language and be run on any platform. Transparency means that the user won't know whether at any given moment she is interacting with a local or remote process, or switching between remote processes. Scalability means that the applications can add participating processes without changing the architecture and underlying protocols.

The web of HTML documents is the most successful of all distributed architectures, beating the pants off all competition. Servers and clients can be written in many languages for all possible platforms, switching from one server to another is completely transparent (unless the server is down), and it has scaled from less than a thousand to millions of servers without skipping a beat. The two main pillars of this success are the HTTP protocol and the uniform naming system of URLs. Recall the first line of an HTTP request.

```
GET http://some-host.org/index.html HTTP/1.0
```

Apart from the protocol version, this has two items: an HTTP command and a resource specified by a URL. Many people call them a verb and a noun. In response to such a command, the server does what's expected and the client transfers to another state that, in the simplest case (no cookies) is completely unburdened by any memories of the preceding state. The new state is immediately represented (displayed) in the client's window. The whole process is called Representational State Transfer or REST.

## REST and HTTP Verbs

REST advocates say that the Web is interoperable and scalable in large part because HTTP has few verbs and a consistent syntax and meaning, forming a structured system. There are seven HTTP verbs in common use: GET, PUT, DELETE, POST, HEAD, TRACE, and OPTIONS. We use the last three of these for support, metaconversations, and debugging. The first four perform real actions. What are those actions? Here we have to distinguish between the intended practice of pure REST and the actual practice. In pure REST, the following principles apply:

- GET is only for information retrieval.

- PUT is for placing or replacing information on the server. PUT and GET are related; if you execute PUT with a certain resource and then execute GET with the same resource, you should GET exactly what you PUT.

- DELETE is for deleting a resource. It is an inverse of PUT; if you PUT and then DELETE a resource, you end up exactly where you started.

- POST is less precisely defined but it should be used primarily for appending multiple resources.

For instance, a POST to a discussion list or message board implies that you're adding to it, rather like appending to a file. REST usage follows this analogy. Ideally, the HTTP command line

```
POST http://some-host.org/messages HTTP/1.0
```

would create (and report) a new URL, such as perhaps `http://some-host.org/messages/15` or `http://some-host.org/messages/2003-09-27-23-59-59/1`.

In our case, we use POST to indicate INSertion into a table. This is much closer to the spirit of REST than using POST to send SOAP messages, with an essentially arbitrary meaning.

In practice, of course, POST is used for sending parameters to programs, and worse yet, GET is commonly used that way also, by attaching parameters in the HTTP query string. In pure REST, GET is not supposed to have any side effects and its query-string parameters, if any, should also be search parameters. In practice, it is used to run any kind of program because of the convenience of creating a clickable URL to run it rather than putting up a form every time.

These practices aside, HTTP does standardize a small set of verbs that all participants of the system know and implement. By contrast, every SOAP application that does a remote procedure call (including method invocations) in effect creates a new verb with its own syntax (signature or arguments and return values) and its own meaning. To use a SOAP application, one must learn the verb and its syntax and semantics. Such a system cannot be scalable (say the REST people) and it will result in "Balkanizing the Internet" into areas that speak different languages altogether. This is the crux of the argument. For more information (and spirited exchanges) see Paul Prescod's `http://www.prescod.net/rest` and Costello's tutorial at `http://www.xfront.com`.

## REST Version Code

If we were to use REST instead of SOAP, how would we implement the DBService? A REST implementation requires surprisingly little code, but it necessitates some design decisions. In particular, how do we send SQL query parameters? HTTP offers two mechanisms, the URL proper and the HTTP query string that consists of name/value pairs of strings. The choice between the two is the subject of best practices. For instance, to send the ASIN over, we could say

```
GET /amabooks?asin=123
```

We could also say

```
GET /amabooks/123
```

The second version, of course, assumes that the Web server administrator has created a mapping between URLs and resources that fits a standard hierarchy.

With PUT, POST, and DELETE we have a different choice to make. They do not use a query string but they have an HTTP body. (A GET message, by contrast, can have a query string but cannot have a non-empty body.) So we can put the ASIN into the URL, we can put it in the body of the message (in XML, of course), or we can do both. Redundancy here is bad because it does not add new information and can be a source of error. On the other hand, if we don't repeat the information in the body of the HTTP message for PUT, what we PUT will be different from what we GET, violating one of REST's main principles. Our choices may not be approved by all REST adherents, but it would not be difficult to readjust them to a different set of best practices.

The choices we make in the implementation are as follows:

- The ASIN is part of the URL.

- The ASIN information is not repeated in the PUT message body.

- The HTTP command name is included with the query parameters.

On the client, the changes are minimal; we just say method="PUT" or method="DELETE," as appropriate. On the server, the HTTP request is processed as before by doHttpTransaction() (see Listing 5-1), which calls readHttpData() to produce a hashtable, httpData, containing the headers and the body (if any) of the message. httpTransaction() examines the HTTP command and calls the appropriate method to process it. Listing 5-13 repeats the relevant part of doHttpTransaction().

*Listing 5-13. Dispatch on HTTP Command*

```
// if Authorization exception is not thrown, process HTTP data
    String cmd=(String)httpData.get("METHOD");
    if("POST".equals(cmd)) doPost(httpData,pW);
    else if("GET".equals(cmd)) doGet(httpData,pW);
    else if("PUT".equals(cmd)) doPut(httpData,pW);
    else if("DELETE".equals(cmd)) doDelete(httpData,pW);
    else
      throw new Exception("unknown command ["+cmd+
                                    "]; POST,GET,PUT,DELETE are supported");
```

All four doXX() methods (including doPost() when it's used as part of REST rather than SOAP implementation) call doREST() with two arguments: the name of the action to perform and the hashtable of HTTP data. The action is the same as the HTTP command except for POST, where the action is INSERT. The methods are shown in Listings 5-14 to 5-16; doPut() and doPost() require additional comment.

*Listing 5-14.* doGet() *and* doDelete()

```
public void doGet(Hashtable httpData,PrintWriter pW)throws Exception{
  doREST("GET",httpData,pW);
}
public void doDelete(Hashtable httpData,PrintWriter pW)throws Exception{
  doREST("DELETE",httpData,pW);
}
```

doPut(), which replaces existing data, performs two actions, first a DELETE then an INSERT.

*Listing 5-15.* doPut()

```
public void doPut(Hashtable httpData,PrintWriter pW)
    throws Exception{
  ArrayList deletionParams=getRESTParams("DELETE",httpData);
  doSQL(deletionParams,httpData);
  doREST("INS",httpData,pW);
}
```

Finally, doPost() is used both within the SOAP and REST implementations so we have to check (using the SOAPAction header) which one to do. Within REST, POST is used for the INSERT action.

*Listing 5-16.* doPost()

```
public void doPost(Hashtable httpData,PrintWriter pW)throws Exception{
  String soapAction=(String)httpData.get("SOAPACTION");
  if(soapAction==null) // we are in REST
    doREST("INS",httpData,pW);
  else // we are in SOAP
    if("DBServerCall".equals(soapAction))
    doDBServerCall(httpData,pW);
  else throw new
    Exception("POST with unknown SOAPAction:["+soapAction+"]");
}
```

What does doREST() do? It calls getRESTParams() to get an ArrayList that is expected by doSQL(), calls that method, and writes the result as an XHTML page (shown in Listing 5-17).

*Listing 5-17.* doREST()

```
public void doREST(String method,Hashtable httpData,PrintWriter pW)
  throws Exception{
  ArrayList paramList=getRESTParams(method,httpData);
  String sqlResult=doSQL(paramList,httpData);
  writeXHTMLPage(sqlResult,pW);
}
```

Our REST implementation assumes a mapping between URLs and database tables or table rows. A URL of the form /tableName is mapped to a table; a URL of the form /tableName/ASIN is mapped to the row or rows of that database table that have to do with the ASIN.

Only GET is supported on URLs that refer to entire tables, so we map GET /aTable to the PreparedStatement object named GETALL_aTable, which runs a query that retrieves everything from that table. Other HTTP commands also correspond in obvious ways to database queries, so we map them to PreparedStatements and their ASIN parameter as in Table 5-1.

*Table 5-1. URLs and PreparedStatements*

| HTTP Command | PreparedStatement |
|---|---|
| GET /XXX/123 | GET_XXX |
| DELETE /XXX/123 | DELETE_XXX |
| PUT /XXX/123 (with body) | PUT_XXX |
| POST /XXX/123 (with body) | INS_XXX |

The database administrator will have to define those PreparedStatements. The first SOAP parameter in every case is now provided within REST by the last component of the URL, with HTTP bodies of PUT and POST messages possibly providing more SOAP parameters. Because we use substitutions that include the ordinal number of the SOAP parameter (remember those $1, $2, etc.), the order of SOAP parameters as submitted by SOAP or REST does not have to be the same as the order of SQL parameters in the PreparedStatement.

The getRESTParams() method (shown in Listing 5-18) extracts all those SOAP parameters from the URL and the HTTP body (if any) and returns the ArrayList that is required by doSQL().

*Listing 5-18. getRESTParams*

```
protected ArrayList getRESTParams(String method,Hashtable hashtable)
    throws Exception{
  if("POST".equals(method))method="INS";
  String url=(String)hashtable.get("URL");
  String[]methodKey=url.substring(1).split("/");
  ArrayList arrayList=new ArrayList();
  if(methodKey.length<2 || methodKey[1].trim().length()==0)
    arrayList.add(method+"all_"+methodKey[0]);
  else{
    arrayList.add(method+"_"+methodKey[0]); // e.g., GET_AmaAuth;
    arrayList.add(methodKey[1]);            // Asin, always the key value here.
  }
  if(!"INS".equalsIgnoreCase(method))return arrayList; // called within PUT.
  String docString=(String)hashtable.get("HTTP_BODY");
  if(null==docString || docString.length()==0)
    throw new Exception("no body to HTTP request");
  Document doc=readDocument(docString);
  NodeList nodeList=doc.getElementsByTagName("dbParam");
  for(int i=0;i<nodeList.getLength();i++){
   Node child=nodeList.item(i).getFirstChild();
   String param=child!=null?child.getNodeValue():"";
   System.out.println("param("+(1+i)+")="+param);
   arrayList.add(param);
   }
  return arrayList;
}
```

That's all there is to our REST implementation of the DBService. As you can see, although very different in spirit, it shares a lot of its code with the SOAP version because the differences are all in the transport, not in the internal workings of the service.

## The HTTP Query String Implementation

For completeness, we also provide an implementation that (ab)uses GET and the HTTP query string to implement all the actions of the service. Let's go back to readHttpData() (see Listing 4-7), which reads the METHOD and the URL from the first line of HTTP data, reads the rest of the headers, and then reads the HTTP_BODY. In the DBAuthService version of Listing 5-19 we add a conditional that checks to see whether a readRequestURL configuration parameter has been set by the sysadmin.

*Listing 5-19.* readHttpData(), *Selections*

```
public Hashtable readHttpData(Reader reader)throws Exception{
  ...
  String cmdLine=readLine(reader);
  ...
  hashtable.put("METHOD",cmdLine.substring(0,firstBlank));
  hashtable.put("URL",cmdLine.substring(1+firstBlank,lastBlank));
  ...
  hashtable.put("HTTP_BODY",readUpToLength(reader,len));
  if(null!=readRequestURL)
    addURLArgs(hashtable,(String)hashtable.get("URL"));
  ...
}
```

If readRequestURL has been set, we're to do something called addURLargs() (shown in Listing 5-20), combining the hashtable and the URL that's stored within it.

*Listing 5-20.* addURLargs() *for Combining HTTP Data with Query String Data*

```
public static void addURLArgs(Hashtable hT,String url)throws Exception{
  int qLoc=url.indexOf('?');
  if(qLoc<0)return;
  URLDecoder decoder=new URLDecoder();
  String[]nVs=url.substring(1+qLoc).split("[&=]");
  hT.put("URL",url.substring(0,qLoc));
  for(int i=1;i<nVs.length;i+=2)
    hT.put(nVs[i-1],decoder.decode(nVs[i],"utf-8"));
}
```

Here we look to see if there are any query parameters in the URL; if not, we have nothing to add. If they are present, they will have been URLEncoded. Blank will have been replaced with "%20," "<" characters by "%3C," and so on, to make a long but legal URL representation of the parameters, in the form

```
http://localhost:65432/amaauth/123?METHOD=PUT&HTTP_BODY=%3CparamList%3E...
```

We split these at every "&" indicating a new parameter and at every "=" dividing a parameter's name from its value. We end up with a string array forming pairs.

```
[METHOD, PUT,
 HTTP_BODY, %3CparamList%3E%3CdbParam%3E%0D%0A...]
```

We go through this array pair by pair, executing

```
hT.put("METHOD", "PUT");
hT.put("HTTP_BODY","<paramList><dbParam>\r\n...");
```

At this point the httpData hashtable is exactly as it would have been for an xmlHttp() invocation with the appropriate body. As a security issue, and especially as a firewall issue, you may prefer not to do this; it violates the basic notion that HTTP GET does not change anything on the server side and is therefore safe. However, it's extremely common because it's convenient. If you don't want to use it, don't set the readRequestURL value in the configuration file.

## Conclusion

In Chapters 4 and 5, you saw the inner workings of a simple but self-contained SOAP/REST Web Service. In Chapter 4, we developed a basic functionality of DBService and used it to implement a book club application. In this chapter, we added user authentication and then re-implemented DBService as a REST application. The difference between SOAP and REST approaches to Web Services is important. Both have strengths and weaknesses; Amazon provides support for both precisely because it is too early to tell which one is better, and in what circumstances.

Most Web Services are not self-contained; they are built on top of a Web Service framework like Apache Axis, which is in turn built on top of a Web server like Apache Tomcat. Most Web Services are created using a Web Service framework or toolkit, and this is the context in which we will operate in the remaining chapters of the book. Those Web Service frameworks are great time-savers but they are hard to understand even when the source code is available because the source is huge. With DBAuthService, you can understand every detail of the code, so it's not only a way to implement a minimal-footprint Web Service, but also a start on understanding the larger systems out there.

# CHAPTER 6

# Restructuring Results with XSLT

**SOAP** MESSAGES AND **REST** query results come from the server to the client as XML data. In previous chapters, we either displayed them as raw XML (tags and all) or used Javascript to restructure the results. In this chapter, we'll use XSLT to transform XML data into HTML presentations. This is probably the most common way to use XSLT, and it's a good way to learn because you see the results of your code right away. We won't go far into XSLT, but we will provide a self-contained introduction.

XSLT can be applied to XML messages on either the server or the client. Amazon's Web Services, in fact, offer users an option to use an XSLT stylesheet located anywhere on the Internet to format query results before they are sent to the client. This is a very useful feature, which we will add to DBAuthService. We think most Web Services should consider offering this feature because it allows the construction of extremely thin client-side code. The end user sees only a series of Web pages constructed by XSLT from XML query results. Each page contains constructed links that will invoke more queries and apply XSLT to their results so that it all works even in older browsers or one that has Javascript disabled. If this feature is not offered or if you want to develop and test your stylesheet before uploading it to the server, you can perform the transformation in your client code (we'll show you how later in this chapter). All you need is a recent version of IE or Mozilla that supports client-side XSLT processing.

We'll present XSLT through a graduated series of examples, solved in a variety of ways. First, we'll look at DBService results: the simple updateCount and then the table. Then we'll look at Amazon results, both light and heavy. Finally, we will use XSLT to combine DBService and Amazon data on a single page.

In this chapter, we cover the following:

- Introduction to XPath and XSLT

- XSLT for Amazon Data

- Combining Data Sources in XSLT

## Introduction to XSLT and XPath

One way to describe XSLT is to say that it is like an SQL for XML. That is, it allows you to formulate queries that produce different views of the same data. For historical reasons, XSLT queries are called stylesheets. The two Web pages shown in Figure 6-1 and Figure 6-2 are produced by the same Amazon query filtered through two different XSLT stylesheets.

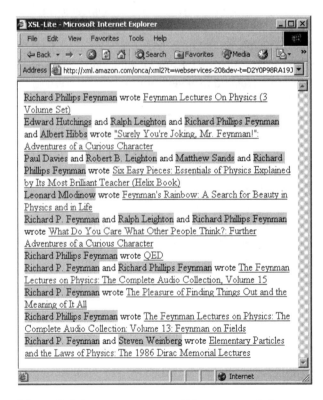

*Figure 6-1. Amazon query result in paragraph form*

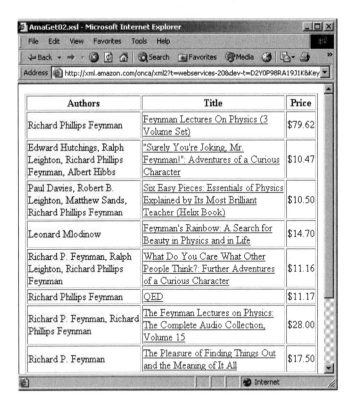

*Figure 6-2. Amazon query result in tabular form*

In this section, we will work with very simple data. We won't show you the stylesheets for Figures 6-1 and 6-2 until the next section. XSLT stylesheets are XML documents with namespaces, and until you have a grasp of their overall structure, they might appear to be a jumble of syntactic constructs. An additional complication is that they use yet another language to formulate the equivalent of SQL query conditions. Just as the WHERE clause in SQL SELECT queries uses a number of Boolean and other operators to select the columns and rows of the table(s) that you want to appear in the resulting view, in XSLT, the same function is performed by XPath. XPath is a language that can select sets of nodes in the tree. To help you understand how XSLT works, we will cover the following concepts:

- Trees, especially DOM trees and XPath trees

- XPath expressions

- Programming by matching and instantiating templates

We covered trees in general and XML trees in particular in Chapter 2. Here is a recap of that material.

## What's a Tree?

A tree is a set of **nodes** connected by **parent-child relationships**. Every node except the **root** has exactly one parent node. In computer science (and genealogy), trees are always drawn upside down, with the root on top and leaves at the bottom. If you start from any node that is not a root, go up to its parent, and continue up the tree, sooner or later you get to the root. The **path** you follow is unique: there's no other way to get from the chosen node to the root. The nodes you encounter along the way are called the **ancestors** of that node. The root is an ancestor of all nodes in the tree, and all nodes in the tree are its **descendants**. If node P is parent of node C then C is usually called a **child** of P. Children of the same node are called **siblings**. Nodes that have no children are called **leaves**.

Common examples of trees include a book's tables of contents, the hierarchy of the Catholic Church, the chains of command in the military, and (closer to our interests) the directory structure of a hard drive.

XML data has two main types of representation: XML as text with markup, and XML as a tree data structure. The process of converting XML text to XML data structure is called **parsing**, and converting XML data structure to XML text is called **serializing**. Usually, an object or software library, called an **XML parser**, performs both operations, serving as an intermediary between a linear XML text (that is easy to send over the wire) and an XML data structure that conforms to a standard API and can be processed by portable code which references that API (see Figure 6-3).

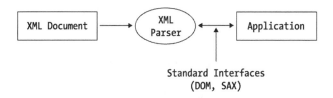

*Figure 6-3. An XML document, a parser, and an application*

## DOM Trees and XPath Trees

The XML trees we used in preceding chapters are DOM trees that are processed using DOM APIs. In addition to DOM trees, XML also has XPath trees that are used in XSLT and in other tools. XPath trees are different from DOM trees in very minor details—so minor that we won't even discuss them. Here is an example of a simple XML document (shown in Listing 6-1) and its XPath tree (shown in Figure 6-4).

*Listing 6-1. Hello, XML*

```
<?xml version="1.0"?>
<!-- A simple example (and this is a comment) -->
<encounter>
  <greeting>Hello, XML!</greeting>
  <response>Hello, what can I do for you?</response>
</encounter>
```

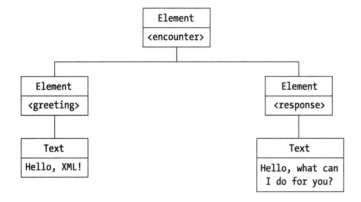

*Figure 6-4. Tree diagram for Listing 6-1*

XPath trees follow these conventions.

- There is a root node that is parent to the root of the element tree and to any top-level comments.

- The text content of an element is wrapped in a text node.

## The Node Types of the XPath Tree

As you can see, there are several different types of nodes in an XPath tree. The most important for our purposes are as follows:

- The unique root node

- Element nodes that correspond to XML elements

- Attribute nodes that correspond to XML attributes

- Text nodes that contain the text content of an XML element

We repeat (because it bears repetition) that the element nodes of an XPath tree form a tree of their own, a subtree of the entire tree. The root of the element tree is a child, often the only child, of the root of the entire tree.

## The XPath Language

XPath is a language used for navigating a tree and selecting a set of nodes for processing. Using XPath, it is easy to issue commands like "Give me the text content of the second child of my next sibling in the tree" and "Give me all the element nodes in the tree whose tag name is 'section' and whose parent's tag name is 'chapter'." XSLT (eXtensible Stylesheet Language for Transformations) uses XPath expressions to access sets of nodes in an XML tree and use them for building an output structure. Neither XPath nor XSLT modify their XML data source in any way.

There are two forms of the XPath language—the full form and the abbreviated form. The abbreviated form is easier to learn but it does not express the full power of the language. In this chapter, with a couple of easy-to-understand exceptions, we use only the abbreviated form.

### XSLT and Directory Paths

XML elements in a document and file directories on a hard drive form a tree structure. The abbreviated form of XPath uses expressions for referring to nodes in a tree that are similar to the way directory paths are expressed in Unix. Since the function of XPath within XSLT is to select a set of nodes for processing, we say that an XSLT expression "selects" a set of nodes. In the examples below, we give XPath expressions and the node sets that those expressions will select. The set can be empty or it can contain a single node. For our examples, we use a simplified tree structure based on the play *Macbeth*, adapted from Jon Bosak's complete Shakespeare in XML, found at `http://www.oasis-open.org/cover/bosakShakespeare200.html`. In this markup, the play consists of acts that consist of scenes; each scene is a sequence of character speeches, and each speech is a sequence of lines. Speech elements have a `Speaker` attribute whose value is the name of the speaker. For simplicity, we ignore lists of characters, prologues and epilogues, and stage directions.

Each item in the following list shows an XPath expression and the corresponding node set.

- `/` selects the root of the XPath tree. Remember that the root of the element tree is a child of the root of the XPath tree.

- `/play` selects a single element that is the child of the root and is itself the root of the tree of elements.

- `/book` selects an empty node set because the root element of our document is play, not book.

- `/play/act` selects a set of elements that correspond to an act of the play.

- `/play/act[2]` selects a single element, the second act.

- `/play/act[position()>1]` selects a set of all act elements except the first act. (In the actual document, we would have to encode the character > as &gt;.)

- `/play/act[2]/scene[3]/speech` selects all speech elements in the third scene of the second act.

- `/play/act[2]/scene[3]/speech[@Speaker='Macbeth']` selects all Macbeth's speeches from that scene, using the `Speaker` attribute.

You will probably agree that abbreviated XPath expressions are quite intuitive and easy to read.

## Absolute and Relative XPath Expressions

Just like directory paths, XPath expressions can be absolute (starting from the root) or relative (starting from the current position in the tree). XPath expressions also use a similar syntax: a single dot refers to the current position, and two dots refer to the parent of the current position. The current position is established by the application that uses XPath, in our case, XSLT. So we'll have to wait until we pick up a little XSLT before we can explain how the "current node" is established. In the meantime, we can look at a few relative XPath expressions, similar to the absolute ones of the preceding section.

- `./act` selects a set of act elements. Depending on where you are in the tree, it can be the empty set or a set of several acts.

- `../act` selects a set of act elements that are children of the parent of the current element. In other words, it selects all siblings of the current element whose tag name is act.

- `../act[2]` selects a single element, the second act element in the set selected in the preceding example.

- `/play/act[position()>1]` selects a set of all act elements except the first act. (In the actual document, we would have to encode the character > as &gt;.)

- `../play/act[2]/scene[3]/speech` selects all speech elements of the third scene of the second act if the current element is a child of the play element.

- `../play/act[2]/scene[3]/speech[@Speaker='Macbeth']` selects all Macbeth's speeches from that scene if the current element is a child of the play element.

It might be useful to think of absolute paths as relative paths with the root of the XPath tree as the current node.

## The Star and the Double Slash

Two more characters and three more abbreviations need to be noted.

- The asterisk (*) stands for "all children of the current node that are element nodes." So `/*` selects the set of all children of the root, `./*` selects the set of all children of the current element, and `./*/speech` selects the set of all grandchildren of the current element whose name is speech.

- The * can be combined with the @ character to refer to attributes. Therefore, `./@*` selects all attributes of the current node.

- The special double-slash (`//`) notation refers to all descendants of the current node, not necessarily direct descendants (that is, children). So `//scene` selects the set of all scenes in a play, and `.//speech[Speaker='Macbeth']` selects all descendants of the current node that are speech elements such that the speaker is Macbeth. If, for instance, the current node is the second act element in the element, this expression will select all Macbeth's speeches in Act II.

With this information about XPath, we can start working through simple examples of XSLT. For XML data, we will use the XHTML output from the REST version of DBAuthService in Chapter 5, as produced by the writeResultCount() and writeResultSet() methods. As you recall, writeResultCount() outputs an integer within a <span> and writeResultSet() outputs a ResultSet as an XHTML table. XSLT of course can work on any XML data, including XHTML, as long as it conforms to the XML syntax.

## The First Stylesheet

We will start with an XSLT that improves the appearance of a result count returned by DBAuthService. The stylesheet will change the content and appearance in two ways: it will place the title of the output XHTML file into the body of the page, and it will transform a lowly <span> into an <h3> within a <div>, adding two words of explanation to it. With Listing 6-2 as input, DBAuthService produces Listing 6-3 as output.

*Listing 6-2. Input to the First Stylesheet, upData01.htm*

```
<?xml version="1.0?>
<!-- input to updateCount01.xsl -->
<?xml-stylesheet type="text/xsl" href="updateCount01.xsl"?>
<html><head><title>DBAuthService Result 1</title></head><body>
<span class='updateCount'>1</span>
</body></html>
```

*Listing 6-3. Output of the First Stylesheet, upOut01.htm*

```
<html>
  <head>
    <meta http-equiv="Content-Type" content="text/html; charset=utf-8">
    <title>updateCount01.xsl Output</title>
  </head>
  <body>
    <div>
      <h3>Original Title: DBAuthService Result 1</h3>
```

```
      <h3>Rows affected: 1</h3>
    </div>
  </body>
</html>
```

The stylesheet itself, updateCount01.xsl, is partially shown in Listing 6-4. The gap in the middle of it contains a single `xsl:template` element that we will discuss shortly.

*Listing 6-4. The Very First Stylesheet*

```
<xsl:stylesheet
    xmlns:xsl="http://www.w3.org/1999/XSL/Transform"
    version="1.0">
<xsl:output method="html" />
<!-- a template element goes here -->
</xsl:stylesheet>
```

Because this is our first stylesheet, we are going to work through it tag by tag. The root element is always either `xsl::stylesheet` or `xsl:transform`, where the xsl prefix is mapped to the namespace identified by the URL `http://www.w3.org/1999/XSL/Transform`. The prefix doesn't have to be xsl, but it usually is. The two attributes of the root element declare the namespace and specify the version. After that, an XSLT program might have some top-level elements before the first template is defined. In this case, the `xsl:output` element specifies that the output will be HTML, not necessarily conforming to the XML syntax. (The other output possibilities are xml, (plain) text, and user-defined.)

What do we mean by "output" here? The purpose of an XSLT program is to take in XML data and output a transform (or a view) of that data. An XSLT program is itself an XML document. An XSLT processor thus receives two XML documents (an XML source and an XSLT program), and both already parsed into XPath trees. (XPath trees are almost identical to DOM trees. The differences are irrelevant here.) The XSLT program produces an output that can be XML, HTML, plain text, or some other format specified by the user. In all our examples, the output is HTML, as shown in Figure 6-5.

To compute the output, the XSLT processor works through the stylesheet element by element, starting at the root. All elements that are not in the XSLT namespace (that is, those whose tag names do not have the xsl: prefix) are passed on to the output unchanged. Those that have the xsl: prefix are processed according to the rules of the language. Their processing, just as in any programming language, can influence the order in which the contents of the stylesheet is evaluated and sent to output.

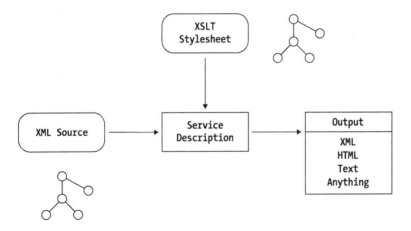

*Figure 6-5. XSLT processor inputs and output*

The most important XSLT element is xsl:template. Most XSLT computations are done by matching a template and instantiating its content in the context created by the match. Let's take a look at our first xsl:template element in Listing 6-5.

*Listing 6-5. The Template Element of Our First Stylesheet*

```
<xsl:template match="/">
  <html><head><title>updateCount01 Output</title></head><body>
 <div>
    <h2>
      <xsl:text>Original Title: </xsl:text>
      <xsl:value-of select="html/head/title"/>
    </h2>
    <h3>
      <xsl:text>Rows affected: </xsl:text>
      <xsl:value-of select="html/body/span"/>
    </h3>
  </div>
  </body></html>
</xsl:template>
```

The effect of match= "/ " is that the root is established as a starting point (the current node) from which we will be making references to those parts of XML data that we want included in the output. However, the first thing to do is to output the standard structural elements of an HTML page: html, head, and body. Within the body, the <div> and <h> tags are not in the XSLT namespace and so they are passed to the output unchanged. Within the <h2> element, there are two elements that *are* in the XSLT namespace: xsl:text and xsl:value-of. The first is used to create new text content for output that is not present in the input—it simply sends its text content to the output. An xsl:value-of tag always has a select attribute that specifies an XPath expression. The processor finds the node that this expression selects and computes its value. In our example, the XPath expression is html/head/title. It is a relative path that starts from the current node, which is the root. As all paths, it can in principle select more than one element, but in this case, in a properly constructed HTML page, the path is unique and leads to the <title> element. The value of an input element as returned by xsl:value-of is the text content of the entire subtree that is under that element. If title had more children elements that contained text, the value of title would be the concatenation of all those texts, in document order. In our example, <title> has no children and its value is exactly its text content in the XML source document.

Proceeding in the same manner, we output more HTML markup to close <h2> and open <h3>. Within <h3> we insert new text and the content of (the value) html/body/span. Finally, we output the remaining HTML markup and close xsl:template.

## Computing with Templates: Pull and Push

XSLT is not an imperative programming language like C, Basic, Java or Javascript; it is a declarative language like pure LISP or Prolog. To say that another way, XSLT does not have an assignment operator. You can give a name to a value, but that name is not a variable in the programming sense because you cannot change its value. (XSLT does have something called variables but they are like variables in mathematics: after you give it a value, that value is fixed.) XSLT does not have statements like x=5 (set the value of x as 5); it has expressions such as x+3 or 17 > position(). XSLT expressions are evaluated in context and the results of the evaluation build the output document. The context of evaluation is typically created by matching a template. Most of XSTL computation is done by matching nodes to a template's match attribute and evaluating the body of the template in the context created by the match. The result of the evaluation becomes part of the output document.

In the stylesheet of Listing 6-4, a single template produces the entire output document. When the template needs additional material from the XML source, it pulls that material by using XPath expressions and xsl:value-of. There is an alternative way of constructing XSLT programs that brings out the unusual nature of XSLT more clearly. Listing 6-6 produces exactly the same output as the template of Listing 6-4. (We show only the templates; the surrounding material of Listing 6-4 remains unchanged.)

*Listing 6-6. Same Result, Push Style*

```
<xsl:template match="/">
  <html><head><title>updateCount02 Output</title></head><body>
  <div>
    <xsl:apply-templates select="*"/>
<!-- apply whatever templates are available and place output here -->
  </div>
  </body></html>
</xsl:template>
<xsl:template match="title">
   <h2>
     <xsl:text>Original Title: </xsl:text>
     <xsl:value-of select="."/>
   </h2>
</xsl:template>
<xsl:template match="span">
   <h3>
     <xsl:text>Rows affected: </xsl:text>
     <xsl:value-of select="."/>
   </h3>
</xsl:template>
```

The key concept here is in the fourth line of code, xsl:apply-templates. This instructs the XSLT processor to visit all the nodes that are selected by XPath's select attribute, and to look for a matching template for each one. If a template is found, the XSLT processor will evaluate the template and place the result in the position indicated by the <apply-templates> tag. In our case, the nodes to look through are selected by an asterisk (*), which matches all element nodes of the source. When we look through all element nodes, we find one that matches the title, so its position in the output tree is filled with the value of the title template. Then we find one that matches span, so its position in the output tree is filled with the value of the span template. The result, as we said, is the same as before, but it is achieved in a much more relaxed, unconstrained manner. In Listing 6-4, the lines of code in the body of the template precisely follow the desired output. In Listing 6-6, the order of templates is immaterial; the process of matching determines the order of evaluation. Even if we switch the last two templates around, the title template will be evaluated first because the <title> element precedes the <span> element in the XML source.

More precisely, matching element nodes to templates is done in document order, which is the order of elements' opening tags. In tree terms, document order is called **depth-first tree traversal**: we go as deeply as we can into the tree until we bottom out, then we back up until there is a sibling on the right that we have not yet visited, and move to that sibling.

## Variations and Default Templates

There is a little bit of cheating in Listing 6-6 that we are now going to expose. Let's take the same XML source (see Listing 6-2) and add another element that contains some text data. For instance, we can add a line that says `<p>nothing in particular</p>`. If we run `updateCount02.xsl` on this modified data, we will see that the new element's contents have been passed on to the output. The body of the output with some white space removed is shown in Listing 6-7. (The new line is shown in bold.)

*Listing 6-7. Unmatched Material Passed to Output*

```
<body>
   <div>
      <h2>Original Title: DBAuthService Result 1</h2>
      <h3>Rows affected: 1</h3>
      nothing in particular
   </div>
</body>
```

What happened? There is no template in our stylesheet that matches a <p> node, and yet its contents were added to the output. The answer is default templates. Generally speaking, when a node is sent out to look for a template that will match and process it, three outcomes are possible.

- There is exactly one template that matches the node.

- There is more than one template that matches the node.

- There are no templates that match the node.

The first case is easy. (The cheat in Listing 6-6 is that it provides only those easy cases.) In the second case, the processor uses the standard conflict-resolution policy to select the best match. In this brief overview, we are not going to give the complete set of rules (see our *XML Programming*, Apress 2002), but you will see an example shortly. In the third case, a default template is applied.

## Default Templates

There is a default template for each node type, as shown in Table 6-1. The attribute default rarely gets used because attributes are not children of their element and it takes a special effort to get to them. Defaults for element and text nodes are used routinely to output text values.

*Table 6-1. Node Types and Default Templates*

| Node Type | Default Template Action |
| --- | --- |
| root | Applies available templates to children, in document order |
| element | Applies available templates to children, in document order |
| text | Copies the text content |
| attribute | Copies the attribute value as text |

This explains what happened to our new <p> node: because it is an element node, it was on the list of nodes to be matched, and we asked to check out all of them. When no match was found, the default template was applied. This template said to apply all available templates to the children of this node. The only child of the <p> node in the XPath tree is the text node that contains its text. Again, the default template was applied and the text was sent to output.

A good way to see default templates in operation is to submit some XML data to the empty stylesheet whose <xsl:stylesheet> element has no content. All default templates will be applied and the output will be the entire text content of the input run together, in document order, with no markup.

## Two More Variations; Overriding the Defaults

The preceding discussion should raise at least these three issues in your minds. Issue 1: If default templates are applied anyway, why did we have to specify select= "* " and explicitly put all element nodes on the list to be matched? Simply put, we didn't. We could simply have said <xsl:apply-templates/> and the result would have been the same.

Issue 2: How do we override default templates and prevent unwanted material from reaching the output? By adding a template that matches all element nodes and tells them to do nothing if they are matched. The following should be added to Listing 6-6:

```
<xsl:template match="*">
  <!-- do nothing -->
</xsl:template>
```

But now we seem to have another problem. When a <title> or a <span> node looks for a match, it finds two possible matches: the specific match for that type of element node, and the generic match that we just added, which matches all element nodes. This is where conflict resolution rules step in. In this kind of conflict, the more specific rule wins. (XSLT has detailed rules for deciding whether one match is more specific than another, but if your program relies on those rules too much it will become difficult to maintain. We recommend that you redesign the program to make its logic explicit rather than hidden in conflict-resolution rules.)

Issue 3: Our problems with unwanted matches by default templates arise because in the initial selection of nodes to be matched (`<xsl:apply-templates select= "* "/>`), we put too many nodes on the list. Can we restrict that list so that only those nodes for which we provide additional templates are put on it? The answer is yes; our top-level template that uses `xsl:apply-templates` to create node lists to match can be more selective, as in Listing 6-8.

*Listing 6-8. Restricting Selection of Nodes to Match*

```
<xsl:template match="/">
  <html><head><title>updateCount05 Output</title></head><body>
  <div>
    <xsl:apply-templates select="html/head/title"/>
    <xsl:apply-templates select="html/body/span"/>
  </div>
  </body></html>
</xsl:template>
```

Now all additional material will be ignored.

At this point, we have probably done all the useful variations on update counts and can move on to more interesting data. We are also ready to learn a little more XPath and XSLT.

# XSLT for Amazon Data

In this section, the source of XML data for our stylesheets will come from Amazon searches, implemented in pure REST, with the GET command and the query string. We will run the search from the HTML form of Listing 6-10, which is a simplified and customized version of the form offered by Amazon as a sort of developer scratch pad at `http://www.amazon.com/gp/browse.html?node=3427431`. Our form submits HTTP GET requests with URLs of the following form (shown in Listing 6-9).

*Listing 6-9. URLs with Query Strings for Amazon REST Web Service*

```
http://xml.amazon.com/onca/xml2
      ?t=webservices-20
      &dev-t=[developer's token]
      &KeywordSearch=[subject keyword(s)]
      &mode=[product line: books, video, ...]
      &type=[lite or heavy]
      &page=[page #]
      &f=[URL of the XSLT stylesheet to use]
```

The form's action attribute sends the request to the right place at Amazon. The entry fields, one of them hidden, provide the parameters of the query string (shown in Listing 6-10).

*Listing 6-10. HTML Form for Submitting Requests to Amazon REST Web Service*

```
<form METHOD="GET" action="http://xml.amazon.com/onca/xml2">
<input type="hidden" name="t" value="webservices-20"/>
<table border="1">
<tr>
  <td>developer's token: <em>Please</em> use your own!</td>
  <td><input type="text" name="dev-t" value="USE_YOUR_OWN"/></td>
</tr><tr>
  <td>keywords</td>
  <td><input type="text" name="KeywordSearch" size="40"
                              value="Hernando de Soto Capitalism"/></td>
</tr><tr>
  <td>mode</td>
  <td><input type="text" name="mode" value="books"/></td>
</tr><tr>
  <td>type</td>
  <td><input type="text" name="type" value="lite"/></td>
</tr><tr>
```

```
  <td>page</td>
  <td><input type="text" name="page" value="1"/></td>
</tr><tr>
  <td>"xml", or XSL page URL</td>
  <td><input type="text" name="f" size="40"
              value="http://www.n-topus.com/xslt/AmaGet01.xsl"/></td>
</tr></table>
<input type="submit" value="search"/></form>
```

As the default value for the f parameter indicates, our stylesheets are stored at
http://www.n-topus.com/xslt/. (You have to place your stylesheet in a public location so that Amazon can access it.) The effect of submitting the form is that a
query is run at Amazon and its output is formatted using the specified stylesheet.
Although we are now using REST rather than SOAP, query results are, of course,
exactly the same as in Chapter 3. To remind you what they look like, Listing 6-11
shows a typical light record, with just a single Details element. (We write "..."
where the actual record shows lengthy URLs for images.)

*Listing 6-11. Amazon Light Record*

```
<?xml version="1.0" encoding="UTF-8"?>
<?xml-stylesheet type="text/xsl" href="AmaGet01.xsl"?>
<ProductInfo>
  <Details url="http://www.amazon.com/exec/obidos/ASIN/039480001X">
    <Asin>039480001X</Asin>
    <ProductName>The Cat in the Hat</ProductName>
    <Catalog>Book</Catalog>
    <Authors>
      <Author>Seuss</Author>
      <Author>Theodor Seuss Geisel</Author>
      <Author>Dr. Seuss</Author>
    </Authors>
    <ReleaseDate>June 1957</ReleaseDate>
    <Manufacturer>Random House</Manufacturer>
    <ListPrice>$8.99</ListPrice>
    <OurPrice>$8.99</OurPrice>
    <UsedPrice>$6.95</UsedPrice>
    <ImageUrlSmall>...</ImageUrlSmall>
    <ImageUrlMedium>...</ImageUrlMedium>
    <ImageUrlLarge>...</ImageUrlLarge>
  </Details>
</ProductInfo>
```

We will develop several stylesheets for Amazon light records like this one, assuming that they might contain more than one Details element.

## Tables Using Push

We want to output query results like this as a table of three columns. The first column will show a comma-separated list of authors. The second will show the product's title, which will be a link to the product's record at Amazon. The third column will show Amazon's price for the product. Our stylesheet will consist of three templates: the top-level template that matches the root, a template for the Details element, and a separate template to process Author elements and output their contents as a comma-separated list of names.

The first template (shown in Listing 6-12) should be completely familiar except that it sets up an HTML table for output and outputs its header row.

*Listing 6-12. Top-Level Template*

```
<xsl:template match="/">
  <html><head><title>AmaGet02.xsl</title></head>
    <body>
      <table border="1">
        <tr><th>Authors</th><th>Title</th><th>Price</th></tr>
        <xsl:apply-templates select="ProductInfo/Details" />
      </table>
    </body>
  </html>
</xsl:template>
```

The second template (shown in Listing 6-13) introduces two new XSLT constructs. The first new construct is variables. You can name a value and then refer to that value by its name prefixed by a dollar ($) sign. For instance, you can say `<xsl:variable name= "eight " select= "3+5 "/>` and the expression $eight will refer to number 8 (or perhaps string 8, depending on context). XSLT variables are like mathematical variables or variables in other declarative programming languages in that they vary from one subroutine call to another but can't be changed within a subroutine call. They are, in effect, local temporary constants. Most of the time we use variables to refer to node sets, as in our second template.

The second new construct in our template is output attributes that contain material from XML source. Remember that attribute values have to be quoted, and if we put an XSLT expression inside those quotes, it will remain unevaluated. So a special syntax is required to tell the XSLT processor that there is an expression that needs to be evaluated inside those output quotes. That special syntax is curly brackets, as you can see in the template of Listing 6-13.

*Listing 6-13. Template for Details Elements*

```
<xsl:template match="Details">
  <xsl:variable name="url" select="@url"/>
  <xsl:variable name="productName" select="ProductName"/>
  <tr><td>
      <xsl:apply-templates select="Authors/Author"/>
    </td><td>
      <a href="{$url}">
        <xsl:value-of select="$productName"/>
      </a>
    </td>
    <td><xsl:value-of select="OurPrice"/></td>
  </tr>
</xsl:template>
```

The template creates two variables and outputs a table row with three cells. The first cell's content is produced by yet another template. (You can see how XSLT templates are like subroutine calls in other languages—you can even give your template a name and parameters just as you would to a function or procedure.) The second and third cells are created in place, pulling in material from the XML source as needed. As is often the case, our stylesheet is not pure push, but combines pull and push styles in a reasonable compromise. Within the second cell, we construct an a element with an href attribute whose value comes from the XML source. This is where the curly-brackets syntax is used.

The final template for Author elements (shown in Listing 6-14) uses a conditional to see whether the element being processed is the first. If it's not, a comma and a space are inserted. Here we catch a glimpse of internal XSLT machinery. The result of a matching process is an ordered list of nodes. The function position() with no arguments indicates the position of each node in that list. To see whether the node is the first, we evaluate the expression position() > 1. Because an XSLT stylesheet is an XML document, we cannot use the character > as data; we use &gt; instead, which is replaced by the appropriate value during parsing.

*Listing 6-14. Template for Author Elements*

```
<xsl:template match="Author">
  <xsl:if test="position() &gt; 1">, </xsl:if>
  <span style="font-weight:bold"><xsl:value-of select="."/></span>
</xsl:template>
```

This concludes the push version for tabular Amazon output. Note that this stylesheet will work correctly whether the XML source contains one or many Details elements. However many there are, they will all be placed by matching in a list of elements to be processed, in their document order, and each one will be processed by the same templates that we have just worked our way through.

An alternative approach, closer in spirit to the more familiar programming languages, would be to say "Select all Details elements using an XPath expression and perform the following action **for each of them**." This is very much like using a loop.

## Creating Tables Using Pull and Sorting

We are going to produce the same output but we will use the pull style of programming (as shown in Listing 6-15). As a bonus, we will also sort the table by Amazon's price, which will require some string functions. As before, we are not going to be purists and use some push programming in the middle of pull. In particular, we will reuse the Author template from the preceding stylesheet.

*Listing 6-15. Tables Produced in the Pull Style and Sorted*

```
<xsl:template match="/">
  <html><head><title>AmaGet03.xsl</title></head>
    <body>
      <table border="1">
        <tr><th>Authors</th><th>Title</th><th>Price</th></tr>
<!-- the next line pulls all Details elements into the template -->
        <xsl:for-each select="ProductInfo/Details" >
    <!-- a line of code goes here to sort the output table by price -->
          <tr>
            <td><xsl:apply-templates select="Authors/Author"/></td>
            <td><a href="{@url}"><xsl:value-of select="ProductName"/></a></td>
            <td><xsl:value-of select="OurPrice"/></td>
          </tr>
        </xsl:for-each>
<!-- end of processing of Details elements -->
      </table>
    </body>
  </html>
</xsl:template>
```

Unsurprisingly, the body of the xsl:for-each element is the same as the body of the Details template in the preceding version, except for the new line of code for sorting. (We could have inserted the same line in the Details template and seen the same result.)

## Sorting, String Functions, and Data Types

The line that does the sorting looks like this.

```
<xsl:sort select="substring-after(OurPrice,'$')" data-type="number"/>
```

Several details need explaining, beginning with data types. XPath has four data types: string, number, Boolean, and node set. We have been largely preoccupied with node sets, but sometimes we have to deal with strings as well. XPath provides a number of string functions; they have names that are descriptive enough to give you an idea of what they do.

- string concat(string, string, ...)

- boolean starts-with(string, string)

- boolean contains(string, string)

- string substring-before(string, string)

- string substring-after(string, string)

- string substring(string, from-position)

- string substring(string, from-position, to-position)

- number string-length(string)

Sorting in XSLT is done by the xsl:sort element, which has to be the first child of an xsl:for-each or an xsl:template.

# Combining Data Sources in XSLT

In our final example, we will show how an XSLT stylesheet can combine material from multiple XML sources, similar to the way SQL join can combine material from several tables. In particular, we will combine material from DBAuthService and from Amazon itself. Remember that although DBAuthService holds some Amazon data locally, it does not contain all the data that is produced by an Amazon "heavy" query. For instance, it does not have a book's Amazon sales rank. In our example, we will output both the locally stored information about a given book (including reviews) and its Amazon sales rank. The output, assuming only one review is available, will look as shown in Figure 6-6.

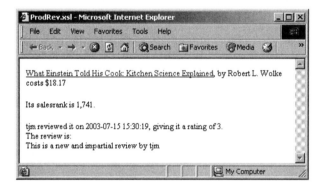

*Figure 6-6. Local reviews and the Amazon sales rank*

As you can see, our information comes from different tables at DBAuthService and from Amazon. Listing 6-16 shows the tables we are combining, with their fields listed.

*Listing 6-16. Information Sources*

```
ProdRevs: AsinUserID,Asin,UserID,dtime,Rating,Keywords,Review
AmaBks:   Asin,ProductName,ReleaseDate,Manufacturer,OurPrice,Url
AmaAuth:  Asin,Author
Amazon: heavy, contains /ProductInfo/Details/SalesRank
```

Note that we are making three calls to DBAuthService to retrieve data from three different tables. Because DBAuthService is a single-threaded process, this presents a logistical problem. If the first call is not finished, the second one cannot start. (It's like calling yourself on the phone—the number will always be busy.) One way to get around this problem would be to run each JDBC database access in a separate thread, but this would complicate the Java programming. Another possibility, and the one we have chosen, is to open a second copy of DBAuthService. This second copy will use a configuration file that is identical in every respect except for the port number. The first copy, on port 65432, can use a stylesheet that invokes the second copy on port 65431, but the second copy must not invoke either. It just returns XHTML pages.

The XSLT tool for combining XML sources is the document() function. This function takes a URL string as its argument. The URL can contain a query string, so the document retrieved by the function can be dynamically constructed, for example, the result of a database query. Our stylesheet will go through the same pattern several times: construct a URL for a query, call the document() function, save the result in a variable, and use XSLT and XPath to extract values from that variable. For instance, suppose we have a book specified by an ASIN and the value of that ASIN is stored in the XSLT variable asin. To extract the authors of that book from the AmaAuth table of the DBAuthService, we go through the steps shown in Listing 6-17.

*Listing 6-17.* document() *Call with Constructed URL*

```
<xsl:variable name="baseRef"  select="'http://localhost:65431/'" />
<xsl:variable name="audoc"
  select="document(concat($baseRef,'AmaAuth/',$asin))"/>
<xsl:variable name="authorTable" select="$audoc/html/body/table" />
```

Note that the port number is specific to this particular DBAuthService access because it is done in the middle of another one. We can now go through the code of the stylesheet in order. Because it is fairly long, we will start with an outline.

## The Top-Level Template

In outline, our stylesheet proceeds as follows. The XML source on which the stylesheet operates is created by a REST DBService call such as

```
http://localhost:65432/ProdRevs/0393011836?xslt=ProdRevs.xsl
```

The top-level template outputs the basic HTML structure (html, head, body) and calls `<xsl:apply-template select= "* "/>` in the middle of the `<body>` element. There are two other templates, one for `<table>`, the other for `<tr>`. Most of the work is done in the `<table>` template. The `<tr>` template specifies output for each review of the book (which will be stored in a row of the XHTML table returned by an SQL query via a REST Web Service query) from the ProdRevs table of DBAuthService. The skeleton of the stylesheet is shown in Listing 6-18. Recall that the XHTML tables returned by REST calls on DBAuthService have a header row, and XSLT numbers nodes on a node list starting with 1, so the first data row is `tr[2]`.

*Listing 6-18. Skeleton of ProdRevs.xsl*

```
<xsl:stylesheet xmlns:xsl="http://www.w3.org/1999/XSL/Transform"
                version="1.0">
<xsl:output method="html" />
<xsl:template match="/"><!-- top-level match -->
  <html><head><title>ProdRevs.xsl</title></head>
    <body>
      <xsl:apply-templates select="*" />
    </body>
  </html>
</xsl:template>
<xsl:template match="table"><!-- most of the code here -->
  <xsl:variable name="asin" select="tr[2]/td[2]"/>
  <xsl:if test="$asin">
<!-- code to extract data from DBService and Amazon here -->
  <div>
<!-- produce output other than review data here -->
<!-- call xsl:apply-templates to produce review data -->
  <xsl:apply-templates select="tr[position()&gt;1]"/>
  </div>
  </xsl:if>
</xsl:template>
<xsl:template match="tr">
<!-- output review data here -->
</xsl:template>
</xsl:stylesheet>
```

The next subsection shows how the data is extracted and combined.

## Pulling in XML Data

The <table> template starts out, as we just saw in Listing 6-18, by extracting the ASIN from the table element and checking to see that it is not null. Almost the entire body of the template is within the xsl:if element. The first three blocks of code follow the same pattern, as shown in Listing 6-17, which is, in fact, the first of those three blocks. The pattern, to recapitulate, is to construct a URL, call the document() function, and extract information from the returned document. Listing 6-19 shows the first two blocks, both accessing DBAuthService.

*Listing 6-19. Pulling in XML Data, Part 1*

```
<xsl:template match="table">
  <xsl:variable name="asin" select="tr[2]/td[2]"/>
  <xsl:if test="$asin">
<!-- extract authors from AmaAuth table at DBAuthService;
        same as Listing 6-17 -->
  <xsl:variable name="baseRef"
    select="'http://localhost:65431/'" />
  <xsl:variable name="audoc"
    select="document(concat($baseRef,'AmaAuth/',$asin))"/>
  <xsl:variable name="authorTable" select="$audoc/html/body/table" />
<!-- extract other book data from AmaBks table at DBAuthService -->
  <xsl:variable name="bkdoc"
    select="document(concat($baseRef,'AmaBks/',$asin))"/>
  <xsl:variable name="bkRow"
    select="$bkdoc/html/body/table/tr[2]"/>
  <xsl:variable name="prodName" select="$bkRow/td[2]"/>
  <xsl:variable name="releaseDate" select="$bkRow/td[3]"/>
  <xsl:variable name="manufacturer" select="$bkRow/td[4]"/>
  <xsl:variable name="ourPrice" select="$bkRow/td[5]"/>
  <xsl:variable name="url" select="$bkRow/td[6]"/>
```

The next block of code (shown in Listing 6-20) extracts the book's sales rank from the Amazon Web Service using the same form and XSLT stylesheets as Listing 6-12 to Listing 6-14. The difference is that this time around we construct the URL as a string inside another stylesheet and invoke the service using document().

*Listing 6-20. Pulling in XML Data, Part 2*

```
  <xsl:variable name="devT" select="USE YOUR OWN"/>
  <xsl:variable name="amaBase"
    select="'http://xml.amazon.com/onca/xml2?t=webservices-20'"/>
```

```
<xsl:variable name="amaURL"
   select="concat($amaBase,'&amp;dev-t=',$devT,
               '&amp;AsinSearch=',$asin,
                '&amp;type=heavy&amp;f=xml')"/>
<xsl:variable name="amaDoc" select="document($amaURL)"/>
<xsl:variable name="salesRank"
   select="$amaDoc/ProductInfo/Details/SalesRank"/>
```

With all the data now packaged into variables, we can produce output as desired.

## Producing the Output

Instead of a table, we are going to create a <div> with paragraphs and line breaks. The code is in two parts. The first part (shown in Listing 6-21) is still within the <table> template. It outputs all book information other than reviews. If there is more than one author, we will sort them alphabetically and separate them by <and>. This is done with the xsl:for-each element. Remember that author names will be in the second column of the returned XHTML table, beginning with row 2 of that table.

*Listing 6-21. Output Code, Part 1*

```
<div> <p>
   <a href="{$url}"><xsl:value-of select="$prodName"/></a><br/>
      <xsl:text>, by </xsl:text>
      <xsl:for-each select="$authorTable/tr[position() &gt; 1]/td[2]">
<!-- select second cell in each row after the first, i.e., author names -->
         <xsl:sort select="substring-after(.,' ')"/>
         <xsl:if test="position()&gt; 1"> and </xsl:if>
         <xsl:value-of select="."/>
      </xsl:for-each><br/>
      <xsl:text> costs </xsl:text>
      <xsl:value-of select="$ourPrice"/>
   </p><p>
      Its Amazon sales rank is
      <xsl:value-of select="$salesRank"/>.
   </p>
   <xsl:apply-templates select="tr[position()&gt;1]"/>
   </div>
   </xsl:if>
</xsl:template><!-- end of the table template -->
```

The rest of the output is produced by the <tr> template that handles reviews and the sales rank (shown in Listing 6-22). Note that we extract more data items into variables than we need, just in case we'll need them in a later revised and expanded edition.

*Listing 6-22. Output Code, Part 2*

```
<xsl:template match="tr">
  <xsl:variable name="asin" select="td[2]"/>
  <xsl:variable name="userID" select="td[3]"/>
  <xsl:variable name="dTime" select="td[4]"/>
  <xsl:variable name="rating" select="td[5]"/>
  <xsl:variable name="keywords" select="td[6]"/>
  <xsl:variable name="review" select="td[7]"/>
  <p>
      <xsl:value-of select="$userID"/> reviewed it on
      <xsl:value-of select="$dTime"/>, <br/>giving it a rating of
      <xsl:value-of select="$rating"/>; <br/>the review is
      <br/>
      <xsl:value-of select="$review"/>
  </p>
</xsl:template>
```

This concludes the code of ProdRevs.xsl. Of course, our use of SalesRank is just for illustration; you'll do better in performance terms if you cache all the Amazon data you need into your own database and just refresh it from Amazon every 24 hours per the Amazon license agreement. However, there will always be data that you didn't think you would need, there can be new kinds of data on Amazon, or you might need to access your user's shopping cart from the current session. In all these cases, something like ProdRevs.xsl might well be useful.

## Conclusion

In this chapter, we scratched the surface of XSLT and found it to be interesting and useful. We will see more XSLT in the next chapter. Our hope is that this brief introduction will give you ideas for further exploration and perhaps even lead to more in-depth study. We can again recommend our *XML Programming*, (Apress 2002), as a possible next step before you take up a dedicated XSLT book such as Michael Kay's *XSLT Programmer's Reference*, (WROX 2001).

Notice that we ended Chapter 3 with a SOAP application that dealt with Google, Amazon, and a weather service. Here we have a REST application that deals with Amazon and a REST/SOAP application of our own—but it can't communicate to Google or a weather service unless those services are wrapped in REST front ends. In the next chapter, we'll work with server tools for REST, and we'll show a uniform way of writing REST front ends (with XSLT if needed) for SOAP services.

# Tomcat, JSP, and WebDAV

COMMUNITY-ORIENTED WEB SERVICES for sharing or jointly authoring documents, such as blogs, RSS, and Wikis are becoming an increasingly important part of the Internet. These and other collaborative technologies are improving every day, but they still need greater standardization. Underneath reasonably uniform functionality, they are implemented in vastly different ways that are difficult to exchange or extend. The closest thing to a standard *protocol* for distributed authoring is WebDAV, an IETF-sponsored set of extensions to HTTP. In this chapter, we will develop a WebDAV-based community Web Service/client.

WebDAV (or simply DAV for short) stands for Distributed Authoring and Versioning. You'll find a description, FAQ, and resources for WebDAV at http://www.webdav.org/. The FAQ defines WebDAV as "a set of extensions to the HTTP protocol that allows users to collaboratively edit and manage files on remote Web servers." The versioning part of WebDAV is still in the works, but the authoring part has been stable for some time. It is, in fact, an under-used starting point for community software; it is adequate for many purposes and it can be easily extended. All you need in order to start is a WebDAV server on a computer that all your users can reach and WebDAV clients on your users' computers. At this point, you may be thinking: "Yet another set of clients and servers? No way!" But given that WebDAV servers (most of them are free) include both Tomcat and the Apache Web server (with mod_dav module), and WebDAV clients include Microsoft Word, OpenOffice.org, and Dreamweaver (with Dreamweaver 4.01 Updater) it is very likely that you and your friends already have all the software you need to start using WebDAV.

In this chapter, we build a Tomcat-based WebDAV service. Once it is configured, you can use any WebDAV client (Microsoft Word or OpenOffice.org ) to save HTML pages on the service. That part is almost trivial—you just need to know how to configure Tomcat—and does not require any programming. In our service, when you save an HTML page, it will be intercepted by a filter that we'll write in Java. The filter will convert the saved HTML into XHTML with a program called Tidy (http://tidy.sourceforge.net/). The "tidied" HTML can be given as an XML source to an XSLT processor (that would have choked on the initial untidied HTML, especially if it has been produced by Microsoft Word's Save as HTML feature).That's as far as this chapter will go, but in the next chapter, we will revise the filter to do much more. First, it will call an XSLT stylesheet that will restructure the initial HTML into a hierarchical XML structure. The restructured XML can then be written (again using our filter) into a database. Once in the database, the initial HTML data will be searchable and linkable in very detailed and elaborate ways that go far beyond string-matching searches through HTML pages. In effect, we'll build a Wiki based on structure found within HTML markup, or inferred from that markup. We don't know if this will revolutionize Wiki technology, but something will, someday soon, and this system, summarized in Figure 7-1, might give you ideas.

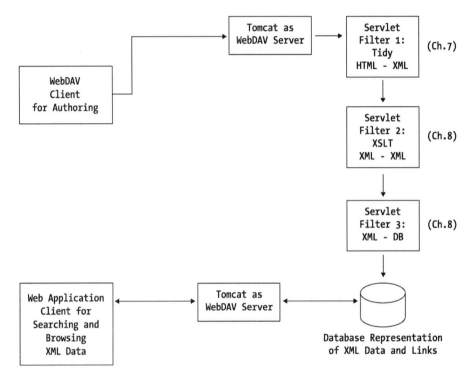

*Figure 7-1. WebDAV with filtering and database*

Before we can build this system, we'll need a little more familiarity with Tomcat itself, JSPs, WebDAV, and the notion of servlet filters.

In this chapter, we will cover the following:

- Tomcat basics, including configuration

- JSP basics: dealing with requests and responses

- JSP for putting SOAP to REST and back

- WebDAV basics

- Building the filter chain: Tidy, XSLT, and JDBC

We'll start with Tomcat, a remarkable piece of open-source software that is getting better all the time.

## Tomcat and JSP

Tomcat is "the official reference implementation for the Java Servlet and JavaServer Pages technologies." These are the standard approaches for building dynamic pages in Java, whether HTML or XML or any other Web resource. Virtually all the dynamic-page building logic of DBAuthService is contained within the logic of Tomcat, and the Tomcat source code is available. We hope and believe that your experience with DBAuthService will give you good starting-points in working with the Tomcat code from the inside.

Tomcat can be used as a standalone Web server (with Servlet and JSP capabilities) or as a Servlet/JSP processor attached to another server, such as Apache or IIS. The early versions of Tomcat could only function as a Web server for small projects or prototypes, but Tomcat's Web server powers have grown with each new release so it's now a plausible basis for large-scale projects.

We will not go into the details of Tomcat installation except to say that it results in a directory tree. The path to the root of that tree is stored in the TOMCAT_HOME system or environment variable. The root of the Tomcat tree has these children.

- bin: A bunch of executable files, including startup.[sh,bat] and shutdown.[sh,bat]

- blurb: License and release notes

- common/lib: jar files shared by all Web applications

- conf: General server configuration files

- logs: Log files

- server/lib: jar files used by the server itself

- webapps: This is the most important directory for Tomcat users. Each individual Web application is a subdirectory of webapps. Connecting to the URL of the host and port on which Tomcat is running puts you into the webapps directory.

- work: This is the directory where the actual code of JavaServer pages is placed, as explained in the next section.

Each individual webapp subdirectory also has a specific structure: a configuration file, web.xml, and a subdirectory called WEB-INF. This subdirectory may have subdirectories to hold Java code of the application, including classes (for Java .class files) and lib (for Java .jar files). The entire directory structure is summarized in Figure 7-2.

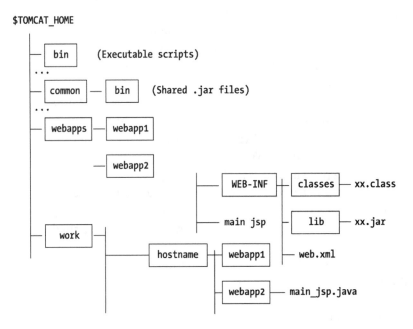

*Figure 7-2. Tomcat and Web application directory structure*

As we go through the workings of JSPs and WebDAV within Tomcat, we will make frequent references to this directory structure.

## JSP Basics

Like any Web server, Tomcat can serve plain HTML pages, but its main strength is its ability to run servlets and JSPs. We will go through two "educational" JSPs—one very basic and another that provides a REST wrapper for a SOAP call.

## *testJSP.jsp*

We start with a page that looks at the request information and echoes some of it, just to show how HTML and Java work together in a JSP. The page, testJSP.jsp, contains the date, information about the client, information about the HTTP header (the URL and the method), and the value of the parameter named "Q," as shown in Figure 7-3.

*Figure 7-3. testJSP.jsp output*

If you were to click the "Try again" link, the page would be invoked with a parameter Q=hello, and the last line of the output would change, unsurprisingly, to

```
The value of the parameter named "Q" is hello.
```

Let's take a look at the code, breaking it in three parts (shown in Listings 7-1 to 7-3). As you read the code, consult Figure 7-3 to see its effect. The testJSP.jsp page starts like this.

*Listing 7-1. testJSP.jsp, Part 1*

```
<%@ page import="java.util.Date" %>
<html><head><title>testJSP.jsp</title></head><body>
<h1> This is the page testJSP.jsp </h1>
<p>
   It's <%= new Date() %>.
   You called from <%= request.getRemoteHost()      %>
   (IP Address      <%= request.getRemoteAddr()      %>);
   with browser <i><%= request.getHeader("user-agent") %></i>.
</p>
```

As you can see, the file begins with a page declaration that identifies it to the JSP processor as possibly containing JSP code and tells the processor do an import of the java.util.Date class. Then we can start with the top-level HTML tags—in fact, we just write the page in plain HTML, but with the following variations. When we write Java code for execution, we place it within <% ... %> , and when we want to include a Java string value, we place that value within <%= ... %>. (As you will see in a moment, we can put any Java expression within those brackets, but it will be converted to string when it is included in the resulting Web page.)

Next, we extract more information from the request object to construct the URI at which the page is found (see Listing 7-2).

*Listing 7-2. testJSP.jsp, Part 2*

```
<%
   String uri= request.getScheme()+"://";
   uri       +=request.getServerName()+":"+request.getServerPort();
   uri       +=request.getRequestURI();
%>
<p>
  You found this page at <%= uri  %>.
  Your request method was <%= request.getMethod() %>.
</p>
```

Finally, we check the value of parameter Q. Because we did not specify any such parameter, its value will be the null object. When it appears within <%= ... %>, it is converted to the string "null" that you saw in Figure 7-3. We construct a "retryURI" that has ?Q=hello attached to the initial URI, and invite the user to click it (shown in Listing 7-3).

*Listing 7-3. testJSP.jsp, Part 3*

```
<%
    String qParam=request.getParameter("Q");
%>
<p>
  The value of the parameter named "Q" is
      <b><%= qParam %></b>.
<%
    if( qParam==null || qParam.length() == 0){
      String retryURI = request.getRequestURI() + "?Q=hello";
%>
      <a href="<%= retryURI %>" >Try again with Q="hello"</a>
<%
    }
%>
</body></html>
```

Now that we have seen a JSP and the dynamic Web page that it produces, we can take a peek at how the computation is done.

## The JSP and its Java Code

The complete URI of testJSP.jsp is http://localhost:8080/wsbk/testJSP.jsp. This means that it is found in the $TOMCAT_HOME$/webapps/wsbk directory, and when we refer to it by its URI in the browser window, we tell the Web server to run the program created and compiled in the first run-through. Its source code can be found at TOMCAT_HOME/work/Standalone/localhost/wsbk/testJSP_jsp.java. This is what happens with all JSPs: their "code" is converted in to pure Java and placed in a subdirectory of the work directory, which is right underneath TOMCAT_HOME.

We are going to look selectively at the code of testJSP_jsp.java, beginning with package and import statements in Listing 7-4.

*Listing 7-4. The Java Code for testJSP.jsp, Package and Import Statements*

```
package org.apache.jsp;
import javax.servlet.*;
import javax.servlet.http.*;
import javax.servlet.jsp.*;
import org.apache.jasper.runtime.*;
import java.util.Date;
public class testJSP_jsp extends HttpJspBase {
```

As you can see, we're defining a class within a package and importing a good many utilities (including the java.util.Date utility at the top of the JSP file). The rest of the code defines the method.

```
public void _jspService
    (
      HttpServletRequest request,
      HttpServletResponse response
    )
```

The request argument of this method is precisely the object we've been using to obtain the header and parameter information; the method itself contains the code of the JSP.

```
out.write("\r\n");
out.write("<html>");
out.write("<head>");
out.write("<title>testJSP.jsp");
out.write("</title>");
out.write("</head>");
out.write("<body>\r\n\r\n");
out.write("<h1> This is the page testJSP.jsp ");
out.write("</h1>\r\n\r\n");
out.write("<p>\r\n    It's ");
out.print( new Date() );
out.write(".\r\n   You called from ");
out.print( request.getRemoteHost() );
```

It's rather monotonous code, full of out.write() for string constants and out.print() for computed string values, but you can see how it relates to the JSP file. When you make an error in your JSP file, the error message comes with references to line numbers in this generated Java file and an estimate for the line number in the JSP. In JSP, you work with a request object and a response object. Usually, you read parameters and headers from the request object (although you can read its body, for example, XmlHttp actions) and write to the response object via the out object, a Java character stream. There's a great deal more to it, and many books (including our own *XML Programming*, Apress, 2002 ) that go into further details, but this should be enough to get you started. We'll show you just a few more JSP features and present a JSP that connects SOAP with REST.

# SOAPxslt.jsp

In the first three chapters, we developed a soapUtil.XmlHttp.sendSoap() method to send a soap action and payload to a given URL, and we used it within an applet. This makes SOAP usable from within a browser even if it doesn't have Javascript enabled or its Javascript does not have an XmlHttp object. However, an applet is a fairly heavyweight client. We have shown the convenience of REST with XSLT, allowing very lightweight clients—no applets, indeed no client-side code at all; just a browser. How can we just construct a lightweight client to work with Google even though Google does not offer a REST interface? JSP is an answer. We can write a dynamic Web page that takes the parameters needed by sendSoap(), runs the SOAP message exchange, and if an xslt parameter is provided, passes the result through an XSLT stylesheet. This is not "pure" REST in the sense that we are again misusing the HTTP GET method, but it's very convenient. (We can check the request object's method, of course, and accept only POST, but this would be less convenient.)

The application is an ordinary Web page, googleREST.html. It contains a form in which to enter arguments for a SOAP call, most of them defaults (shown in Figure 7-4).

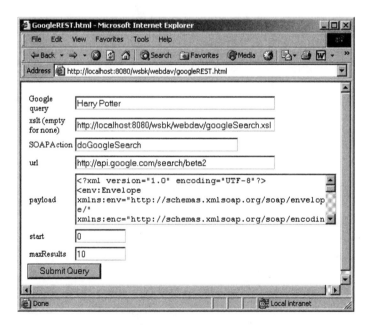

*Figure 7-4. The Google REST client,* googleREST.html

One of the parameters of the form is the URI of an XSLT stylesheet, which can be on the local host; the provided default is googleSearch.xsl. If we enter "Harry Potter" as the query term, we get the output shown in Figure 7-5.

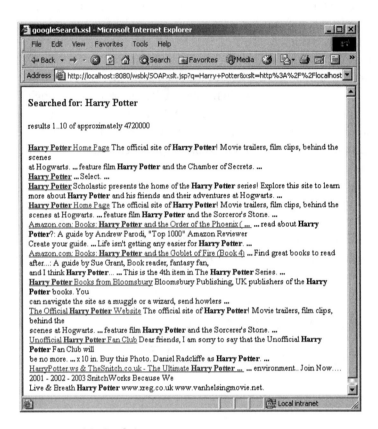

*Figure 7-5. SOAPxslt.jsp output*

There are four phases of processing going on in this submission.

- The form of Listing 7-5 has an onSubmit() method that uses Javascript to construct the payload from the other parameters. We could ask the JSP to do this, but it would have to be specialized to Google. As it is currently written, SOAPxslt.jsp doesn't know anything about Google.

- SOAPxslt.jsp invokes SOAP and obtains the result, which is XML containing escaped HTML strings (in which, for example, < is represented by &lt;).

- If a stylesheet URI has been indicated, SOAPxslt.jsp applies the stylesheet to that result—but HTML strings will still be entitized. XSLT doesn't have good tools for converting the entity representation into the actual characters.

- The HTML page constructed by the stylesheet has an onload() method that converts the entitized characters into characters in the input strings. This approach provides a simple solution to a problem that is quite common. Often, XML tools work with well-formed XML containing HTML that has been entitized for safety. Somehow, you have to get back from &lt; to <, and interpret the result syntactically.

In the next four subsections, we will go over each of the four phases, beginning with the HTML client.

## The HTML Client Page

As we said, the client is an ordinary Web page, googleREST.html (shown in Listing 7-5). It contains a form to enter arguments for a SOAP call and two Javascript functions. The first, fixEnvelope(), collects the arguments from the form and calls the second function, which is good old doGoogleSearchEnvelope() of the early chapters. (See, for example, doAmazonKeywordSearchEnvelope() of Listing 3-5 for comparison.) The result of this search is stored in the payload field of the form, so it gets submitted to the JSP page on the server.

*Listing 7-5.* googleREST.html

```
<html><head><title>GoogleREST.html</title>
<script>
var key="Use Your Own";
function fixEnvelope(theForm){
  with(theForm)
    payload.value=doGoogleSearchEnvelope(key,q.value,start.value,max.value);
  return true;
}
function doGoogleSearchEnvelope(key,q,start,maxResults){
  var env='<?xml version="1.0" encoding="UTF-8"?>\n';
  env+='<env:Envelope xmlns:env="http://schemas.xmlsoap.org/soap/envelope/"';
<!-- same as in early chapters;
    see doAmazonKeywordSearchEnvelope(), Listing 3-5 -->
  env+='</env:Envelope>';
  return env;
}
```

```
</script>
</head><body>
<form name="googleForm" ...>
  action="http://localhost:8080/wsbk/SOAPxslt.jsp"
  onSubmit="return fixEnvelope(document.googleForm)" >
  <!-- see Listing 7-6 below -->
<input type="submit"/>
</form>
</body></html>
```

The function returns true because it's used as the form's onSubmit() method, which customarily returns true to proceed with submission or false to cancel it. Here is the form (see Listing 7-6).

*Listing 7-6. The Form of* googleREST.html

```
<form name="googleForm" method="GET"
  action="http://localhost:8080/wsbk/SOAPxslt.jsp"
  onSubmit="return fixEnvelope(document.googleForm)" >
<table>
<tr>
  <td>Google query</td><!-- enter query terms here -->
  <td><input type="text" name="q" value="Harry Potter" size="50"/></td>
</tr><tr>
  <td>xslt (empty for none)</td>
  <td><input type="text" name="xslt"
      value="http://localhost:8080/wsbk/webdav/googleSearch.xsl"
  size="50"/></td>
</tr><tr>
  <td>SOAPAction</td>
  <td><input type="text" name="SOAPAction" value="doGoogleSearch"
      size="40"/></td>
</tr><tr>
  <td>url</td>
  <td><input type="text" name="url" value="http://api.google.com/search/beta2"
size="50"/></td>
</tr><tr>
  <td>payload</td>
  <td><textarea name="payload" rows="5" cols="50"></textarea></td>
</tr><tr>
<!-- other parameters for Google Web service query -->
</tr></table>
<input type="submit"/>
</form>
```

This form, including the payload computed by fixEnvelope(), is submitted to the SOAPxslt.jsp page. The page, as you recall, runs the SOAP call and pipes the result through an XSLT stylesheet.

## The JSP Page

That page consists of three blocks of code. It begins with a <%@ page ... %> declaration that imports a variety of standard Java classes and one user-defined class (where the "user" is us). The class, soapUtil.XmlHttp, is the equivalent of the xml-http objects of the earlier chapters. Next we see a <% .. %> Java code block that does the calculation and output using methods from the imported classes and two local methods. Finally, there is a <%! .. %> Java code block that defines the local methods. There is no HTML markup in this JSP page because all the output comes from the method results.

### Local Methods of the JSP

Let's look at SOAPxslt.jsp's local methods first. We have a method to perform an XSLT transformation (shown in Listing 7-7) and another to show errors (shown in Listing 7-8).

*Listing 7-7. The JSP Local Method to Invoke XSLT Transformer*

```
public static String transform(String xslt,String soapResult)
    throws Throwable{
  Transformer transformer=null;
  TransformerFactory tFactory = TransformerFactory.newInstance();
  StreamSource xsltSrc = new StreamSource(xslt);
  transformer = tFactory.newTransformer(xsltSrc);
  StreamSource streamSrc = new StreamSource(new StringReader(soapResult));
  StringWriter resultStrWriter=new StringWriter();
  StreamResult streamResult=new StreamResult(resultStrWriter)
  transformer.transform(streamSrc,streamResult);
  return outStrW.toString();
}
```

Since the release of the javax.xml package, this is the standard Java way of running an XSLT stylesheet from within Java code. (A very similar block of code runs XSLT in DBAuthService.) Basically, we obtain a new javax.xml.Transformer object that has the intended XSLT already compiled and imprinted on it at creation time.

We perform the transformation by invoking the transformer's transform() method. The method takes two arguments, the XML Source and the Result to dump output to. Both the source and the result can be simply Java streams, although the source can also be a DOM tree or a number of other things. In our code, we use a Stream-Source (one byte at a time) both for the XML source (which is the SOAP result) and the output (and, in fact, also for the stylesheet itself). The StreamSource constructor can take either a stream or the name of a resource (file or URI) as an argument, to which it would open a stream itself. With the SOAP result, we have the string value, which we have to convert to a character stream before we can use it as an argument of transform().

Next we look at the method for showing exceptions, or more generally throwable values (shown in Listing 7-8). It hides a rather complicated situation in which errors can be wrapped within errors. Syntactic errors are common in the XML of the stylesheet, as you will discover on your own as soon as you start testing your own XSLTs. showThrowable() looks inside the error object to see if it's wrapping another error, then looks inside that, and so on. If it finds that the innermost error is indeed a SAXParseException thrown by the XML parser, we show that; otherwise we show just the top-level error. The reason we are trying to get to the parser-thrown exception is that it identifies the line and column number of the error within the file being parsed.

*Listing 7-8. Unwrapping Exceptions with* showThrowable()

```
public static void showThrowable(Throwable t,PrintWriter out){
  // if the problem is just a SAXParseException of one of the
  // StreamSources, show that; otherwise show the top throwable.
  Throwable th=t;
  while(t!=null){
    if(t instanceof TransformerException)
      t=((TransformerException)t).getException();
    if(t instanceof SAXParseException)break;
    if(t instanceof SAXException)
      t=((SAXException)t).getException();
  }
  SAXParseException spe=(SAXParseException)t;
  if(spe!=null){
    out.println(""+spe+"\n"+
                "publicID="+spe.getPublicId()+";systemId="+spe.getSystemId()+
                "; line:col="+spe.getLineNumber()+":"+spe.getColumnNumber());
    spe.printStackTrace(out);
  }else th.printStackTrace(out);
}
```

## The Rest of the JSP

Given the two local methods, the rest of the Java code of SOAPxslt.jsp is pretty straightforward (shown in Listing 7-9). It reads the parameters provided by googleREST.html and it asks the soapUtil.XmlHttp object to do the SOAP invocation. If a stylesheet has been requested, it applies that stylesheet. Otherwise, it returns the raw XML value after overriding the response object's default "text/html" content-type with "text/xml."

*Listing 7-9. Java Code of* SOAPxslt.jsp

```
try{
   String xslt=request.getParameter("xslt");
   String soapAction=request.getParameter("SOAPAction");
   String url=request.getParameter("url");
   String payload=request.getParameter("payload");
   String soapResult=XmlHttp.sendSoap(url,soapAction,payload);

   if(xslt==null || xslt.length() == 0) {
     response.setContentType("text/xml");
     out.println(soapResult);
   }
   else {
     String outStr=transform(xslt,soapResult);
     out.println(outStr);
   }
}catch(Throwable t){
   showThrowable(t,new PrintWriter(out));
}
```

As you can see, the SOAPxslt.jsp page has no knowledge of any particular SOAP service; it's up to the client to tell it what service to use and what stylesheet should be applied to the result. In this case, we're using the wsbk/webdav/googleSearch.xsl stylesheet, which just happens to be our next subject.

## The Stylesheet

The stylesheet of this section works on Google search output. We haven't looked at that output since Chapter 2, so here's a reminder of its basic structure. Listing 7-10 (identical to Listing 2-12) shows the top-level elements.

*Listing 7-10. Top-Level Elements of Google Search Response*

```
<?xml version='1.0' encoding='UTF-8'?>
<SOAP-ENV:Envelope
  xmlns:SOAP-ENV='http://schemas.xmlsoap.org/soap/envelope/'
  xmlns:xsi='http://www.w3.org/1999/XMLSchema-instance'
  xmlns:xsd='http://www.w3.org/1999/XMLSchema'
>
<SOAP-ENV:Body>
<ns1:doGoogleSearchResponse
  xmlns:ns1='urn:GoogleSearch'
  SOAP-ENV:encodingStyle='http://schemas.xmlsoap.org/soap/encoding/'
>
  <return xsi:type='ns1:GoogleSearchResult'>
<!-- see Listing 2-13 for the contents of return -->
  </return>
</ns1:doGoogleSearchResponse>
</SOAP-ENV:Body>
</SOAP-ENV:Envelope>
```

Notice that the top-level elements of the stylesheet's input declare and use namespaces (SE and NS1) that the stylesheet will have to match. Therefore, they have to be declared in the stylesheet, as shown in Listing 7-11.

*Listing 7-11. Stylesheet Header with Namespace Declarations*

```
<xsl:stylesheet
  xmlns:xsl="http://www.w3.org/1999/XSL/Transform"
  xmlns:SE="http://schemas.xmlsoap.org/soap/envelope/"
  xmlns:ns1="urn:GoogleSearch"
  version="1.0"
>
```

Now we come to something new: the stylesheet is forming a page with Javascript code in it. Let's take a look at the top-level match, shown in Listing 7-12.

*Listing 7-12. Top-Level Match of* googleSearch.xsl

```
<xsl:template match="/">
  <html><head><title>googleSearch.xsl</title>
<script language="javascript">
  function unescapeAll(){
    ...
```

```
</script>
  </head>
  <body onload="unescapeAll()">
    <xsl:apply-templates
      select="SE:Envelope/SE:Body/ns1:doGoogleSearchResponse/return"
    />
  </body>
</html>
</xsl:template>
```

The Javascript function unescapeAll(), defined within the <script> element, will be executed as soon as the page loads. As we promised earlier, we will "unescape" character codes within HTML/Javascript. First, let's pursue the templates as they dig into the XML source tree. In Listing 7-12, apply-templates selects the elements of the input, of which there is exactly one. The template that matches return (shown in Listing 7-13) is a combination of pull and push. It pulls in a few children of return before pushing the action out to another template. Before you read through the code, you may want to review Figure 7-5, which shows the output of the stylesheet, or better yet, run the application and see the output on screen.

*Listing 7-13. Template to Match the* return *Element*

```
<xsl:template match="return">
  <h3>Searched for: <xsl:value-of select="searchQuery"/></h3>
  <p>results
    <xsl:value-of select="startIndex"/>..<xsl:value-of select="endIndex"/>
    of
    <xsl:if test="'false'=string(estimateIsExact)"> approximately </xsl:if>
    <xsl:value-of select="estimatedTotalResultsCount"/>
  </p>
  <xsl:apply-templates select="resultElements"/>
</xsl:template>
```

The only thing left is to generate the output for the list of item subtrees found within resultElements (shown in Listing 7-14). Each subtree contains a URL, a title, and a snippet, where both the title and the snippet are entitized HTML data. Because XSLT doesn't have any tools for removing the entities, we wrap them into span elements with class="escData" so the Javascript can find them easily and move on. To separate elements of the resulting page, we output   which is the same character as   but XML doesn't recognize nbsp.

*Listing 7-14. Template to Match* item *Elements*

```
<xsl:template match="item">
  <div>
    <a href="{URL}">
      <span class="escData"><xsl:value-of select="title"/></span>
    </a>
    <xsl:text> </xsl:text>
    <span class="escData"><xsl:value-of select="snippet"/></span>
  </div>
</xsl:template>
```

That's all there is to the template, except for the Javascript code that will do the unescaping (shown in Listing 7-15). In order to understand how it works, remember that the DOM tree of an HTML document holds the text content of an element in a special text node that is the first child of that element's node. So, for instance, a span holding text will be represented in the tree by a node of type Element whose first child will be a node of type Text, which holds the text content of the span. To retrieve that content, you would get the nodeValue of the text node.

> **NOTE** *If the text content of an element exceeds a certain limit, it may be broken into two or more TEXT nodes. To retrieve the entire text content, we would loop through the "next siblings" of the first child. This does not apply to the titles and small snippets of Google output.*

As you read through the code, notice the &lt; and &amp;&amp; symbols, representing the Javascript < and && operators.

*Listing 7-15. Javascript Function for Unescaping*

```
function unescapeAll(){
  var spans=document.getElementsByTagName("span");
  for(var i=0;i &lt; spans.length;i++){
    var span=spans.item(i);
    if(span.className=="escData" &amp;&amp; span.firstChild) {
      var parsedContent=span.firstChild.nodeValue;
      span.innerHTML=parsedContent;
    } // end if
  } // end for
}
```

We are looking at each span in the document to see if it has been marked as (non-empty) escaped data. If so, we replace its innerHTML (escaped data) with the nodeValue, created by the HTML parser as it was building the DOM tree, replacing in the process all escaped characters with actual data. This does the parsing for us. We can now use REST (with a little Javascript) to access a SOAP service—provided you use a modern browser with Javascript enabled. If you are attracted to REST in part because you want to use less Javascript, you may want to make two changes and move two computations to the server. On the way out, you would have to find a way to build the payload inside the JSP and pass all the necessary parameters. On the way back, you would have to do the unescaping, also on the server. A possible approach would be to generate the result of the XSLT transformation as a DOMResult rather than as a StreamResult. You can then traverse the DOM tree yourself and unescape the characters before sending the result to the client. (Java, of course, has an unescape() function.)

This completes our discussion of a REST wrapper for SOAP. It is time to extend REST to WebDAV.

## WebDAV in General and in Tomcat

Before we look at the mechanics of getting WebDAV to work in Tomcat, let's talk a little more about what WebDAV is, where it comes from, and what its prospects are in the crowded field of Web Services.

### *WebDAV Overview*

From the beginning, the Web was intended to be a read-write network of cooperatively authored resources. This is why the very first standard version of HTTP (1.0) included PUT and DELETE with GET and POST. However, PUT and DELETE were left unimplemented by browsers and servers because they required additional support before they would work. This is the origin of WebDAV, which is, as we said in the Introduction, "a set of extensions to the HTTP protocol which allows users to collaboratively edit and manage files on remote Web servers." (www.webdav.org) The extensions include both new methods (PROPFIND, PROPPATCH, LOCK, UNLOCK, and others) and new headers. These are invisible to the user; we don't have to write an HTML form whose method is PROPPATCH.

Although WebDAV uses XML (a W3C specification) extensively, it is not part of W3C activity because W3C tries (wisely) to stay away from protocols, which have been traditionally developed by the IETF (Internet Engineering Task Force). The official documents of the IETF are called RFC (Request for Comment); after a certain amount of time and a number of procedural steps, an RFC can become a standard. RFCs are all numbered and stored as `http://www.ietf.org/rfc/rfcNNN.txt`, where NNN is the RFC's number. Some of the RFCs related to the Web are RFC2068 for HTTP 1.1, RFC2396 for URIs, and RFC2518 for WebDAV.

It may surprise you to see that HTTP and URIs are in such wide use, whereas WebDAV is relatively unknown even though its status as a protocol is exactly the same. This is partly because WebDAV took a little longer to implement and partly because of a lack of publicity and media buzz. SOAP has been actively pushed by very powerful interests, and the much simpler RSS and Wiki have gained wide grassroots support, but WebDAV has languished a bit. This is a pity because with many new technologies, the promise and publicity are often far ahead of what's implemented and available, but with WebDAV, it's the other way around: there is a strong infrastructure support that is just waiting for new applications to be built.

In the area of Web servers, the two main players are Microsoft and Apache. (Apache, although completely independent and open-source, is strongly backed by Sun and IBM, among others.) So it is significant that both Microsoft and Apache, along with Adobe, Macromedia and many others, vigorously support WebDAV. For our purposes, it is important that Apache Tomcat is a WebDAV server because this is what we are going to use in our example applications.

## WebDAV in Tomcat

In your Tomcat distribution you'll find `$TOMCAT_HOME/webapps/webdav/index.html`, which explains that "Tomcat includes built-in support for WebDAV level 2, which enables remote authoring of the website." It suggests various WebDAV clients, points you to further information, and then says that "This test context ... can be put in read-write mode by editing the web application descriptor file (`WEB-INF/web.xml`)." This is the file `$TOMCAT_HOME/webapps/webdav/WEB-INF/web.xml`.

This is a configuration file for the webapp, but it isn't the same type of configuration that we used for DBAuthService. It's more like the XML version of an old-style properties file, full of initialization parameters. The top part of the file (shown in Listing 7-16) associates a servlet program to use for any HTTP access to the webapp. The middle of the file associates MIME types such as text/html with filenames, and the end of the file sets up security. The servlet class is

`org.apache.catalina.servlets.WebdavServlet`

You'll find its description in the Tomcat javadocs, at

`$TOMCAT_HOME/webapps/tomcat-docs/catalina/`
`                    docs/api/org/apache/catalina/servlets/WebdavServlet.html`

If you've downloaded the source, you'll also find the code itself at

```
$TOMCAT_HOME/src/catalina/src/
                   share/org/apache/catalina/servlets/WebdavServlet.java
```

Listing 7-16 shows the beginning of the webapp description. It names the servlet class, provides some initialization parameters that the servlet can read as Tomcat starts the webapp, and it associates that particular servlet with a URL-pattern so that Tomcat knows when to invoke it. In particular, this servlet is to be invoked whenever someone uses a URL matching "/", in other words: anything within the WebDAV Web application. The most important initialization parameter for our purposes is of course the one that is commented out in the distribution: the readonly parameter, which defaults to true and needs to be set to false to unleash the collaborative authoring powers of WebDAV.

*Listing 7-16. The Beginning of Tomcat's WebDAV Descriptor File*

```
<web-app>
  <servlet>
    <servlet-name>webdav</servlet-name>
    <servlet-class>org.apache.catalina.servlets.WebdavServlet</servlet-class>
    <init-param>
      <param-name>debug</param-name>
      <param-value>0</param-value>
    </init-param>
    <init-param>
      <param-name>listings</param-name>
      <param-value>true</param-value>
    </init-param>
    <!-- Uncomment this to enable read and write access -->
<!--
    <init-param>
      <param-name>readonly</param-name>
      <param-value>false</param-value>
    </init-param>
-->
    <!--load-on-startup>1</load-on-startup-->
  </servlet>

  <!-- The mapping for the webdav servlet -->
  <servlet-mapping>
    <servlet-name>webdav</servlet-name>
    <url-pattern>/</url-pattern>
  </servlet-mapping>
```

All we need to do is uncomment the `readonly` parameter to get things going. But what about security? For that, we look at the end of the web.xml file (shown in Listing 7-17), which is also commented out in the distribution. This specifies a security constraint that says anyone who signs on using basic authentication with a user ID that plays the "role" (usergroup) of "tomcat," as specified in `$TOMCAT_HOME/ conf/tomcat-users.xml`, can get in.

*Listing 7-17. Security Constraints in the WebDAV Descriptor File*

```
<!--
  <security-constraint>
    <web-resource-collection>
      <web-resource-name>The Entire Web Application</web-resource-name>
      <url-pattern>/*</url-pattern>
    </web-resource-collection>
    <auth-constraint>
      <role-name>tomcat</role-name>
    </auth-constraint>
  </security-constraint>

  <login-config>
    <auth-method>BASIC</auth-method>
    <realm-name>Tomcat Supported Realm</realm-name>
  </login-config>

  <security-role>
    <description>
      An example role defined in "conf/tomcat-users.xml"
    </description>
    <role-name>tomcat</role-name>
  </security-role>
-->
```

Going to the `tomcat-users.xml` file, we find one or more user IDs, each given a password, and some given the role "tomcat." If you simply uncomment the security-constraint from this web.xml file, you'll be able to start editing a file in Microsoft Word and save it as HTML to `http://localhost:8080/webdav/testSave.html` or some such name. You will be prompted for the user ID and password in the standard way. That's good, but suppose for the moment that we have one or more trusted users who have write privileges, but all users have read privileges. In other words, we want to distinguish between users with write-access and users with read-access. To do this, add `http-method` elements (as shown in Listing 7-18) after the `url-pattern` within the security constraint.

*Listing 7-18. Specifying Access by HTTP Method*

```
<url-pattern>/*</url-pattern>
<http-method>PUT</http-method>
<http-method>LOCK</http-method>
<http-method>POST</http-method>
<http-method>DELETE</http-method>
```

Now the security constraint applies only to the specified HTTP methods. It will not prevent any user from GETting your WebDAV files and linking to them, but they can only PUT, LOCK, DELETE, or POST their own material if you give them a user ID and a password with an appropriate role. You can put a list of user IDs into the tomcat-users.xml file and give each one a writable subdirectory inside the WebDAV webapp just by editing the URL-pattern for each. Each user can have write access to his or her own subdirectory, and read access to all subdirectories. There are examples of how to do that at `http://www.orbeon.com/oxf/doc/tutorial-authentication`, and further information at `http://jakarta.apache.org/tomcat/tomcat-4.1-doc/realm-howto.html`.

Many other security configurations, including HTTPS, can be set up within the Tomcat server whether it is used standalone or as a servlet/JSP container for Apache or IIS. As always, you can also design your own security schemes because the entire source code is available, as well as documentation and mailing lists of people who can help you (and who you can help).

The remainder of this chapter presents a WebDAV project that is set up as a separate Web application called "oxdav" (Open-Xml-DAV). We will present it in three stages in the next three sections of the chapter. We begin by making the oxdav directory a simple copy of the WebDAV directory, and then we start changing things. In particular, in the configuration file where the servlet was called "webdav," we'll call it "oxdav" for consistency, although it's still an instance of the WebdavServlet class. We could add the functionality we want by coding a modification or subclass of the WebdavServlet class, but Tomcat (and the servlet specification) offers a much better approach: a filter that we can associate with the servlet. So our stages are actually three progressively more complex versions of the filter chain inserted between the user's WebDAV submission and what is finally stored on the server. The first version takes incoming HTML files and applies Tidy to them, but mainly it's there to indicate that the filter has been invoked into the Tomcat log. The second version goes through the process of transforming those Tidied HTML files with XSLT as they come in. Finally, the third version puts data from the transformed input into a database and allows us to write a JSP interface to run database queries that find pages within the collection.

# TidyFilter.java

This is our first filter application. The application itself is quite simple—the HTML input is passed through the Tidy program—but the notion of a filter chain of servlets is new, so we'll spend some time looking at what it does and how it is set up. In the next section, we will see that, although simple, the TidyFilter can serve an important purpose.

## *Filter Chains in General and in Tomcat*

Filter chains are part of the servlet functionality. They are a set of APIs that allow us to insert a Java class or a sequence of classes that work on the incoming request before it gets to the destination servlet. Remember that the destination servlet is specified in the URI of the HTTP request. If your URI is `http://localhost:8080/examples/servlet/HelloWorldExample`, your request is passed as an HttpServlet object to `HelloWorldExample.class` (a servlet) within the `webapps\examples\WEB-INF\classes` directory. If that servlet has a filter chain associated with it, your request will first go to the first filter in the chain, specifically to its `doFilter()` method. That method receives both the request and the response objects as arguments (see Listing 7-20). It can handle the request itself and send back a response, in which case the request's intended recipient servlet will never see it, or it can send both the request and the response down to the next object in the chain, which may be the next filter or the intended recipient servlet.

In the case of the WebDAV servlet, an additional conceptual difficulty is that you don't really see the request URI; it will be something you type in the Save As dialog box of your WebDAV client. However, remember that every Tomcat-based Web application is, at heart, a servlet, and it is to this servlet (the `oxdav` servlet, to be precise) that we are going to attach a filter chain, consisting of just one filter, TidyFilter.

## *Filter Chain Setup in Tomcat*

As you might have guessed, a filter chain for a servlet is set up and configured in the servlet's descriptor, which is the web.xml file. Listing 7-19 illustrates how a filter is set up. After the `<servlet>` and `<servlet-mapping>` elements, (within which we have just changed the `servlet-name` from `webdav` to `oxdav`) we say the following:

*Listing 7-19. Setting Up a Filter*

```
<filter>
    <filter-name>Announcement</filter-name>
    <filter-class>webdavFilters.TidyFilter</filter-class>
    <init-param>
      <param-name>srcPrefix</param-name>
      <param-value>oxdav</param-value>
    </init-param>
    <init-param>
      <param-name>targetPrefix</param-name>
      <param-value>res/</param-value>
    </init-param>
</filter>
<filter-mapping>
    <filter-name>Announcement</filter-name>
    <servlet-name>oxdav</servlet-name>
</filter-mapping>
```

This means that the input for the oxdav servlet will be filtered by the TidyHTML filter, which will be an object of class TidyFilter in the webdavFilters package. It has two initialization parameters, one called srcPrefix with value oxdav, and one called targetPrefix with value res/. These prefixes specify the directories that will contain the incoming HTML files and their Tidied transforms.

According to rules for Java class naming and packaging, the webdavFilters.TidyFilter class has to be declared in file TidyFilter.java within a webdavFilters directory. We will place the source code in the same directory as the binary .class file, which, according to the rules of servlet containers, has to be in the WEB-INF/classes subdirectory of the Web application directory. Putting it all together, the source code for the filter is in

```
$TOMCAT_HOME/webapps/oxdav/WEB-INF/classes/webdavFilters/TidyFilter.java
```

Like the others to follow, the TidyFilter filter implements the javax.servlet.Filter interface, which you can find in Tomcat's javadocs; your distribution also has several examples of filter definition and use. Any Tomcat filter implementation must define three methods: init(), doFilter(), and destroy().

## *The Three Methods*

The signature of the init() method is as follows:

```
public void init(FilterConfig filterConfig) throws ServletException
```

Tomcat (or any standard servlet container) calls this method when the filter is to be placed into service. In our example web.xml file, this takes place when Tomcat begins to run. The FilterConfig object has access to initialization information.

The doFilter() method does all the work; it is the equivalent of doGet() and doPost() in regular servlets. Just like those two methods, it takes the Request and Response objects as its arguments as well as the FilterChain object within which it operates.

*Listing 7-20. Signature of* doFilter()

```
public void doFilter
  (
    ServletRequest request,
    ServletResponse response,
    FilterChain chain
  ) throws java.io.IOException, ServletException;
```

An important difference between a filter and an HTTP servlet is that servlets operate on objects that implement the HttpServletRequest and HttpServletResponse interfaces, whereas doFilter() operates on objects that implement the more generic ServletRequest and ServletResponse. In a typical Web application, the communication protocol is indeed HTTP or its extension WebDAV, so the request and response objects are HTTP specific. If doFilter() wants to do something with them before sending them down the filter chain, it casts in the beginning of doFilter(), as in these two lines of our code from the TidyFilter.

```
HttpServletRequest hsr=(HttpServletRequest)servletRequest;
final HttpServletResponse resp = (HttpServletResponse)servletResponse;
```

It is up to each filter to decide whether it should pass the message further down the chain. To pass something down the chain simply means to invoke doFilter() on the filterChain object.

```
filterChain.doFilter(servletRequest,wrappedResp); // pass it through
```

Finally, the destroy method is simply

```
public void destroy()
```

This method is called by Tomcat when it's time to quit; that is, when Tomcat shuts down. In TidyFilter.java, it simply logs a farewell message.

## The Beginning of TidyFilter.java

The file naturally begins with a package declaration (webdavFilters) and imports, which are largely familiar. The only new ones are those relating to the org.w3c.tidy package.

```
import org.w3c.tidy.Tidy;
import org.w3c.tidy.OutImpl;
import org.w3c.tidy.Configuration;
```

We begin the TidyFilter.java code with the initialization (shown in Listing 7-21). We use the FilterConfig object for two purposes: to obtain the ServletContext so we can use its log() method, and to get initialization parameters.

*Listing 7-21. Beginning of TidyFilter and the* init() *Method*

```
public class TidyFilter implements Filter {
  private ServletContext ctx; // for logging
  private String srcPrefix,targetPrefix;

public void init(FilterConfig filterConfig)throws ServletException{
  ctx=filterConfig.getServletContext();
  srcPrefix = filterConfig.getInitParameter("srcPrefix");
  targetPrefix = filterConfig.getInitParameter("targetPrefix");
  ctx.log("Filter "+filterConfig.getFilterName()+
    "; map webapps/"+srcPrefix+" to "+ctx.getRealPath(targetPrefix));
}
```

All we do in the ini() method is retrieve the initialization parameters from the web.xml file and log the prefix mapping information. Depending on your configuration of Tomcat, the logged data may appear in a console window or in a log file within $TOMCAT_HOME/logs.

The `destroy()` method is even simpler.

```
public void destroy(){ ctx.log("Destroying filter..."); }
```

By contrast, `doFilter()` has a lot to do.

## The Central Method of TidyFilter

Before we dive into the code, let's remind ourselves that we are not in the familiar HTTP situation where the request comes from the browser, but in the WebDAV situation, where the request comes from a WebDAV client, such as Microsoft Word. One difference is that you don't really see the URI address to which the request is sent (unless you set up a TCP tunneling utility, which is discussed in Chapter 9). In our application, the URI will be `http://localhost:8080/oxdav/`, which will send the request to the `oxdav` servlet (which is actually a `webdav` servlet, renamed). However, because the servlet has a filter chain associated with it, the request will first arrive at the first filter of the chain. In our case, it is the first and only TidyFilter. Therefore, the first piece of software that will see the incoming request is the `doFilter()` method we are about to inspect. What does it need to do?

Our filter does two things. First, it passes the request and response down the filter chain so the servlet (which is the next station in the chain) can do its work. Second, it determines whether it should apply Tidy to the current request. Tidy is to be called only if the following conditions hold:

- The request's method is PUT

- The submitted file has the .htm or .html extension

- The submitted file is placed into the directory indicated by srcPrefix (oxdav in our case)

The filter extracts the relevant information from the request and if all the conditions check out, it invokes Tidy (see Listing 7-22).

*Listing 7-22. The* doFilter() *Method of TidyFilter*

```
public void doFilter(
            javax.servlet.ServletRequest servletRequest,
            javax.servlet.ServletResponse servletResponse,
            javax.servlet.FilterChain filterChain)
    throws java.io.IOException, javax.servlet.ServletException {
// cast request and response arguments to HTTP versions
  HttpServletRequest hsr=(HttpServletRequest)servletRequest;
  final HttpServletResponse resp = (HttpServletResponse)servletResponse;
// log the information about response and its method
  String strReq=httpReqLine(hsr)+" "+hsr.getMethod();
  ctx.log("Accessing filter for "+strReq);
// pass both request and response down the chain
  filterChain.doFilter(servletRequest,servletResponse);
// check the conditions and apply Tidy if warranted
  if("PUT".equals(hsr.getMethod().toString())){
     String url=hsr.getRequestURL().toString();
     if(url.endsWith(".htm") || url.endsWith(".html")){
       int prefixLoc=url.lastIndexOf(srcPrefix); // check the directory
       if(prefixLoc >= 0) { // HTML file submitted to oxdav directory
          url=url.substring(prefixLoc+srcPrefix.length());
// apply Tidy after obtaining real directory paths from ServletContext
          cleanUpFile(ctx.getRealPath(url), ctx.getRealPath(targetPrefix+url));
          }
       }
    }
  ctx.log("Finished with filter for "+strReq);
}
```

Now we have the cleanUpFile() method to consider.

## *Tidying Up HTML*

The cleanUpFile() method cleans up the HTML file using Tidy. Tidy is an amazing program that covers all sorts of possible eventualities. (Think of all the ways in which an HTML file can be screwed up either by a human or by a piece of software that cares little about HTML correctness.) To help Tidy in its truly Herculean efforts, and also to direct those efforts to the desired outcome (for example, HTML 4.01 or XHTML or some other XML format), there is a configuration file that sets Tidy's many parameters. Sample files are provided with the distribution, but we provide our own, which the method reads in before invoking Tidy (shown in Listing 7-23). Tidy's output is a DOM tree that we don't use in this application but will use in the next one.

*Listing 7-23. The* cleanUpFile() *Method of TidyFilter*

```
public String cleanUpFile(String srcFileName,String targetFileName){
  try{
    Tidy tidy=new Tidy();
    tidy.setMakeClean(true);
    tidy.setXmlTags(false);
// get a Configuration object; reset it from our config file
    Configuration configuration=tidy.getConfiguration();
    File cfgFile=new File(ctx.getRealPath("TIDY/tidy.cfg"));
    String cfgFileText=cfgFile.toString();
    tidy.setConfigurationFromFile(cfgFileText);
    configuration.adjust();
// open streams to Tidy source and target, call tidy.parseDOM()
    FileInputStream fis=new FileInputStream(srcFileName);
// the next line assumes that the output directory has been created
    FileOutputStream fos=new FileOutputStream(targetFileName);
    org.w3c.dom.Document tidyOut=tidy.parseDOM(fis,fos);
// return the empty string for now
    return "";
    } catch(Exception ex){
  ctx.log("cleanUpFile err: ",ex); return "err: "+ex;}
}
```

The key operation, after the `tidy` object is configured is `tidy.parseDOM()`, which returns a document object. As a side effect, it transforms the input HTML file into an output XML file. It checks character encodings, deals with defined entities, and deals with whatever else it's told to deal with by the `TIDY/tidy.cfg` file.

## Tidy Configuration File

Listing 7-24 is yet another configuration file, and it's not even XML. It's a plain text list of properties.

*Listing 7-24. Configuration File for Tidy*

```
indent=auto
indent-spaces=2
wrap=72
markup=yes
clean=yes
output-xml=yes
input-xml=no
show-warnings=yes
numeric-entities=yes
quote-marks=yes
quote-nbsp=yes
quote-ampersand=no
break-before-br=no
uppercase-tags=no
uppercase-attributes=no
smart-indent=yes
output-xhtml=no
char-encoding=latin1
word-2000:yes
```

Aside from `input-xml=no` (this is incoming HTML) and `output-xml=yes` (we want XML output because we will be running an XSLT stylesheet on it soon), the most important setting is `word-2000=yes`. This warns the Tidy utility that its input might be produced by Word's Save As HTML feature, which does not necessarily create legal HTML at all. As a well-behaved application, Tidy is not very happy about that, but it can cope if given a proper warning.

## Conclusion

In this chapter, we covered a variety of topics, all of which help us build a complete Web application rather than just a client to an existing service. In order to do that, we have to bring in a Web server and a server technology for running back-end applications. Our choices are Apache Tomcat for the server and JSP for the back-end technology. Even relatively basic familiarity with those technologies yielded a significant result. We developed a capability to connect to the Google Web Service (and other SOAP-only Web Services) using only HTTP.

Once we have a Tomcat server running, it would be foolish to ignore its WebDAV support, especially because WebDAV directly relates to our subject matter. In many areas, especially collaborative authoring, WebDAV may well be preferable to either SOAP-based Web Services or RSS/Wiki type collaborative frameworks. So we introduced WebDAV, first as a simple read/write Web environment, and then in combination with a filter chain. Our filter chain consists of a single filter, TidyFilter, that applies the Tidy program to the saved file. Tidy converts the saved HTML file (perhaps containing grammatically incorrect HTML) into a file that conforms to XML syntax.

At this point, if we use a WebDAV client to save an HTML file in the oxdav webapp, that is, save it as `http://localhost:8080/oxdav/test.html`, the `webdavServlet` object will deposit it as required in the directory `$TOMCAT_HOME/webapps/oxdav/test.html` and then the TidyFilter object will put an XML-syntax version of that file in `webapps/oxdav/res/test.html`. This useful because now we can apply an XSLT stylesheet to it. The next chapter explains what kind of stylesheet to apply and what we are going to do with its output.

# CHAPTER 8

# WebDAV Client to Database via XML

IN THIS CHAPTER, we present two more filters. XsltFilter transforms the output of TidyFilter to build a more meaningful XML structure. DBFilter stores the resulting XML structure in a database to simplify searching and linking. Together, these two filters build a fairly complex system that is not just an example for this book but a simple version of an application that we believe is well motivated and potentially quite useful.

In this chapter, we will cover the following:

- XsltFilter: motivations and an example

- Tomcat configuration

- More information about XSLT and XPath

- The code of hierdiv.xsl

- DBFilter: motivations and the structure of the database

- The code of CollectTopics.java

## XsltFilter: Motivations and an Example

Why is the Web great? One can think of many answers to this question, but we are looking for a basic foundational architectural feature that makes all the other wonderful Web features possible. More precisely, What *makes it possible* for the Web to be great? Here's the answer we're looking for: Everything on the Web—every Web resource—has a name based on a simple and uniform naming scheme. This makes it possible to use just a couple of simple verbs (GET, PUT) to perform all Web actions. To get a Web page, all you need to know is its URI/URL. You don't have to worry about where it is exactly, what kind of machine it's on, what program was used to write it, and so on.

What if we want to get at parts of a page? Suppose your Web page is a Shakespeare play, and you want to find the second speech of the third scene of the first act. Now things are getting tricky because most likely your first act has a header, such as `<h2>Act I</h2>`, but you don't know where it ends unless you search through the page for `<h2>Act II</h2>`. (Let's assume that there is only one `<h1>` element in the entire document, for the main title in the very beginning.) The scenes within the act probably have a well-marked beginning like `<h3>Scene3</h3>`, but you'd have to look for the next `<h3>` to find where your scene ends. And even if your speeches within a scene are paragraphs that have a marked beginning and end, how would you count them?

Now imagine that your Shakespeare play is not marked up in HTML but in XML, as in the early XPath examples of the preceding chapter. Imagine further that people know what the XML tags are because you have published the DTD (Document Type Definition) of your page, or perhaps a RELAX NG grammar or an XML Schema. Suddenly, every single speech in your play has a name—it is the concatenation of your play's URL and the unique XPath to that speech, something like

```
http://MyShakespeare.org/Henry_V#/act[1]/scene[3]/speech[2]
```

As you can deduce from our discussion of XPath, you have an even finer control. You can ask for the second stage directive in Act 4 of Hamlet in which the word "skull" is mentioned. This is one of the reasons why the XML Web of tomorrow will be even more powerful than the HTML Web of today. Not just every document, but every structural component of a document (element or attribute) has a name—and a URI. Better still, you can link to each such component without inserting any markup (such as `<a name="linkToMe">`) into the target document because you can link using a structural description of your target expressed in the XPath syntax.

Actually, the language we are describing is not XPath but a simplified version of XPointer, a special language for naming document fragments that is based on XPath but defined in a separate W3C specification, `http://www.w3c.org/TR/xptr`. XPointer is used by yet another language called XLink (`http://www.w3c.org/TR/xlink`) for linking as described.

This is a vision of the future. It is held back by a simple problem: who is going to do all that XML markup? HTML has gotten to the point where it is widely known and the tools are good, but you cannot expect the multitudes who can put together a Web page (perhaps by typing it up in Microsoft Word first and Saving As HTML) to learn XML, XPath, Xpointer, and XLink. This is where we derive our motivation for the XsltFilter.

## From Headers to Structure

No authoring tool on the planet has more users than Microsoft Word. Word, like HTML, is presentation oriented rather than structure oriented. Word styles describe how the text should look instead of how it is structured. There is markup for paragraphs (hard return), and you can see words because they are separated by white space or punctuation, but sentences are difficult, and the only structure indications above the paragraph are in the headers, just as in HTML.

Our goal is to go from a Word document to XML structure. We'll do it with WebDAV, Tidy, and XSLT.

A user creates a document in Word, maintaining a correct header structure: a Header 1 is used once in the entire document, and major divisions are indicated by a Header 2. Header 2 can be followed by a Header 3 to indicate subdivision or by another Header 2 to indicate a sibling, and so forth. The user then saves her document as HTML in a WebDAV directory. The document is picked up by the TidyFilter and cleaned up so an XSLT can work on it. The XsltFilter of this section will convert the structure implied by the headers into an explicit XML-type tree structure.

In a complete application of this sort, the content of initial headers would provide metadata from which XML tags could be constructed, so that `<h2>XML Security</h2>` would become `<section name="XML_Security">...</section>`. Also, the linking would be as described in the preceding section, without any additional markup in the target document. Unfortunately, both XPointer and XLink were developed very recently so the browsers are unaware of them, and specialized XLink software is sparse and immature. In this book, we do not provide a complete XML+XPath+XLink solution, but something simpler: we will wrap each structural component implicitly indicated by headers into an HTML div element. We will preserve the existing headers and insert them into the resulting div element. We will also insert a "self link" into each header so that a later application (`CollectTopics.java`) can use it to form an old-fashioned `<a href="...">` link to the header. The output for our <h2> header will be

```
<div style="margin:10" class="h2"><!-- margin for indent to show nesting -->
<h2> <a class="selfLink">_</a>XML Security</h2>
...
</div><!-- inserted before the next h2 or the end of document -->
```

## An Example

Let's work through an example that goes through all the steps. We start with a file that is legal HTML but not legal XML because the <br> tag would be <br/> or <br></br> in XML (see Listing 8-1).

*Listing 8-1. An HTML File That is Not XML*

```
<html><head><title>Testing oxdav</title></head>
<body>
<h1>Top Header</h1>
  Top-level text, <br> including <em>emphasized</em> text,
  with links to <a href="http://www.google.com">google</a>
  and to the local <a href="openXMLhelp.htm">help file</a>.
<h2>Section 1</h2>
  part of section 1.
<h3>Section 1.1</h3>
  This is in section 1.1
<h3>Section 1.2</h3>
  This is in section 1.2.
<h4>Section 1.2.1</h4>
  This is in section 1.2.1.
<h2>Section 2</h2>
  This is in section 2.
<h3>Section 2.1</h3>
  This is in section 2.1
</body>
</html>
```

We save this as `http://localhost:8080/oxdav/hierarchy.html` (or to wherever on the Web your WebDAV server is located.) Tidy is invoked and produces the output of Listing 8-2. It is almost identical except Tidy inserted a label identifying itself as the generator of this content, and it has done as little as possible to the HTML in order to make it legal XML; in this case, it has replaced the `<br>` tag with `<br/>`.

*Listing 8-2. Tidy Output*

```
<html>
  <head>
    <meta name="generator" content="HTML Tidy, see www.w3.org" />
    <title>Testing oxdav</title>
  </head>
```

```
<body>
  <h1>Top Header</h1>
  Top-level text, <br />
   including <em>emphasized</em> text, ...
```

Tidy also returned the DOM structure for this result, and our XSLT file, hierdiv.xsl, will use this file to generate the transformed output in the res subdirectory.

```
$TOMCAT_HOME/webapps/oxdav/res/hierarchy.html
```

This file can now be reached as http://localhost:8080/oxdav/res/hierarchy.html, shown in Figure 8-1. Note the link to section 1.2 in the status bar.

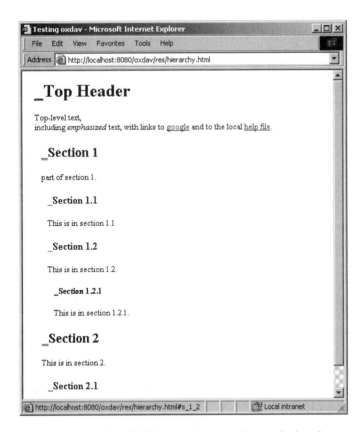

*Figure 8-1. Result of XSLT transform, res/hierarchy.html*

You can see from the indentations in Figure 8-1 that all sections and subsections have become div elements that represent the nested structure of headers. Also, each header has a self link anchor (a blue underscore(_) character) that points to that header, so it's easy to create links to parts of this file. Our output so far is as shown in Listing 8-3.

*Listing 8-3. XSLT Output*

```
<html>
<head>
<META http-equiv="Content-Type" content="text/html; charset=UTF-8">
<meta content="HTML Tidy, see www.w3.org" name="generator">
<title>Testing oxdav</title>
</head>
<body>
<div class="div_h1" id="divs" style="margin:10">
<h1>
<a href="#s" name="s">_</a>Top Header</h1>
<span class="textCollection">Top-level text,
<br> including <em>emphasized</em> text,
with links to <a href="http://www.google.com">google</a>
and to the local
<a href="openXMLhelp.htm">help file</a>.
</span>
...
</html>
```

The h1 element (from <h1> to </h1>) has been placed inside a div element, with a self-link inserted into the h1. The same div element contains all the material from the original document that is logically included under the original h1 heading. Logical inclusion as visible to a human reader has become data inclusion between the start and end div tags, visible to a parser. In the original document, the h1 element is followed by some introductory text, which we see has been copied into a span element within the div. The introductory text is followed by one or more h2 elements, each of which has received the same treatment as the h1: each h2 element has been placed inside a div element, with a self-link inserted into the h2 and so on. The XSLT has done a lot of restructuring. We are going to see the two stages in which it is done. First the changes to the filter that invokes the XSLT, and then the XSLT itself.

## Filter Configuration

First, we will add another initialization parameter to the filter class within our
web.xml file so that Tomcat knows where to find the XSLT file.

```
<init-param>
    <param-name>xslUri</param-name>
    <param-value>openXML/CODE/hierdiv.xsl</param-value>
</init-param>
```

That's actually a reference to the file webapps/oxdav/openXML/CODE/hierdiv.xsl.
The init() method of XsltFilter.java is the same as in TidyFilter.java except we
will add one line to it.

```
xslUri=ctx.getRealPath(filterConfig.getInitParameter("xslUri"));
```

The doFilter() and destroy() methods will not change at all, but the core of
the cleanUpFile() method shown in Chapter 7 (see Listing 7-24) will change, as
shown in the **highlighted** lines of Listing 8-4.

*Listing 8-4. Revised* cleanUpFile() *Method*

```
public String cleanUpFile(String srcFileName,String targetFileName){
  try{
// create Tidy object as before
...
// get a Configuration object; reset it from our config file, as before
...
// open streams to Tidy source and target, call tidy.parseDOM()
    FileInputStream fis=new FileInputStream(srcFileName);
    FileOutputStream fos=new FileOutputStream("tmp.xml");
    org.w3c.dom.Document tidyOut=tidy.parseDOM(fis,fos);
    transform(tidyOut,xslUri,targetFileName);
// return the empty string as before
    return "";
    } catch(Exception ex){
  ctx.log("cleanUpFile err: ",ex); return "err: "+ex;}
}
```

We're still creating the Tidy output file, but now it's just tmp.xml, which we use for debugging. The real output of Tidy is the DOM document object that TidyFilter simply threw away. We take that output and pass it on to the transform() method (shown in Listing 8-5), which at this point should look rather familiar.

*Listing 8-5. The* transform() *Method of XsltFilter*

```
public void transform(
        org.w3c.dom.Document doc,
        String xslUri,
        String outFileName)    throws Exception{
  TransformerFactory tFactory = TransformerFactory.newInstance();
  Transformer transformer = tFactory.newTransformer(new StreamSource(xslUri));
  transformer.transform(new DOMSource(doc), new StreamResult(outFileName));
}
```

Now we can use XSLT to do whatever we want with the HTML input, and the XSLT output will appear in the output directory specified by the web.xml file, where users can look at it. For this chapter's application, the stylesheet hierdiv.xsl will create a hierarchical structure implicit in the HTML headers. Because the stylesheet uses a fair amount of new XPath and XSLT material, we will introduce the new material before working through the code.

## New XPath and XSLT

The main new XPath feature in this section is the **full form of XPath expressions**. The full form is based on the concept of the **axes** of the XPath tree. There are also two new functions: the generate-id() function that generates a unique ID for an XPath tree node, and the key() function that extracts values from key tables created by xsl:key elements.

The new XSLT features, in addition to xsl:key, are the mode attribute that makes it possible to match the same node more than once with different templates, and template parameters.

In the rest of this section, we present the new material, first XPath, then XSLT.

## Axes

Imagine that you are sitting on a node in the middle of an XPath tree with other nodes all around you. This is, of course, a two-dimensional tree, drawn on a sheet of paper, and the nodes are ordered from left to right by their order in the document. Other than looking at yourself, there are four directions for you to look: up, down, right, and left. Imagine that you can regulate the scope and angle of your vision: how far and how wide you can see. For instance, if you look up, you can choose to see only your parent node or the entire path of your ancestors, all the way up to the root. If you look down, you can choose to see only your immediate descendants (children nodes) or you can see all your descendants all the way down to the leaves. If you look to the right, you can choose to see only the nodes on your level (your siblings that follow you in document order), or you can choose to see those siblings and all their ancestors and descendants, that is, the entire part of the tree that is to the right of you. Similarly, if you look to the left, you can choose to see only the nodes on your level (your siblings that precede you in document order), or you can choose to see those siblings and all their ancestors and descendants, that is, the entire part of the tree that is to the left of you.

These are the **axes** of the XPath tree; here is the list of those we have already mentioned.

- self

- parent

- ancestor

- child

- descendant

- following-sibling

- following (following-siblings plus their ancestors and descendants)

- preceding-sibling

- preceding (preceding-siblings plus their ancestors and descendants)

As Figure 8-2 shows, for any given node, the entire XPath tree is the sum of itself, its ancestors, descendants, and the preceding and following axes.

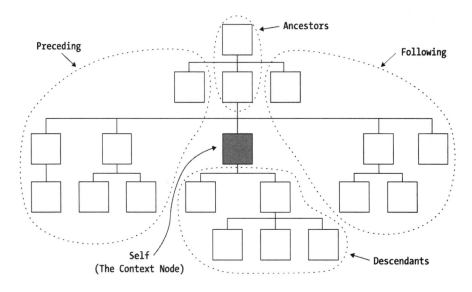

*Figure 8-2. XPath tree and axes*

Another useful way to look at the axes is to switch to the linear view and divide all elements into groups by the position of their tags. There are four elements.

- **Ancestors** of element E are all elements whose start tag precedes the start tag of E and whose end tag follows the end tag of E so that ancestor elements completely contain E.

- **Descendants** of element E are all elements whose start tag follows the start tag of E and whose end tag precedes the end tag of E so that descendant elements are completely contained in E.

- **Preceding** elements of E are all elements whose end tag precedes the start tag of E.

- **Following** elements of E are all elements whose start tag follows the end tag of E.

These are the only possibilities because XML elements cannot overlap. (This is what it means to say that they form a tree.)

For convenience, there are also several disjunctive axes: ancestor-or-self and descendant-or-self. Finally, there is a special axis for attributes and another one for namespaces. We will cover the attribute axis but not the namespace one.

**An important note on ordering**: When you select an axis, you get an ordered node set. However, the ordering is not always the same as the document order; it radiates out from the current node. In practice, this means that the ancestor axis is ordered from parent up to the root and the preceding sibling is ordered from the current node to the left, beginning with its immediately preceding sibling.

With axes defined, we can proceed to the full form of XPath expressions.

## The Full Form of XPath Expressions

Just like short-form expressions, full-form expressions can be relative or absolute. Absolute expressions start with the slash (/) character; relative expressions don't. Relative expressions are evaluated relative to the context node; absolute expressions are evaluated with the context node set to the root of the XPath tree. Here is an example of an absolute full-form path expression.

```
/child::play/child::scene[position()=3]/child::speech[attribute::speaker="King"]
```

Stepping through the expression from left to right, we first select all play elements that are children of the root (there can be only one, according to XML rules). We next select the third scene element that is a child of play, and finally all the speech elements that are children of the third scene and have a speaker attribute whose value is "King." Sometimes, reading from right to left is clearer: this location path selects all the speeches by King in the third scene of the play.

### Location Steps and Their Components

A path expression consists of one or more **steps** separated by a slash. There are three location steps in our example. A location step consists of three parts, two required, one optional.

- axis: In what direction are we going?

- node test: What nodes are we selecting while going in that direction?

- additional predicate (optional): further conditions on nodes to be selected.

The axis name is separated from the node test by the double colon (::) separator. The additional predicate, if any, appears in square brackets.

## Node Tests

A node test is either a **name test** or a **node-type** test. The simplest name test is a literal; it tests for the name of an element or attribute node. For instance, `child::speech` selects all the children of the context node that are `speech` elements, and `attribute::speaker` selects all the attributes of the context node whose name is speaker (of which there can be at most one, according to XML rules). The expression

```
child::speech/attribute::speaker
```

selects all `speaker` attributes of all `speech` elements that are children of the context node. If the context node is a `scene`, the expression will select all the speakers within that scene, with repetitions.

## Deriving Abbreviated Form from Full Form

As we know, some (but not all) full-form expressions can be also written in an abbreviated form. There are abbreviated forms for predicates, axis specifiers, steps, and entire path expressions. Here are the main rules.

### Abbreviated Predicates

Predicates of the form `[position()=3]` can be abbreviated to `[3]`.

### Abbreviated Axis Specifiers

Abbreviations are provided for two most common axes, `child` and `attribute`. If the axis specifier is abbreviated completely out of existence, the default `child` axis is assumed. The `attribute::` specifier is abbreviated to `@`. Here is an earlier example repeated next to its abbreviated form.

```
/child::play/child::scene[position()=3]/child::speech[attribute::speaker="King"]
/play/scene[3]/speech[@speaker="King"]
```

### *Abbreviated Steps*

Two UNIX directory path conventions, the period (.) for the current directory, and the double period (..) for the parent directory, are adopted to represent `self::node()` and `parent::node()`, respectively. For instance, the following will select all descendants of the context node that have both attributes a1 and a2:

```
./descendant-or-self::node()/*[@a1 and @a]
```

The next example returns true if there is no parent node. This is the way to test whether a given node is the root. (There is no `root()` predicate in XPath.)

```
not(..)
```

To find the position of the parent node within the list of its siblings, you can say

```
count(../preceding-sibling::node()) + 1
```

`count()` is a node-set function. It takes a node-set and returns the number of nodes in it.

This is as much XPath as we need to know for our stylesheet.

## XSL Keys as Elements and Functions

A simple usage of `xsl:key` looks like this.

```
<xsl:key name="root" match="h1" use="'h1key'" />
```

This creates a hashtable called root and adds all h1 elements to it as a node-set of h1 element nodes, in the order in which they appear in the document. The node-set is keyed by a key, the string h1key. Note that the constant string h1key is in single quotation marks, which is inside the double quotation marks of the XML attribute. What would happen if we omitted the single quotation marks, saying use="h1key"? This would be interpreted as an XPath expression to evaluate and find the nodes it refers to, that is, element nodes whose name is h1key.

More formally, this is what the attributes of xsl:key mean.

- The name of the hashtable is the value of the name attribute.

- The node-set stored in the hashtable consists of nodes that match the match pattern.

- The key for a given node-set is the value of the use attribute evaluated as an XPath expression.

The accompanying key() function takes two arguments: the name of the hashtable and a key value. The function returns the node-set of all nodes that are keyed by the given value. To retrieve the node-set of all h1 elements in the document, of which there should be only one, we would say

```
key("root","h1key")
```

To retrieve the first h1 element itself, we would say

```
key("root","h1key")[1]
```

It is important to realize that the table of keys created by xsl:key is created **at parse time**, before the stylesheet starts running. What this means is that the Transformer object will take a little extra time building a table as it reads the input. At run time, when we say something like <xsl:value-of select="key('root','h1key')[1]"/>, it takes a constant amount of time to retrieve the content of the h1 element, no matter where it is in the tree. This is made possible by the hashtable.

## *Parameters and Variables*

We have already seen some of the uses of XSLT variables, now we'll see more of the ways they can be used. We will also use XSLT parameters. Parameters and variables have many properties in common. Both xsl:param and xsl:variable are used to associate a name with a value. The values are specified in exactly the same ways.

## Parameter and Variable Values

The value can be specified in two ways.

- If the element (xsl:param or xsl:variable) is empty, it must have a select attribute that specifies the value.

- If the element is not empty, it cannot have a select attribute. The body of the element specifies the value.

Listing 8-6 shows a few examples. In all of them, xsl:param can be replaced with xsl:variable resulting in correct XPath expressions.

*Listing 8-6. Examples of* xsl:param

```
<xsl:param name="example" select="person/name" />
<!-- $example is a node-set -->
<xsl:variable name="str" select="'a literal string'"/>
<!-- $str is a string -->
<xsl:param name="num" select="275*3-23"/>
<!-- $num is a number -->
<!-- next example is a non-empty xsl:param element -->
<xsl:param name="anotherExample">
  <xsl:copy-of select="person/name" />
</xsl:param>
```

As we already mentioned (but it bears repetition), if you want to supply the value as a literal string, you need two levels of quotation marks.

```
<xsl:param name="country" select="'Benin'"/>
```

If you leave the inner quotation marks out, the processor will look for the child of the current element whose name is Benin. The outer quotation marks are for the XML parser; the inner quotation marks are for the XSLT/XPath processor.

## Position and Usage

Parameters and variables can be **top-level** or **local to a template**. The difference is in scope: top-level parameters and variables are visible everywhere in the stylesheet, whereas local parameters and variables are visible only within their template. (Remember that XSLT templates are like subroutines in more familiar languages.)

Other than scope, top-level and template-level variables work exactly the same way. Their function is to hold a value for future reference. Parameters are for receiving parameter values either for the entire stylesheet (top-level parameters), or for a template (template-level parameters). In either case, the values of parameters are defaults that can be overridden by values supplied from the outside.

The way parameters are passed to the entire stylesheet is implementation-specific. We don't use top-level parameters in this book so we won't spend any more time on them.

Within a template, variables can appear anywhere but parameters must be listed in the very beginning, before anything else, for instance

```
<xsl:template match="*" mode="section">
  <xsl:param name="parentPath" select="''"/>
...
</xsl:template>
```

This sets the value of the parentPath parameter to the empty string. To override this value, xsl:apply-templates must be non-empty and contain a child element xsl:with-param.

```
<xsl:apply-templates select="h3" mode="section">
  <xsl:with-param name="parentPath" select="$path"/>
</xsl:apply-templates>
```

This sets the value of the parentPath parameter to the value of the variable path and passes that value into the matching template that has this parameter declared. Note that matching templates must have a mode attribute whose value has to be section.

## The Mode Attribute

The mode attribute and its value are part of the pattern that has to be matched for a template to be applicable. The possible uses and side effects of mode are quite interesting.

One side effect of the mode attribute is that it blocks default templates. If you say

```
<xsl:apply-templates select="*"/>
```

all the element nodes will be placed on the current node set, and if you don't provide matching templates for some of them, they will be processed by default templates. However, if you say

```
<xsl:apply-templates select="*" mode="section"/>
```

only the modes and the matching templates you provide will apply to the nodes placed on the current node set. The nodes for which you provide no matching templates will simply go unmatched and forgotten.

Perhaps the most interesting use of mode is to create the equivalent of a **recursive procedure**. A procedure is recursive if it calls itself. A simple example is the following Javascript function to compute factorial:

```
function factorial(n) {
  if(n==0) return 1;
  else return n*factorial(n-1);
}
```

To see how mode can imitate the effect of recursion, assume that Listing 8-7 is the only template in your stylesheet that has mode="collectText".

*Listing 8-7. Mode Matching to Imitate Recursion*

```
<xsl:template match="node()" mode="collectText">
  <xsl:if test="not(string-length(name(.))=2) or
                not(starts-with(name(.),'h'))">
    <xsl:copy-of select="."/>
    <xsl:apply-templates mode="collectText"
                     select="following-sibling::node()[1]"/>
  </xsl:if>
</xsl:template>
```

Assume the template is always invoked with the first child of an element. (The first child is matched by a template with a different mode attribute.) Then the effect of Listing 8-7 is to apply itself to all the following siblings of the first child. It applies itself to a node as directed and then applies itself (as the only template to match mode="collectText") to the next sibling. An important detail is that the internal xsl:apply-templates of Listing 8-7 puts only one node, the next sibling, on the current node-list.

Listing 8-7 is actually part of `hierdiv.xsl`, and we are ready to look at its code in full.

## The Code of `hierdiv.xsl`

In outline, `hierdiv.xsl` consists of key definitions followed by three templates. The first of the three is the top-level template that outputs the top-level HTML structure and pushes the rest of the action to any other template whose `mode` attribute is `section`. There is exactly one such template, and we arrange things so that it applies only to h1 through h6 header elements. (We will sometimes refer to them all as "hN" elements.) Finally, there is the template of Listing 8-7 that applies to all elements unless the matched element is hN, in which case it does nothing because of its `xsl:if` condition.

So how do we arrange things so that only hN elements get processed by the `mode=section` template? This is where `xsl:key`, in combination with `generateID()`, can be extremely helpful. Before we start looking at the keys, let's review the rules of how hN elements are placed in the initial document.

- All hN elements are at the top level: none are embedded in a paragraph or a table or anything else.

- An hN element cannot be followed by any h(N+2) or h(N+3) etc. elements.

- An hN element can be followed by an h(N), h(N+1), or h(N-1) element.

For instance, an h3 can be followed by another h3 to indicate a sibling section at the h3 level. It can also be followed by an h4 to indicate a child subsection at the h4 level, and it can be followed by an h2 to indicate the end of its parent section at the h2 level and the beginning of the next such section (an uncle? an aunt?). Finally, it can be followed by the end of the document to indicate the end of all its ancestor sections. It cannot, however, be followed by an h5 or an h6 because this would break the regular hierarchical structure of sections and subsections.

> **NOTE** *If the initial HTML is created from a Word document, we assume that Header1 through Header6 styles have been defined and that their placement in the document conforms to the same rules.*

With these conventions in mind, let's take a look at the keys.

## The Key Definitions

There are two keys created in this stylesheet, the root key and the children key. The root key is the key used as an example in our section on xsl:key.

```
<xsl:key name="root" match="h1" use="'h1key'" />
```

The children key is considerably more complex. Before we look at the code, let's go over the header structure one more time. It helps to think of those headers as parents and children. For instance, if we have a sequence of h3 headers, its "parent header" will be the first h2 immediately preceding that sequence. Similarly, for a sequence of h5 headers, its parent header is the first h4 immediately preceding that sequence, and so on.

Our goal is to put every such sequence of sibling headers into a key that is somehow indexed by their parent header node. If we use the node by itself as a hashtable key, we will implicitly be using the string value associated with that node, which may not be unique. This is where the generate-id() function can help. It takes a node as an argument and generates a unique ID for it. That ID can be the hashtable key indexing the sequence.

Finally, given an h3 node, how do we find the first h2 node that precedes it? That's easy: just use the preceding or the preceding-sibling axis. (We can use preceding-sibling because we assume that all hN elements are direct descendants of the body element and therefore siblings. If we want to be more cautious about this, we can use the preceding axis.) Because the nodes of either preceding or preceding-sibling are ordered from right to left, we ask for the first h2 of the axis. Putting this all together, the following xsl:key element will put all h3 nodes into the children key and break them into node-sets such that each node-set is indexed by the unique ID of the immediately preceding parent h2 node.

```
<xsl:key name="children"
    match="h3" use="generate-id(preceding::h2[1])" />
```

We do the same for all hN nodes from h2 to h6, as shown in Listing 8-8.

*Listing 8-8. Key Definitions*

```
<xsl:key name="children"
    match="h2" use="generate-id(preceding::h1[1])" />
<xsl:key name="children"
    match="h3" use="generate-id(preceding::h2[1])" />
<xsl:key name="children"
    match="h4" use="generate-id(preceding::h3[1])" />
```

```
<xsl:key name="children"
    match="h5" use="generate-id(preceding::h4[1])" />
<xsl:key name="children"
    match="h6" use="generate-id(preceding::h5[1])" />
```

Now when we process the source document and look at a header element, say an h4, we can be sure that select="key('children', generate-id(.))" will select a list of all the h5 elements that are the children headers of that h4 element, in order. If we start by selecting the h1 node for match="section" processing and then use only the children key to add nodes for match="section" processing, all and only hN nodes will undergo such processing.

We can now look at the templates, beginning with the top-level one. That's where we select the h1 node for match="section" processing.

## *The Top-Level Template*

In addition to outputting the top-level HTML structure and calling xsl:apply-templates, the stylesheet's top-level template (shown in Listing 8-9) checks whether there is more than one h1 element and outputs a warning if that is the case. In outputting the top-level HTML structure, we use xsl:copy-of to output the "deep copy" (with all descendants) of the source document's head element.

*Listing 8-9. The Top-Level Template*

```
<xsl:template match="/">
<html><xsl:copy-of select="/html/head"/><body>

<!-- output warning if more than one h1 element; copy them to output -->
    <xsl:if test="1 &lt; count(key('root','h1key'))">
        <h1 style='color:red'>
          Warning: This document contains more than one h1 element.
        </h1>
      <div style='color:red'><pre>
        <xsl:copy-of select="key('root','h1key')"/>
      </pre></div>
    </xsl:if>

    <xsl:apply-templates mode="section" select="key('root','h1key')[1]"/>
</body></html>
</xsl:template>
```

We produce an error report if there is more than one h1 element, but even if that's the case, we try to apply templates to the first h1 element and ignore the rest, if any. More precisely, we try to apply templates whose mode attribute is mode="section." If there were more than one such template with the same match pattern and the same mode, the usual rules of conflict resolution would apply and the more specific match would take precedence. Fortunately, there is only one mode="section" template in this stylesheet.

## The Section-Handling Template

This template will apply only to hN header elements. (You will see how we accomplish this in a moment.) For each such element, we want to do two things: restructure the source document to create hierarchical structure and links, and copy unchanged all the material from the current header element to the next one. You can think of the action of this template as unfolding in two dimensions by using two xsl:apply-templates invocations. Vertically, it builds hierarchical structure by going from every hN element to the list of its children headers by using the children key. Horizontally, at each level of the structure being built, it goes from the current hN node to its following sibling, produces a deep copy of it on output, and recursively continues to the next sibling. (This second process, executed by the mode="collectText" template, is described in the section on the mode attribute.)

### Examples of Restructuring the Source

It is helpful to see the effects of restructuring before we discuss its mechanics. Listing 8-10 shows an excerpt from the input file hierdivIn.xml.

*Listing 8-10. Input File with Headers*

```
<h2>Contributions by Daniel Dennett</h2>
probably pretty good.
<h3>sub-contribs by DDennett</h3>
    also excellent
<h4>sub-subs by DD</h4>
  best of all
<h3>more subs by DD</h3>
 good, but not as good as the sub-subs
<h2>Contributions by S.J.Gould</h2>
probably fun to read, but not so good.
```

The h2 elements in this excerpt are the first and the second in the document. This is reflected in the `id` attribute of the output div elements. Listing 8-11 shows how the second h3 element (the second child of the first h2 element) is restructured on the output.

*Listing 8-11. Hierarchical div Elements and Their Attributes*

```
<div class="div_h3" style="margin:10" id="divs_1_2">
   <h3><a name="s_1_2" href="#s_1_2">_</a>more subs by DD
   </h3><span class="textCollection">
      good, but not as good as the sub-subs
   </span>
</div>
```

You can see that the class attribute of the div shows its level in the hierarchy, whereas the string s_1_2, repeated three times in the attributes of the div and anchor elements, shows its "tree address." This "div_h3"   div is the second child of the first child of the root.

Listing 8-12 shows the restructuring of the first h3 element together with its embedded h4 element.

*Listing 8-12. Embedded Hierarchical div Elements*

```
<div class="div_h3" style="margin:10" id="divs_1_1">
   <h3><a name="s_1_1" href="#s_1_1">_</a>sub-contribs by DDennett
   </h3><span class="textCollection">
      also excellent
   </span>
   <div class="div_h4" style="margin:10" id="divs_1_1_1">
      <h4><a name="s_1_1_1" href="#s_1_1_1">_</a>sub-subs by DD
      </h4><span class="textCollection">
         best of all
      </span>
   </div>
</div>
```

In terms of the two processes and two templates, the section template produces the entire structure including div tags, the anchor element, the copy of the hN element, and the span tags. The contents of the span are produced by the collectText template. This template collects more than text; it also preserves structure. If we insert a table or a list between two headers, the table and the list will be copied to the output intact.

## The Code

In outline, the code of the template does the following:

- Constructs the tree address string using a parameter and a variable

- Outputs the div tag and its attributes

- Copies the hN element with an anchor element in it to output

- Invokes the textCollection template

- Recursively invokes this template with the children of the current header selected

Listing 8-13 shows the tree address construction. (In terms of the outline, it shows the first and the last items.) You may want to review the section on parameters and variables earlier in the chapter where a similar example was used for illustration.

*Listing 8-13. Parameter and Variable for Constructing Tree Address*

```
<xsl:template match="*" mode="section">
  <xsl:param name="parentPath" select="''"/>
  <xsl:variable name="path">
    <xsl:choose>
      <xsl:when test="$parentPath">
        <xsl:value-of select="$parentPath"/>_<xsl:number/>
      </xsl:when>
      <xsl:otherwise><xsl:text>s</xsl:text></xsl:otherwise>
    </xsl:choose>
  </xsl:variable>
  <div ...>
  ...
```

```
      <xsl:apply-templates mode="section"
                            select="key('children',generate-id(.))">
        <xsl:with-param name="parentPath" select="$path"/>
      </xsl:apply-templates>
  </div>
</xsl:template>
```

You can see that except for the first time in the top-level template, the section template is always invoked with a string parameter that is the tree address of the current node's parent node. That tree address is stored in the path variable and then selected as the value of the parentPath parameter when the template is recursively invoked. Within the template, the current node's path is constructed as the value of the path variable. That value is the value of an xsl:choose element, which is probably XSLT at its most verbose. The same meaning would be expressed in Javascript pseudocode as

```
if(parentPath) // parentPath is not the empty string
  return concat(parentPath,"_",number());
else return "s";
```

Here number() is a pseudocode rendering of <xsl:number/>, which produces the positional number of the current element among its siblings.

The rest of the code is in Listing 8-14. Remember that if quoted output attribute values contain expressions to be evaluated, we put those expressions in curly brackets.

*Listing 8-14. Restructuring Code*

```
<div class="{concat('div_',name(.))}"
     style="margin:10"
     id="{concat('div',$path)}">
  <xsl:copy>
    <a name="{$path}" href="{concat('#',$path)}">_</a>
    <xsl:copy-of select="node()"/>
  </xsl:copy>
  <span class="textCollection">
    <xsl:apply-templates mode="collectText"
                         select="following-sibling::node()[1]"/>
  </span>
```

```
<xsl:apply-templates mode="section"
                     select="key('children',generate-id(.))">
    <xsl:with-param name="parentPath" select="$path"/>
  </xsl:apply-templates>
</div>
```

The xsl:apply-templates element inside the span tags invokes the remaining collectText template.

## The Text-Collection Template

This template was discussed in the section on the mode attribute (Listing 8-7) as an example of a recursive construct in XSLT. We repeat the code as Listing 8-15 for convenience.

*Listing 8-15. Copying Material Other than Headers to Output*

```
<xsl:template match="node()" mode="collectText">
  <xsl:if test="not(string-length(name(.))=2) or
                not(starts-with(name(.),'h'))">
<!-- do a deep copy of the current element -->
    <xsl:copy-of select="."/>
<!-- recursively apply to the next sibling -->
    <xsl:apply-templates mode="collectText"
                         select="following-sibling::node()[1]"/>
  </xsl:if>
</xsl:template>
```

This concludes our discussion of the XSLT filter that converts HTML headers into an explicit hierarchical structure of div elements with self-links included. Now we are going to store this hierarchical structure with links in a database for powerful querying and linking.

## DBFilter.java

With DBFilter.java, we arrive at a possible framework for a community information management system. The entry point to the system is the index.html page within http://localhost:8080/oxdav (shown in Figure 8-3).

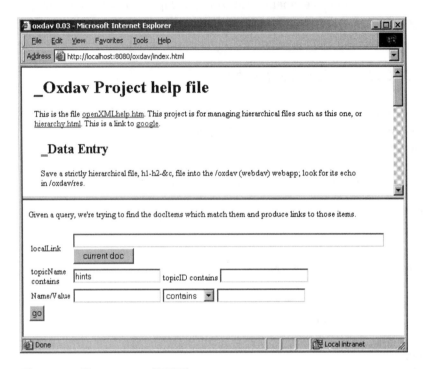

*Figure 8-3. Home page of DBFilter*

This is a two-frame page; the top dataFrame contains one of the documents in the system; the bottom control frame (ctlFrame) contains openXMLctl.jsp with a form for querying the system. If we fill in the topicName contains field with hints (as shown in Figure 8-3) and click go, we will get two matches showing in the control frame, as shown in Figure 8-4.

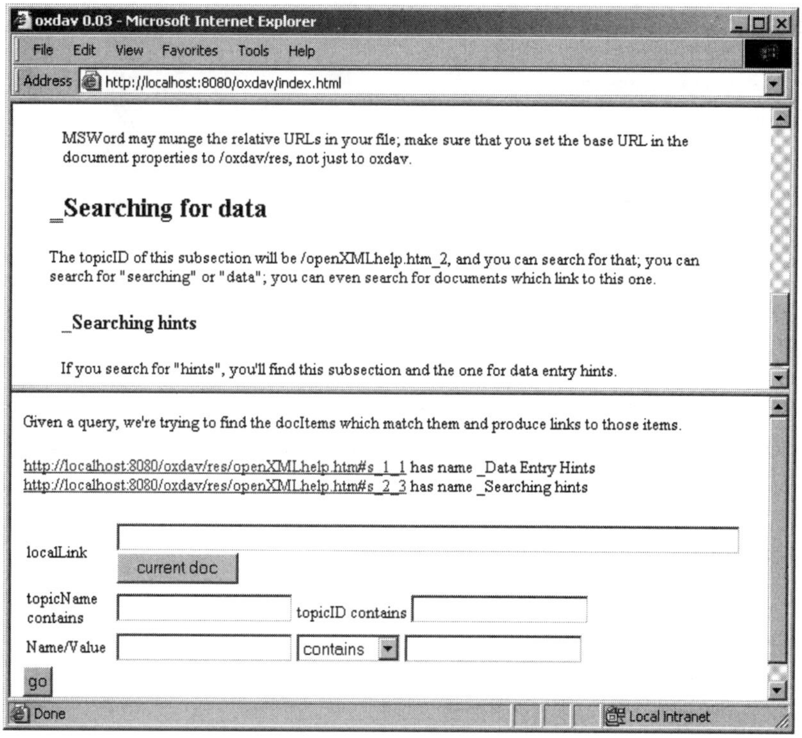

*Figure 8-4. Query result*

The result is that every HTML document (*.html or *.htm) that has been entered into the system is searched, and every section or subsection whose header contains the word "hints" is now shown with its address as a clickable link. If we click the first of these, the data frame shows the corresponding file (which in our example is the same file) scrolled to the clicked topic (see Figure 8-5).

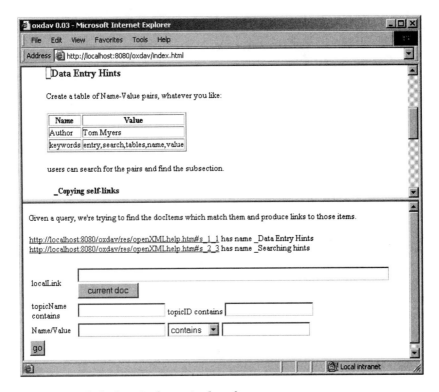

*Figure 8-5. Clicked topic shown in data frame*

The JSP code for openXMLctl.jsp is a straightforward use of JDBC, similar to what you saw in DBService. It does SELECT queries from two database tables: the (topicID, topicName) table and the (topicID, partName, partValue) table, and it maps topicIDs to URIs and vice versa. In effect, it is a very limited kind of topic map construction. Topic maps are beyond the scope of this book, but if you want to find out more, start at http://www.topicmaps.org/.

Our remaining task for this chapter is to review the changes in DBFilter as compared to XsltFilter, with particular attention to the filter's transform() method that traverses the stylesheet's output and adds topics to database tables using putTopicsInDB().

## Changes to web.xml and Filter Methods

Once more we go back to the web.xml file, and just as we changed from TidyFilter to XsltFilter, we now change from XsltFilter to DBFilter. Our DBFilter class will take one more initial parameter, the `localRefPrefix`, which is used to distinguish links to the outside world from links to documents within the system. In this case, the parameter is the same as the webapp location, but it could be a subdirectory of the webapp.

```
<init-param>
    <param-name>localRefPrefix</param-name>
    <param-value>http://localhost:8080/oxdav</param-value>
</init-param>
```

Naturally, the `init()` method will read this parameter. It will also initialize the RDBC driver and use a `ServletContex` object named `ctx` for logging and obtaining directory paths (see Listing 8-16).

*Listing 8-16. The* `init()` *Method of DBFilter*

```
public void init(FilterConfig filterConfig)
    throws ServletException{
  try{
    Class.forName("com.mysql.jdbc.Driver").newInstance();
  }catch(Exception ex){ex.printStackTrace();}

  ctx=filterConfig.getServletContext();
  srcPrefix = filterConfig.getInitParameter("srcPrefix");
  targetPrefix = filterConfig.getInitParameter("targetPrefix");
  xslUri=ctx.getRealPath(filterConfig.getInitParameter("xslUri"));
  if(debugging)
    ctx.log("Filter "+filterConfig.getFilterName()
                    +";\n map webapps/"+srcPrefix+"\n to "
                    +ctx.getRealPath(targetPrefix)
                    +"\n with "+xslUri);
}
```

The `destroy()` method will be the same but `doFilter()` will undergo a small change in the way it invokes `cleanUpFile()`. In the XsltFilter, the argument is simply the file's name, whereas in this filter, the argument is the file's relative URL (that is, the URL with the `http://localhost:8080/oxdav` prefix stripped off).

From `cleanUpFile()` the URL is passed on to `transform()`, and `transform()` has grown significantly.

## Changes to the Transformation Method

Recall that in TidyFilter, Tidy's output was simply dumped into a file, whereas in XsltFilter, we put the same output into a DOM object for further processing by an XSLT stylesheet. We now repeat the same change with the output of XSLT but instead of dumping it into a file, as in XsltFilter, we will put it in a DOM object for further processing. This further processing consists of traversing the DOM and putting topics into the database for searching. We'll explain what we mean by "topics" after we finish with the code of `transform()`.

DBFilter's `transform()` is the same as XsltFilter's `transform()` up to a point. We create a transformer object with an XSLT stylesheet as an argument. Then we need an empty DOM document object to put the XSLT output into. We obtain a `resultDoc` object by calling `generateDOMResultDocument()`. Then we can call `transformer.transform()` with `resultDoc` as output argument, and the same XSLT output as with XsltFilter ends up in that object. To process `resultDoc`, we need another transformer, but not an XSLT-based transformer. We call it a serializer because it traverses the document collecting information and putting it somewhere in a linear text form. Our serializer traverses `resultDoc` twice, once to put its contents into the database, and a second time to dump them into an HTML file (see Listing 8-17).

*Listing 8-17. The* `transform()` *Method of DBFilter*

```
public void transform(Document doc,String xslUri,
                      String outFileName,String url)
    throws Exception{
<!-- start as in XsltFilter -->
  TransformerFactory tFactory = TransformerFactory.newInstance();
  Transformer transformer =
    tFactory.newTransformer(new StreamSource(xslUri));
<!-- obtain a new DOM Document, use for DOMResult -->
  Document resultDoc=generateDOMResultDocument();
  transformer.transform(new DOMSource(doc), new DOMResult(resultDoc));
<!-- create and configure another transformer for resultDoc -->
  Transformer serializer = tFactory.newTransformer();
  serializer.setOutputProperty(OutputKeys.OMIT_XML_DECLARATION,"yes");
  serializer.setOutputProperty(OutputKeys.METHOD,"text");
<!-- this is the punchline: put topics and data into database -->
```

```
      putTopicsInDB(url,resultDoc,serializer);
  <!-- reconfigure the serializer and dump resultDoc into a file -->
    serializer.setOutputProperty(OutputKeys.METHOD,"html");
    serializer.transform(new DOMSource(resultDoc),
                          new StreamResult(outFileName));
  }
```

The generateDOMResultDocument() method simply produces an empty tree with predefined properties (see Listing 8-18).

*Listing 8-18. The* generateDOMResultDocument() *Method of DBFilter*

```
public static Document generateDOMResultDocument()throws Exception{
  DocumentBuilderFactory dfactory = DocumentBuilderFactory.newInstance();
  dfactory.setNamespaceAware(true);
  DocumentBuilder docBuilder = dfactory.newDocumentBuilder();
  Document outNode = docBuilder.newDocument();
  return outNode;
}
```

The rest of the action is in putTopicsInDB() and its supporting methods. Before we can tackle the code, we will explain what topics are and where they come from.

## Topics and the Structure of the Database

For our purposes, a topic is anything that has the following properties:

- It has a name and a unique ID.

- It has some content associated with it that describes its topic.

- It has named properties that have values. (Think of triples that consist of a topic ID, a property name, and a property value.)

- It can be searched for and linked to.

Now we have three questions, at least. Where do the topics and their content come from in our system? Where do their properties come from? How are topics and their properties stored in the database? Here are some preliminary answers; we will use our help page, openXMLhelp.htm for our examples.

The names of topics are the contents of the header elements, h1 through h6, which initially come from whatever WebDAV client the "domain expert" was using to create the initial document. If that was Word, the names of the topics are the contents of Word headers that are section titles. In brief, a topic is a section title in some document and its content is the collected text of that section.

The unique ID of a topic is the concatenation of two strings: the relative URL of the document of which this topic is a section, and the unique tree address of that section in the transform produced by `hierdiv.xsl`. For instance, if the relative URL of our file is `/openXMLhelp.html`, the section in question is the second subsection of the top-level first section (the second h3 after the first h2 in the original document), and the content of the section header is "MSWord base url Warning," the following will be true:

- The topic ID is `/openXMLhelp.html_1_2`

- The topic name is _ MSWord base url Warning

- The topic content is the text of the section (including any HTML markup) collected into a span by the `mode=collectText` template of `hierDiv.xsl`.

It is easy to construct a link to the topic from this information; the `href` attribute of such a link will be `http://localhost:8080/oxdav/res/hierarchy.html#s_1_2`.

## Topic Properties

To create a topic's properties, the user can create a table anywhere within the section of the document that corresponds to that topic. The table has two columns labeled Name and Value. Every row that the user enters into that table becomes a triple (as described in the list just shown): the topic ID of the section, the name, and the value. For an example, consider the excerpt from `openXMLhelp.html` shown in Listing 8-19.

*Listing 8-19. A Section with a Properties Table*

```
<h2>Data Entry</h2>
  Save a strictly hierarchical file, h1-h2-&amp;c, file into the
  /oxdav (webdav) webapp; look for its transform in /oxdav/res.

<h3>Data Entry Hints</h3>
  Create a table of Name-Value pairs, whatever you like:
  <p>
```

```
<table border="1"><tr><th>Name</th><th>Value</th></tr>
      <tr><td>Author</td><td>Tom Myers</td></tr>
      <tr><td>keywords</td><td>entry,search,tables,name,value</td></tr>
</table>
</p>
users can search for the pairs and find the sub-section.
```

In the res directory, the XSLT transform of this excerpt will be saved as shown in Listing 8-20 (with some white space removed).

*Listing 8-20. A Section with a Properties Table, Transformed*

```
<div class="div_h2" id="divs_1" style="margin:10">
<h2><a href="#s_1" name="s_1">_</a>Data Entry</h2>
<span class="textCollection">Save a strictly hierarchical file,
h1-h2-&amp;c, file into the /oxdav (webdav) webapp;
look for its transform in /oxdav/res. </span>
<div class="div_h3" id="divs_1_1" style="margin:10">
<h3>
<a href="#s_1_1" name="s_1_1">_</a>Data Entry Hints</h3>
<span class="textCollection">Create a table of Name-Value pairs, whatever you like:
<p></p>
<table border="1">
<tr><th>Name</th><th>Value</th>
</tr><tr>
<td>Author</td><td>Tom Myers</td>
</tr><tr>
<td>keywords</td><td>entry,search,tables,name,value</td>
</tr></table>
```

Because this material is traversed as a DOM tree, we'll execute commands like

```
addDocTopic('/openXMLhelp.htm#s_1_1','_Data Entry Hints')
```

We will also be creating three-part associations

```
addTopicPart('/openXMLhelp.htm#s_1_1','Author','Tom Myers')
addTopicPart('/openXMLhelp.htm#s','locallink','hierarchy.html')
addTopicPart('/openXMLhelp.htm#s','link','http://www.google.com')
```

Both addDocTopic() and addDocTopicPart() are ultimately called from putTopicsInDB(). Both invoke a PreparedStatement that puts the data into the database table. Listing 8-21 shows addDocTopic().

*Listing 8-21. Adding a Topic to the Database*

```
public void addDocTopic(String topicID, String header,String fullValue){
  if(trace)
    ctx.log("addDocTopic('"+topicID+"','"+header+"')");
  try{ // addTopicPS is a PreparedStatement
   addTopicPS.setString(1,topicID);
   addTopicPS.setString(2,header);
   addTopicPS.setString(3,fullValue);
   addTopicPS.executeUpdate();
  }catch(Exception ex){
    ctx.log("insert of "+topicID+" failed",ex);
  }
}
```

Given this code and the very similar code of addDocTopicPart(), the structure of this particular database table is not very hard to guess.

## The Structure of Database Tables

There are two tables in the database, one for topics and the other for topic properties (also called associations or "parts"). Both have three columns. The topics table has topic ID, topic name, and the full text of the topic. The associations table has topic ID (as a foreign key), property name, and property value. The combination of topic ID and property name serves as the primary key.

We can now do a quick overview of the code.

## Putting the Topics in the Database

One of the variables that putTopicsInDB() has access to is stmt, a statement object that is connected to the topics database. The first thing we do is delete any topics that come from the current document because if we are updating a document, we don't want to keep the results of previous versions. Then we make sure that there is at least one div element in the document, and log a complaint if there isn't. Finally, we invoke putTopicInDB() (note singular "topic" in the method name) on each div element that we found (see Listing 8-22).

*Listing 8-22. Adding a Topic to the Database*

```
public void putTopicsInDB(String url, Document doc,
                          Transformer serializer)throws Exception{
  stmt.executeUpdate("DELETE FROM topics WHERE topicID LIKE '"+url+"%'");
  stmt.executeUpdate("DELETE FROM parts WHERE topicID LIKE '"+url+"%'");
  Element docElt = doc.getDocumentElement();
  NodeList divs = docElt.getElementsByTagName("div");
  if(divs.getLength()==0){
    ctx.log("No divs found in "+url);
    return;
  }
  for(int i=0;i<divs.getLength();i++)
    putTopicInDB(url, (Element)(divs.item(i)),serializer);
}
```

Now the action shifts to putTopicInDB() where we are dealing with an individual div element. First we make sure that the div element was generated by our XSLT, and is therefore a topic in our sense. If that's the case, we do three things.

- Add a topic triple (ID, name, text content) to the topics table of the database. This is done by addDocTopic().

- Add all links to the database so that searches can return clickable links. This is done by putAnchorInDB(), which calls addTopicPart().

- Add the association triples to the database if there are HTML tables within the content that define topic properties. This is done by putTableInDB(), which calls addTopicPart().

Both addTopicDoc() and addTopicPart() invoke PreparedStatements to update the database. Throughout these activities, there is a good deal of string manipulation to extract directory paths and construct correct href attributes. This is not trivial code, but it does not introduce any major new themes or libraries—and of course you can find it all in the code archive. When it's all done, we have our documents packaged away in the database, ready to be queried.

## Conclusion

In this chapter, we used WebDAV's extensions to HTTP to explore Microsoft Word as a client for Web Services. You can also use OpenOffice.org (version 1.1 or later), or even a plain text editor that saves manually edited HTML files to a drive X: that is linked to `http://localhost:8080/oxdav` using WebDrive from `http://www.southrivertech.com/`.

The localhost restriction is only there so that it's easy for you to test and modify your code. We believe that a lot of small organizations could use something like our oxdav filter to make it easy for naïve users (but ones who are willing to follow some formatting guidelines) to create structured documents that can be easily searched with searching techniques that go a long way beyond full-text. Businesses, schools, charitable groups, academic departments, Little League teams—you, Dear Reader, probably know a group of people who use Word or OpenOffice.org to handle .doc files and are having a real problem organizing these files. A Wiki can certainly help, and Save As Html can help a lot more.

# CHAPTER 9

# WSDL and Axis

**SOAP HELPS AUTOMATE ACCESS** to the Web's resources. This chapter goes up a level, presenting a framework and a technique to automate the creation of SOAP applications.

Automatic generation of Web Services clients and services is, in a sense, the Big Idea of Web Services. It has the following goals:

- Writing a SOAP Web Service should be (almost) indistinguishable from writing any other kind of application.

- A SOAP service should be self-describing and use XML for its description.

- It should be possible to automatically generate client code for the Web Service from its XML description. Although generating entire clients may prove impossible, a more realistic goal is to aim for generating parameterized client-side libraries that would simplify client creation.

- It should be possible to automatically and directly generate a description of the Web Service from its code.

In other words, The Big Idea is that you won't need to retrain programmers to write Web Services and you won't need programmers at all to write Web Service clients. (Nor would you need books on client creation such as this one.) What you *will* need is an agreed-upon service description language and a framework that can generate service descriptions and client code; ideally, the same framework can also generate much of the Web Service code from the service's description. With a standard service description language and a compatible framework, it's possible to start with a description and automate much of the programming effort for the SOAP service and all of it for the SOAP client. One popular service description language is WSDL, short for Web Service Description Language.

In this chapter, we will cover the following:

- WSDL and the Web Service construction framework

- The syntax and semantics of WSDL

- The difference between RPC encoding and document/literal encoding

- The power and limitations of the Axis framework

## A Brief History of WSDL and Axis

WSDL version 1.0 started as a proposal by Microsoft, IBM, and Ariba, as part of their effort to promote SOAP-based Web Services. Very early in the development, the originators of the specification sought the backing and the imprimatur of the W3C, and submitted a revised draft, WSDL 1.1, for W3C's consideration. It was published as a W3C Note on 15 March 2001 (`http://www.w3.org/TR/wsdl`).

In the hierarchy of W3C publications, a Note is the lowest of the low: it signifies that no institutional resources have been allocated to the draft and it carries no commitment that any such resources are forthcoming. However, a year later, W3C formed a Working Group its own version, WSDL 1.2, which has been and remains the basis of further development at W3C. You can find the latest draft of WSDL 1.2 at `http://www.w3.org/TR/wsdl12`. In the meantime, Version 1.1 remained a frozen fixed point that supports current development. Our discussion is based on the WSDL 1.1 but it would not change much for 1.2. The following definition is from the 1.1 Note:

> *WSDL is an XML format for describing network services as a set of endpoints operating on messages containing either document-oriented or procedure-oriented information.*

The term "endpoint" in this definition is what we have been calling a Web Service; that is, a named location on the Web that delivers a service in response to a message.

The difference between document-oriented and procedure-oriented information is at the heart of a long-standing controversy within the Web Services community. The controversy is centered around whether Web Services are primarily for RPC (Remote Procedure Call) or for delivering documents, and whether, even when used for RPC, Web Services are still best thought of as delivering XML documents back and forth rather than as making function calls. This difference may seem unimportant—it's a difference within human minds, not in computer code—but it does influence design in important ways. We revisit this controversy when we get to the `style` attribute of the binding element within WSDL.

## *Frameworks in General, Axis in Particular*

In the world envisioned by WSDL creators, the main area of competition among vendors will be development frameworks. Each framework will vie to attract both the allegiance of programmers and the attention of managers who decide which tools to employ. A number of frameworks emerged in the early, hyperactive days of Web Services, but it's probably fair to say that by now the field has narrowed to a few major contenders, Microsoft's .NET, IBM's Emerging Technologies Toolkit, and Apache Axis among them. We are working with Axis because it's Java, free, open source, and in active development.

Axis installation is not completely trivial, but the online documentation is good. To install, download and unzip the latest version from `http://ws.apache.org/axis`, and move the unzipped `webapps/axis` directory into Tomcat's own `webapps` directory (after which you will need of course to restart Tomcat). As the instructions warn you, you may have to move some .jar files around to make Tomcat and Axis happy with each other. If you installed the LE version of Tomcat, which is slightly smaller because it uses utilities from Sun's JDK 1.4, you may even have to reinstall the full edition of Tomcat. At some point you will be able to visit `http://localhost:8080/axis/happyaxis.jsp`, which will verify that all the pieces are in place on Java's classpath or in Java's `lib/ext` directory.

With Axis installed, you can proceed to running our first example of a WSDL-described Web Service.

## The Factorial Service

This example illustrates how WSDL is supposed to work (but currently works only in very simple cases). The steps are as follows:

1. Write a Java class in the usual manner.

2. Make it into a Web Service.

3. Obtain its WSDL description.

4. Use the WSDL description to generate a client.

## Factorial.java

We start with a plain and simple Java class called Factorial, stored in Factorial.java (see Listing 9-1).

*Listing 9-1. A Java Class Defined in a .java File*

```
public class Factorial {
public int factorial (int N) throws Exception {
  if (N < 0 ) throw new Exception("no factorial for "+N);
  if (N < 2 ) return 1;
  return N * factorial(N-1);
}
}
```

How can we make this marvelous utility into a Web Service? The next section explains.

## Factorial.jws

To make a Java class into a Web Service, follow these two steps.

1. Rename your .java file as a .jws file.

2. Put it in the right place.

In our example, we rename Factorial.java as Factorial.jws and put it into the webapps/axis directory within Tomcat. (You will find it there when you unzip our archive.) The SOAP server is ready to receive requests from a SOAP client. But we don't have a client yet, so we proceed to the next step.

## Obtaining a WSDL Description of the Factorial Service

Axis comes with a tool (a Java program) called Java2WSDL. As its name suggests, it takes a Java class on input and produces a WSDL description for it. In our example, we don't really have a Java class, we have a Java source file that is used to create a service class on the fly. In this case, to invoke Java2WSDL, go to http://localhost:8080/axis/Factorial.jws?WSDL and the WSDL description will be shown in the browser. WSDL for the Factorial is shown in Figure 9-1.

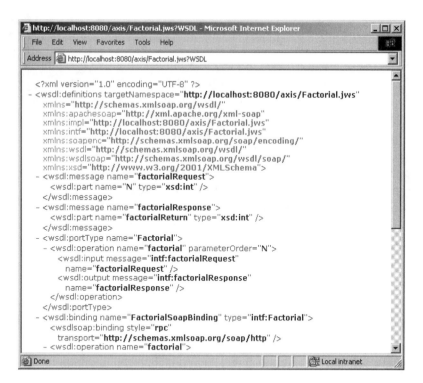

*Figure 9-1. A WSDL file in the browser*

This is our first WSDL example, which we will use to introduce WSDL. Listing 9-2 shows its top-level element in outline form.

*Listing 9-2. A Generated WSDL File in Outline*

```
<wsdl:definitions
   targetNamespace="http://localhost:8080/axis/Factorial.jws" ...>
   <wsdl:message name="factorialRequest">...</wsdl:message>
   <wsdl:message name="factorialResponse">...</wsdl:message>
   <wsdl:portType name="Factorial">...</wsdl:portType>
   <wsdl:binding name="FactorialSoapBinding" type="impl:Factorial">
      ...
   </wsdl:binding>
   <wsdl:service name="FactorialService">...</wsdl:service>
</wsdl:definitions>
```

We will flesh out this outline in the next section, but let's complete the process of deploying the service first.

## Automatic Client Construction for Factorial.jws

A client is usually on another machine, but you may not have another machine handy, so we'll just go into another Web application within the same Tomcat installation, namely wsbk. However, you should pretend that the Axis webapp and the wsbk webapp are on different machines even though the common/lib directory within the Tomcat installation contains jar libraries for both the server and the client.

To recapitulate, on the server, we used the Java2WSDL utility to generate a WSDL description from the Java code of the service. On the client, we have the opposite task of generating Java code from a WSDL description. Unsurprisingly, the name of the utility to do that is WSDL2Java. You can run it from our batch file makeFactorialFromWSDL.bat (shown in Listing 9-3) in the webapps/wsbk/axis directory. It brings in the necessary Axis libraries and then runs WSDL2Java.

*Listing 9-3. A Batch File to Run WSDL2Java*

```
set CL=../../../common/lib/
set AXP=%CL%axis.jar;%CL%commons-logging-api.jar
set AXP=%AXP%;%CL%commons-discovery.jar;%CL%wsdl4j.jar;
set AXP=%AXP%;%CL%jaxrpc.jar;%CL%saaj.jar
set WSDLURI=http://localhost:8080/axis/Factorial.jws?WSDL
java -cp %AXP% org.apache.axis.wsdl.WSDL2Java %WSDLURI%
```

Assuming that you put the Axis distribution jars into Tomcat's common/lib directory, this sets AXP to be the required Axis classpath, and then it sets WSDLURI to be the right URI to retrieve the WSDL. After running this, you will find that WSDL2Java created a subdirectory three levels deep within your current webapps/wsbk/axis directory. The path to the new subdirectory, localhost/axis/Factorial_jws, mirrors the location of the service and also corresponds to a Java package that contains the client classes and interfaces. There are two interfaces, Factorial and FactorialService, implemented by two classes, FactorialSoapBindingStub and FactorialServiceLocator, in that order. All the code files are within the webapps/wsbk/axis/localhost/axis/Factorial_jws directory. The Factorial interface and its implementing class are about how to do the Factorial computation. The interface knows about the factorial function on integers, whereas its SOAP binding stub knows about XML and SOAP messages. The FactorialService interface and its implementing class are about how to connect to the service, invoke the service, and obtain the result. The interface knows about URIs and the Factorial interface, whereas the ServiceLocator class knows about SOAP end-points and the factorial SOAP binding stub.

**NOTE** *A stub, in case this is a new notion for you, is a local proxy for the actual service. The proxy implements the service interface but doesn't do the actual work. Instead it serializes the request into XML and deserializes the result.*

Listing 9-4 shows the Factorial interface file, Factorial.java.

*Listing 9-4. The Factorial Interface*

```
package localhost.axis.Factorial_jws;
public interface Factorial extends java.rmi.Remote {
  public int factorial(int n) throws java.rmi.RemoteException;
}
```

This is the interface implemented by the Web Service; it is a translation into Java-specific terms of the interface defined by the WSDL description. (RMI, in case this is a new acronym for you, stands for Remote Method Invocation, which is a Java package for distributed systems.) Now we have an interface and a Web Service somewhere out there that implements it via SOAP messages. Our task is to write a SOAP message-generating client that can find our service on the Web using WSDL information. In particular, it will use the WSDL excerpt shown in Listing 9-5, which is the last child element of the definition element of Listing 9-2.

*Listing 9-5. The Service: Binding and Location*

```
<wsdl:service name="FactorialService">
  <wsdl:port binding="impl:FactorialSoapBinding" name="Factorial">
    <wsdlsoap:address location="http://localhost:8080/axis/Factorial.jws"/>
  </wsdl:port>
</wsdl:service>
```

This WSDL, through Axis internal magic, results in the getFactorial() method of the generated FactorialServiceLocator class.

```
public localhost.axis.Factorial_jws.Factorial
    getFactorial(java.net.URL portAddress)
    throws javax.xml.rpc.ServiceException;
```

The code of the method calls on several parts of the Axis system as well as the other Factorial_jws classes, but we don't need to look at the code at all. We just have to compile it, along with the rest of generated code, and run it from our FactorialClient class.

## Invoking the Client

Our FactorialClient.class is invoked as follows, where CP is a classpath containing the necessary classes and jar files:

```
C:..>java -cp %CP% FactorialClient 10 http://localhost:8080/axis/Factorial.jws
```

The client produces this output

```
seeking 10! at http://localhost:8080/axis/Factorial.jws
http://localhost:8080/axis/Factorial.jws
   ... says that 10! is 3628800
```

As you can see, the Factorial client connected to the given URL sent 10 as a parameter and then printed the result. Listing 9-6 shows the FactorialClient code. All the important action is within the try block.

*Listing 9-6. FactorialClient.java*

```java
import localhost.axis.Factorial_jws.*;
import java.net.URL;
public class FactorialClient {
public static void main(String[]args){
  if(args.length==0){
    System.out.println("usage: FactorialClient N [ http://... ]");
    return;
  }
  int N=Integer.parseInt(args[0]);
  String uriStr="http://localhost:8080/axis/Factorial.jws";
  if(args.length > 1) uriStr=args[1];
  try{
    System.out.println("seeking "+N+"! at "+ uriStr);
    URL url=new URL(uriStr);
    FactorialServiceLocator fSL=new FactorialServiceLocator();
    Factorial f = fSL.getFactorial(url);
    int res=f.factorial(N);
    System.out.println(uriStr+"\n  ... says that "+N+"! is "+res);
  }catch(Exception ex){ex.printStackTrace();}
} // end main()
} // end FactorialClient
```

There are three objects interacting in this code. The FactorialClient creates an instance of FactorialServiceLocator. This is the object that knows how to connect to the service located at a given URI. It has a getFactorial() method that produces a Factorial object (that is, an object that implements the automatically constructed Factorial interface of Listing 9-4). The method takes the service URI as an argument so that the Factorial object, when it invokes the factorial() method, actually invokes the service and receives back the result.

Notice that in this scenario, we don't have to read any XML at all. We create the .jws file, which is an ordinary Java class but with an unusual suffix, and we automatically construct a WSDL file to describe it in a standardized, non-Java-dependent way. The WSDL is XML, of course, but we needn't look at it. Instead, we use the WSDL2Java tool to construct Java wrapper classes for the service as described in the WSDL. We can use our wrapper classes anywhere—they know about XML data going over HTTP—but we don't have to. We need only to write the initial Factorial.jws and the FactorialClient.java just shown.

## Exceptions From Server to Client

One possible disadvantage is that if something goes wrong, we have limited awareness of the XML. For example, if we look for the factorial of −10, what we get at the client is an error message and the Java exception shown in Listing 9-7. Although you probably realize that the exception is based on a SoapFault structure because you have seen that structure earlier in the book, the message is understandable even if you've never heard of SoapFaults.

*Listing 9-7. Error Message from a SoapFault*

```
C:..>java -cp %CP% FactorialClient -10 http://localhost:8080/axis/Factorial.jws
seeking -10! at http://localhost:8080/axis/Factorial.jws
AxisFault
 faultCode: {http://schemas.xmlsoap.org/soap/envelope/}Server.userException
 faultSubcode:
 faultString: java.lang.Exception: no factorial for -10
 faultActor:
 faultNode:
 faultDetail:
        {http://xml.apache.org/axis/}stackTrace: AxisFault
...
java.lang.Exception: no factorial for -10
        at org.apache.axis.message.SOAPFaultBuilder.createFault...
```

The closest this comes to XML, especially if you're familiar with James Clark's notation for namespaces, is at the line

```
faultCode: {http://schemas.xmlsoap.org/soap/envelope/}Server.userException
```

This notation is now a standard way of expanding `nsprefix:Server.userException`, where `nsprefix` is mapped to the namespace defined by the URL between the curly braces.

Beyond that, the exception seen by our `FactorialClient` is an `AxisFault`, which you can find in the Axis API documentation. It's a subclass of `java.rmi.RemoteException` and it simply shows the subelements of the SOAPFault element. Looking at this, you can easily guess the XML, but it's not really necessary. For simple examples like Factorial, we can forget the XML just as in HTTP we forget the packet structure of TCP/IP.

Unfortunately, most examples, including the later examples in this chapter, are not as simple and require us to be more conscious of the actual XML going over the wire. So before we return to WSDL, we will show you an Axis tool for XML monitoring.

## The Axis TCP Monitor

Axis provides a utility, the Axis TCP Monitor (`org.apache.axis.utils.tcpmon`), which allows you to watch HTTP traffic to a specific server and port. Suppose we want to watch the traffic on `localhost:8080` (as is indeed the case). Instead of specifying `localhost:8080` as the target port for our traffic, we direct it to a `tcpmon` listener on another host and/or port (for example, `localhost:12345`), and instruct the listener to pass on the 12345 traffic to *its* target host-and-port, which we set to `localhost:8080`. Now all messages to and from `localhost:8080` can be intercepted and displayed by the `tcpmon` listener on `localhost:12345`. This is usually called "HTTP tunneling." `tcpmon` serves as a tunnel (with a hidden video camera) that lets HTTP traffic pass through. Although it's a great utility, `tcpmon` is also a potential security hole and should be used with caution.

**NOTE** *There is nothing SOAP-specific about* `tcpmon` *or HTTP tunneling in general. You can establish a* `tcpmon` *mapping from any local port to any Web server, local or non-local, serving either static or generated pages. For instance, you can associate port 8082 with* www.google.com:80, *connect to* `localhost:8082`, *use the engine, and have* `tcpmon` *display your queries going out and HTML coming back.*

To start the TCP Monitor, open a command window in the `TOMCAT_HOME/common/lib` directory where you put the axis.jar library file, and type

```
java -cp axis.jar org.apache.axis.utils.tcpmon
```

This opens a graphical window (shown in Figure 9-2), which we can use to monitor TCP transmissions between this machine and another location. It's described in the Axis user guide. For convenience, we've included a `webapps/wsbk/` `tcpmon.bat` file that (in Windows, assuming that `common/lib` contains axis.jar) can be double-clicked to run this command.

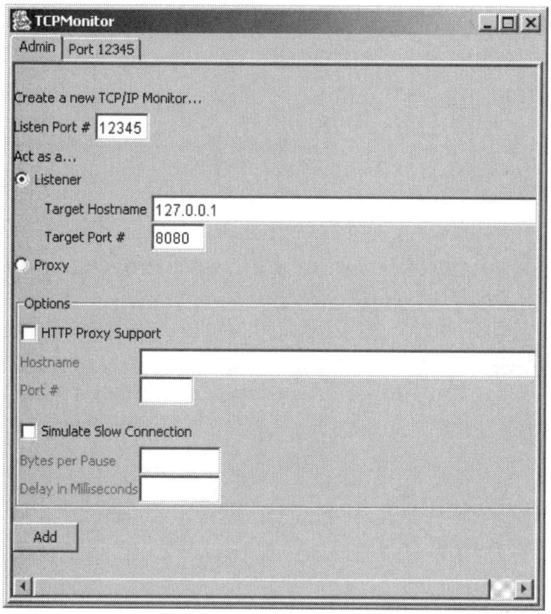

*Figure 9-2. The TCP Monitor in action*

We want to connect to localhost or 127.0.0.1, which is the default `tcpmon` host. We want to talk to Axis itself, found at port 8080, which is the default for both `tcpmon` and Tomcat's port. All we need to do is set 12345 as a listen port, and invoke

```
C:..>java -cp %CP% FactorialClient 10 http://localhost:12345/axis/Factorial.jws
```

Now we can sit back and watch the XML/SOAP traffic go by.

### An XML Exchange

Here's the XML/HTTP, as sent by the client on port 12345 (shown in Listings 9-8 and 9-9). It starts with the command line (POST, of course, with the relative URI of the Web Service) followed by headers. The SOAPAction is empty because the WSDL specified that, and the Content-Length is 438.

*Listing 9-8. Headers of an HTTP Message with SOAP Payload, in the TCP Monitor*

```
POST /axis/Factorial.jws HTTP/1.0
Content-Type: text/xml; charset=utf-8
Accept: application/soap+xml, application/dime, multipart/related, text/*
User-Agent: Axis/1.1
Host: 127.0.0.1
Cache-Control: no-cache
Pragma: no-cache
SOAPAction: ""
Content-Length: 438
```

Next comes the body of the SOAP request (see Listing 9-9), which is of course an XML document: an Envelope containing a Body containing the requested operation.

*Listing 9-9. The Body of a SOAP Message, in the TCP Monitor*

```
<?xml version="1.0" encoding="UTF-8"?>
  <soapenv:Envelope
      xmlns:soapenv="http://schemas.xmlsoap.org/soap/envelope/"
      xmlns:xsd="http://www.w3.org/2001/XMLSchema"
      xmlns:xsi="http://www.w3.org/2001/XMLSchema-instance">
    <soapenv:Body>
      <ns1:factorial
          soapenv:encodingStyle="http://schemas.xmlsoap.org/soap/encoding/"
          xmlns:ns1="http://DefaultNamespace">
        <N xsi:type="xsd:int">10</N>
      </ns1:factorial>
    </soapenv:Body>
  </soapenv:Envelope>
```

Ignore the namespaces for the moment and consider the structure. As always in SOAP, the Envelope holds a Body, but the contents of the Body are specified by the SOAP encoding. It holds a factorial element corresponding to the wsdl:operation element of the description. The children of the wsdl:operation element are the operation's parameters, of which there is one, an xsd:int called N, whose value is 10. With SOAP encoding, there can be any number of parameters and they can be complex objects, but the Body element will always contain one element whose tagname is the name of the operation requested and whose children represent the arguments to that operation.

The response (shown in Listing 9-10) starts with an HTTP success code and headers. The body of the message is again an XML document that contains an envelope that contains a body, but there's one extra nesting level. Instead of specifying that this is a factorialReturn element with the value 3628800, the body contains a factorialResponse that contains that factorialReturn element.

*Listing 9-10. HTTP Response with SOAP Response as Body*

```
HTTP/1.1 200 OK
Set-Cookie: JSESSIONID=6A458A1549C437ED070EF30DF2D54DC3; Path=/axis
Content-Type: text/xml; charset=utf-8
Date: Sun, 03 Aug 2003 13:54:32 GMT
Server: Apache Coyote/1.0
Connection: close

<?xml version="1.0" encoding="UTF-8"?>
  <soapenv:Envelope xmlns:soapenv="http://schemas.xmlsoap.org/soap/envelope/"
          xmlns:xsd="http://www.w3.org/2001/XMLSchema"
          xmlns:xsi="http://www.w3.org/2001/XMLSchema-instance">
    <soapenv:Body>
      <ns1:factorialResponse
          soapenv:encodingStyle="http://schemas.xmlsoap.org/soap/encoding/"
          xmlns:ns1="http://DefaultNamespace">
        <ns1:factorialReturn xsi:type="xsd:int">3628800</ns1:factorialReturn>
      </ns1:factorialResponse>
    </soapenv:Body>
  </soapenv:Envelope>
```

It's extremely verbose, as XML so often is, but you can see how to work with it. In fact, at this point you should be able to look at the XML/HTTP message, put it into Javascript to construct the request for the factorial of whatever number you want, and then use Javascript DOM or XSLT to extract the factorialReturn result.

## XML Response with SoapFault

What about errors? An error comes back with HTTP headers just as before, except that instead of a 200 OK signal we receive a 500 internal server error. The HTTP body of the response is still an XML document, still a SOAP Envelope that contains a SOAP `Body`, but now the `Body` contains a `Fault` element, which contains `faultcode`, `faultstring`, and (possibly) `detail` (see Listing 9-11) elements.

*Listing 9-11. HTTP Response with a SOAP Fault as Body*

```
HTTP/1.1 500 Internal Server Error
Set-Cookie: JSESSIONID=370F21B9B554D4BBDC9B59E5DB30A01E; Path=/axis
Content-Type: text/xml; charset=utf-8
Date: Sun, 03 Aug 2003 15:11:18 GMT
Server: Apache Coyote/1.0
Connection: close

<?xml version="1.0" encoding="UTF-8"?>
<soapenv:Envelope
    xmlns:soapenv="http://schemas.xmlsoap.org/soap/envelope/"
    xmlns:xsd="http://www.w3.org/2001/XMLSchema"
    xmlns:xsi="http://www.w3.org/2001/XMLSchema-instance">
  <soapenv:Body>
    <soapenv:Fault>
      <faultcode>soapenv:Server.userException</faultcode>
      <faultstring>java.lang.Exception: no factorial for -10</faultstring>
      <detail/>
    </soapenv:Fault>
  </soapenv:Body>
</soapenv:Envelope>
```

Now that you have seen the SOAP traffic between a service and its client, you can better appreciate the WSDL description of the service that generates the code that generates the traffic. In the next section, we will go over a WSDL description in detail.

# An Overview of WSDL

As an example, we will use the WSDL description of the factorial service. You saw its top-level outline in Listing 9-2, and it's repeated here for convenience.

```
<wsdl:definitions
  targetNamespace="http://localhost:8080/axis/Factorial.jws" ...>
  <wsdl:message name="factorialRequest">...</wsdl:message>
  <wsdl:message name="factorialResponse">...</wsdl:message>
  <wsdl:portType name="Factorial">...</wsdl:portType>
  <wsdl:binding name="FactorialSoapBinding" type="impl:Factorial">
    ...
  </wsdl:binding>
  <wsdl:service name="FactorialService">...</wsdl:service>
</wsdl:definitions>
```

By the time we reach the last element of this description, we have defined a service called `FactorialService` whose messages (jumping back to the beginning) are called a `FactorialRequest` and a `FactorialResponse`. Being a Web Service, it needs a port where the input (request) will come in and the output (response) will go out. That's a pretty abstract notion of a port that, at this point, is not committed to any specific protocol (it could be e-mail or HTTP or something else). The specifics are developed in the `wsdl:binding` element, which is by far the longest of the elements. We'll take those elements one at a time in the following subsections. All these tags are in the `wsdl:` namespace, defined in `wsdl:definitions` to be `http://schemas.xmlsoap.org/wsdl/`.

## The Factorial Request Message

The message requesting the services of this particular Web Service will consist of one part: the integer N for which we want a factorial calculated. Here's how we say that in WSDL.

```
<wsdl:message name="factorialRequest">
  <wsdl:part name="N" type="xsd:int"/>
</wsdl:message>
```

Notice the type `xsd:int`. This corresponds quite nicely to a Java `int` value, but the type system here is not quite that of Java. Web Service messages have to be acceptable to clients and servers written in any programming language, so the data type specifications could not be taken from any specific language. The meaning of `xsd:int` and other data types has been defined by W3C in the specification of XML Schema (Part II, Data Types).

## The Factorial Response Message

The response message is also an xsd:int, and its name is simply factorialResponse.

```
<wsdl:message name="factorialResponse">
  <wsdl:part name="factorialReturn" type="xsd:int"/>
</wsdl:message>
```

## The Port Type Element

This is an abstract description of the Factorial Web Service that describes the logic of what goes in and out to each operation without specifying that all message exchanges are done over HTTP. In this case, the only operation is the factorial method, with its input and output (see Listing 9-12).

*Listing 9-12. The Port Type*

```
<wsdl:portType name="Factorial">
    <wsdl:operation name="factorial" parameterOrder="N">
      <wsdl:input message="impl:factorialRequest" name="factorialRequest"/>
      <wsdl:output message="impl:factorialResponse" name="factorialResponse"/>
    </wsdl:operation>
  </wsdl:portType>
```

Here you see the previous definitions being included by reference. Let's look at the top-level wsdl:service next—the binding is the most complex, so we'll do it last.

## The Service Element

The service itself, whose name is FactorialService, has a port whose portType is Factorial and whose binding to HTTP will be described as a FactorialSoapBinding. All we need to know now is the specific location (see Listing 9-13).

*Listing 9-13. The Service: Binding and Location*

```
<wsdl:service name="FactorialService">
  <wsdl:port binding="impl:FactorialSoapBinding" name="Factorial">
    <wsdlsoap:address location="http://localhost:8080/axis/Factorial.jws"/>
  </wsdl:port>
</wsdl:service>
```

That's all there is to the top-level service description: the location, the messages that go back and forth, the data carried by those messages (described in a language-independent way), and the portType that places the messages in order. What is left for the FactorialSoapBinding? At this point we are descending to a more precise level of detail.

## The Binding Element

The wsdl:binding element specifies quite a few details, including

- style: How programming data is encoded in XML

- transport: HTTP or something else

- service operations: inputs and outputs for each operation

We begin with the style of the binding. There are two such styles: the RPC (Remote Procedure Call) style and the document/literal style. The difference between them is summarized very clearly and succinctly in the following message from Anne Thomas Manes <anne@manes.net> on the axis-user@ws.apache.org list, July 30, 2003:

> *Document/literal means that you have defined a schema element definition for the SOAP message (the contents of soap:body) and that the message conforms to that schema.*

> *RPC/encoded means that you have defined the types of the message elements that you wish to pass, and you let your SOAP implementation generate the SOAP message structure using the SOAP encoding data model. ... Since the message structure is generated on the fly, there is no schema that defines the message, so you can't validate the message.*

In other words, the document/literal style of XML binding provides an explicit specification of the XML data that is sent over the wire. This specification is written in a formal notation (such as XML Schema or RELAX NG), and there are tools for validating the data; most importantly, you can use the specification for debugging. By contrast, the RPC/encoded style of XML binding relies on implicit datatype encoding rules that are hidden in the implementation of the Web Services framework. The practical consequence of document/literal is that if a client fails to communicate with the server, you can inspect the SOAP messages and tell which one is doing something wrong by checking the messages against the specification. With RPC/encoded, this is a lot harder if not impossible.

The next encoding detail is whether the messages ride on HTTP or some other transport, such as SMTP. For now and the foreseeable future, most of them ride on top of HTTP.

Finally, we define the specifics of each service operation. To define an operation, we specify the soapAction header expected by the service, and then specify the inputs and outputs. It may seem unnecessary to define the bindings of the inputs and outputs any further because we already know that they are xsd:int values. However, the implementation requires that information to travel across the wire (see Listing 9-14).

*Listing 9-14. The Binding Element*

```
<wsdl:binding name="FactorialSoapBinding" type="impl:Factorial">
  <wsdlsoap:binding
    style="rpc"
    transport="http://schemas.xmlsoap.org/soap/http"
  />
  <wsdl:operation name="factorial">
    <wsdlsoap:operation soapAction=""/>
    <wsdl:input name="factorialRequest">
      <wsdlsoap:body
        encodingStyle="http://schemas.xmlsoap.org/soap/encoding/"
        namespace="http://DefaultNamespace"
        use="encoded"/>
    </wsdl:input>
    <wsdl:output name="factorialResponse">
      <wsdlsoap:body
        encodingStyle="http://schemas.xmlsoap.org/soap/encoding/"
        namespace="http://localhost:8080/axis/Factorial.jws"
        use="encoded"/>
    </wsdl:output>
  </wsdl:operation>
</wsdl:binding>
```

Notice that the namespace http:...jws looks like a reference to the service itself—it's not. The point of a namespace is to be unique, and URIs are generally pretty good at being unique. Of course, a localhost URI is not reliably unique, but in order to publish this on the Web we'd need to rename it anyway, so it's not a big worry.

## RPC Encoding vs. Document/Literal

Standard SOAP encoding for RPC, indicated by the use of the namespace URI http://schemas.xmlsoap.org/soap/encoding, involves a set of conventions for representing data as XML. The conventions include, as we mentioned, that the SOAP Body element will always contain one element whose tagname is the name of the operation requested and whose children represent the arguments to that operation. If one of the arguments is an array, it will be encoded as soap:array, and software on both ends will understand what soap:array means. For example, a doGoogleSearchResponse() will come back with an array of item elements wrapped in a resultElements tag. Assuming that the namespace ns1 is mapped to xmlns:ns1="urn:GoogleSearch", we might have

```
<resultElements
    xmlns:ns3="http://schemas.xmlsoap.org/soap/encoding/"
    xsi:type="ns3:Array"
    ns3:arrayType="ns1:ResultElement[3]">
```

What follows is, of course, an XML sequence of three item elements.

With the document/literal style, we would have a schema that defines the type of the returned value, the schema would determine that it is a sequence of elements of a certain type, and those elements would actually be present in the message sent over the wire because the message would have to conform to the schema.

What is this schema we are talking about? There are several schema languages, including DTD, RELAX NG, and XML Schema from W3C. The last one is the most commonly used at the present time. As we mentioned, the XML Schema specification consists of two parts, and we have seen examples of the second part in use in this line from Listing 9-10.

```
<N xsi:type="xsd:int">10</N>
```

This is an example of SOAP encoding, and it uses XML Schema Part 2 to define simple types, but it does not use XML Schema Part 1 to define complex types, such as a sequence of elements. Part of the reason may be that both SOAP and XML Schema Part 2 were ready and waiting for XML Schema Part 1, which was delayed several times. When it came out, it was easily the longest, most controversial, and most impenetrable W3C specification issued to date. Many months and books later, it is still quite impenetrable, and there isn't a single complete implementation. However, simpler sections of it have been absorbed, and as a result, over the past year there has been a trend away from the RPC/encoded style for SOAP invocation and toward the document/literal style. The advantage of document/literal is that if something goes wrong, you can inspect and even validate the XML document that is sent over the wire, whereas with SOAP encoding, when a specific server generates a document that is not accepted by a specific client, you can use the TCP Monitor to look at the XML document, but you cannot tell what it should have been because you do not know which program is doing the wrong thing.

So as we watch the `axis-user@ws.apache.org` discussion list, we see that more and more newbies are told to use RPC/encoded if necessary, but document/literal is preferred. The promise of RPC/encoded has not diminished, but it appears to be limited. The promise of the document/literal style of WSDL will be further enhanced in WSDL 1.2, which allows the use of a RELAX NG grammar instead of XML Schema Part 1 to specify complex XML structures. (RELAX NG offers a much simpler and more intuitive approach in most people's opinion.) In the meantime, we are going to use document/literal for the rest of this chapter, using XML Schema Part 1.

## Document/Literal WSDL

Document/literal is not new. We can find an example in the WSDL 1.1 specification from March 15, 2001.

The table of contents has a link to Example 1 SOAP 1.1 Request/Response via HTTP, which is a stock-quote example: a ticker-symbol such as IBM or MSFT goes in, and a float representing the current stock price comes out. Stock-quotes examples are numerous (the Axis distribution comes with several versions in the samples directory), but we are going to produce yet another one. When we clip the whole example from the WSDL specification, paste it into a text editor, save it as **w3stockquote.wsdl**, and run WSDL2Java on that file, we get an error message.

```
java.io.IOException: Emitter failure.  There is an undefined binding
    (StockQuoteBinding) in the WSDL document.
Hint: make sure <port binding=".."> is fully qualified.
```

All right, we'd better read the WSDL, and it turns out that the problem is quite simple. Look for the port binding for the service section as the hint suggests and you find a reference to a StockQuoteBinding, but what is defined in the binding section is

```
<binding name="StockQuoteSoapBinding" type="tns:StockQuotePortType">
```

We change the port's StockQuoteBinding to StockQuoteSoapBinding, rerun WSDL2Java, and all is well. (Typos are universal, but if you can read code you can deal with them.) So let's read that WSDL before we look at the generated code.

# XML Schema for StockQuote

In the previous section, the WSDL definitions element contained three message tags, a portType, a binding, and a service. This time, we'll see those again, but first we'll see a types section that describes the XML document types—not with reference to SOAP encoding of data structures, but simply as complete, self-contained structures (see Listing 9-15).

*Listing 9-15. The* types *Element in Document/Literal Encoding*

```
<types>
    <schema targetNamespace="http://example.com/stockquote.xsd"
            xmlns="http://www.w3.org/2000/10/XMLSchema">
        <element name="TradePriceRequest">
            <complexType>
                <all>
                    <element name="tickerSymbol" type="string"/>
                </all>
            </complexType>
        </element>
        <element name="TradePrice">
            <complexType>
                <all>
                    <element name="price" type="float"/>
                </all>
            </complexType>
        </element>
    </schema>
</types>
```

Here you see elements of a complex type, defined according to the conventions of XML Schema Part 1. There's an element called TradePriceRequest and another element called TradePrice; each is described as a complexType whose children can be sequence, choice, or, as shown in Listing 9-15, all (meaning that in the document, children elements can appear in any order). We only have one child so it doesn't really matter, but in principle, because the arguments to the procedure call are named, they can appear in any order without causing any confusion. The arguments could be complex types containing sequences of subelements as well, but in this case, the arguments are simple types, string and float, defined in XML Schema Part 2.

> **CAUTION** *This is how things are supposed to work in principle. In actual practice, as of today, many clients are not capable of working with truly complex, deeply nested type definitions, and many services are not prepared to accept any permutation of named arguments, insisting on the order in which they are shown in the Schema. Bear this in mind when working with document/literal encoding.*

## *Messages, PortType, Service*

Now we describe our two messages. The message called `getLastTradePriceInput` (the content of the requesting soap `Envelope`) will contain a body with a `TradePriceRequest`.

```
<message name="GetLastTradePriceInput">
    <part name="body" element="xsd1:TradePriceRequest"/>
</message>
```

Notice that this doesn't look quite like the Factorial example simply because the `message` tag for that example was shown as `wsdl:message` and it was in the `http://schemas.xmlsoap.org/wsdl/` namespace. Are these examples different in some fundamental way? No; from an XML point of view they are not different at all because that namespace is the default namespace for the `GetLastTradePrice` example; in James Clark's namespace notation, we'd write both of these as {`http://schemas.xmlsoap.org/wsdl/`}:"message.

Similarly, the message called `getLastTradePriceOutput` will contain a body with a `TradePrice`.

```
<message name="GetLastTradePriceOutput">
    <part name="body" element="xsd1:TradePrice"/>
</message>
```

What we've described is not very different from what we were describing before. The difference is that with document/literal we are talking about XML, whereas with RPC/encoded, we avoided talking about XML. The abstract `portType` is very similar to what it was before.

```
<portType name="StockQuotePortType">
    <operation name="GetLastTradePrice">
        <input message="tns:GetLastTradePriceInput"/>
        <output message="tns:GetLastTradePriceOutput"/>
    </operation>
</portType>
```

Again we have a single operation for this portType, and it has a single input and a single output, which are already defined. Once more, let's look at the service element before we check the binding.

```
<service name="StockQuoteService">
    <documentation>My first service</documentation>
    <port name="StockQuotePort" binding="tns:StockQuoteSoapBinding">
        <soap:address location="http://example.com/stockquote"/>
    </port>
</service>
```

The service has a documentation element, which looks like a good place for a description but we won't write one to improve the existing "My first service." We're defining a StockQuoteService; it has a port name and binding, and it has a default location that is at http://example.com/stockquote. We've already seen how to override that.

## HTTP Binding for StockQuote

The binding itself (shown in Listing 9-16) is actually a bit simpler than Factorial's. It has a name and a portType and its style is document rather than RPC. Its transport is still HTTP, and it has one operation, GetLastTradePrice. This operation has a soapAction, an input, and an output. The input and output are defined to use literal XML rather than encoded programming-language data, so they don't need to provide an encodingStyle.

*Listing 9-16. The Binding Element for StockQuote*

```
<binding name="StockQuoteSoapBinding" type="tns:StockQuotePortType">
    <soap:binding style="document"
      transport="http://schemas.xmlsoap.org/soap/http"/>
    <operation name="GetLastTradePrice">
        <soap:operation soapAction="http://example.com/GetLastTradePrice"/>
        <input>
            <soap:body use="literal"/>
        </input>
        <output>
            <soap:body use="literal"/>
        </output>
    </operation>
</binding>
```

That's all there is. One difference from Factorial is that we're starting with WSDL, rather than starting with code from which WSDL is generated, but the main difference is that the WSDL talks about the XML as a document. Does this mean the client code (unlike the Factorial client code) will have to work with the XML as a document? No—it can, but that's not necessary. When we ran the WSDL2Java tool on this WSDL, we generated another package of Java client classes; in fact, we created two.

## Generated Client Packages

The com.example.stockquote_xsd package is generated from our types declarations. This package has two classes: _TradePrice and _TradePriceRequest. (Notice the underscores beginning the class names.) These classes are Java beans with getXX() and setXX() methods for the objects they carry. _TradePriceRequest has a setTickerSymbol() method to set the input string, whereas _TradePrice has a getPrice() method by which to receive the resulting float. They also have XML serialization methods, that is, methods by which they can be turned into XML descriptions. The XML descriptions can also be reconstructed by deserialization methods. The fact that they are beans lets us serialize by invoking a general Axis class, called org.apache.axis.encoding.ser.BeanSerializer. Deserialization works in the same way. That means that from the client point of view, you'll be able to deal with programming-language structures instead of with raw XML.

The other package is com.example.stockquote_wsdl. It provides the same facilities that we saw in the Factorial.jws service. As before, there is an interface representing the portType: StockQuotePortType. Any class implementing this interface has the method

```
_TradePrice getLastTradePrice(_TradePriceRequest body);
```

This, of course, is the actual functionality needed: to get a TradePrice from a TradePriceRequest. As before, there's a Locator class that finds a StockQuoteServiceLocator class to implement the portType interface. It has the method you'd expect

```
public StockQuotePortType getStockQuotePort(URL portAddress)
    throws javax.xml.rpc.ServiceException ;
```

The logic in a StockQuoteClient can therefore look a lot like the logic of FactorialClient, but a little more elaborate. We'll build a _TradePriceRequest and call its setTickerSymbol() method; then we'll get a StockQuotePortType for the service's URL and ask it to getLastTradePrice(). This will give us a _TradePrice from which we can call getPrice() and that will be that (apart from exceptions).

There's just one problem in writing this client code: we don't have an actual StockQuote service to follow this WSDL. Fortunately, that's not much of a problem. Even though WSDL2Java doesn't know what a stock quote is, it is happy to generate service stubs for us from WSDL.

## Generated Service Stubs

We will repeat the invocation of WSDL2Java, but instead of invoking it on our (cut-and-pasted) WSDL file, we add two arguments to the invocation.

```
java ..WSDL2Java --server-side --skeletonDeploy true WSDLFile
```

Here we're informing the tool that we want server stubs as well as client stubs, and that we also want deployment and undeployment files, which make it easy for Axis to manage this service. We get the same client files as before, but there are four new files within the com.example.stockquote_wsdl package. Two are Web Service Deployment Descriptor (.wsdd) files; the other two, StockQuoteSoapBindingImpl.java and StockQuoteSoapBindingSkeleton.java, are there to generate the service. The skeleton has metadata describing the service so the Axis server running it will be able to (for example) recognize calls on the available operations. The Impl is an actual implementation of the StockQuotePortType interface, and the central bit of code in it is

```
public _TradePrice getLastTradePrice(_TradePriceRequest body)
  throws java.rmi.RemoteException {return null;}
```

To get a service from WSDL, we have to generate the code and then modify it so that the operations return real information—at least real enough for testing purposes. We'll modify this method, replacing "return null" with a dummy method that returns the length of the tickerSymbol as if it were a stock quote.

```
String stockSym=body.getTickerSymbol();
_TradePrice tP= new _TradePrice();
tP.setPrice(stockSym.length());
return tP;
```

## *The Stock Quote Client*

Now we'll write the StockQuoteClient using a copy of FactorialClient as a starting point. We'll run it with a command-line that will look like the following (broken in two lines for clarity):

```
java -cp %CP% StockQuoteClient MSFT
    http://localhost:8080/axis/services/StockQuotePort
```

The output, following the pattern of FactorialClient, will be

```
seeking MSFT price at http://localhost:8080/axis/services/StockQuotePort
http://localhost:8080/axis/services/StockQuotePort
 ... says that MSFT price is 4.0
```

The URI is where the service will be deployed, but of course we'll also test with the TCP Monitor by using a different listen port for the client to connect with. First we make the imports reflect the newly generated stock quote classes (see Listing 9-17).

*Listing 9-17. Client to Use Generated Code for StockQuote*

```
import com.example.stockquote_xsd.*;
import com.example.stockquote_wsdl.*;
import java.net.URL;
```

Then we produce a main() method that again expects one command-line argument but optionally takes a replacement URI for the SOAP service.

```
public class StockQuoteClient {
public static void main(String[]args){
  if(args.length==0){
    System.out.println("usage: StockQuoteClient sym [ http://... ]");
    return;
    }
  String sym=args[0];
  String uriStr="http://localhost:8080/axis/services/StockQuotePort";
  if(args.length > 1) uriStr=args[1];
```

The rest of the client is an expanded version of the corresponding code from FactorialClient. Construct a new Locator for the service, use its getStockQuotePort() method to find a StockQuotePortType object, construct the argument for this object's getLastTradePrice() method, and report on the result (see Listing 9-18).

*Listing 9-18. Conclusion of Client Code for StockQuote*

```
try{
  System.out.println("seeking "+sym+" price at "+ uriStr);
  URL url=new URL(uriStr);
  StockQuoteServiceLocator sL=new StockQuoteServiceLocator();
  StockQuotePortType serv = sL.getStockQuotePort(url);
  _TradePriceRequest tpr = new _TradePriceRequest();
  tpr.setTickerSymbol(sym);
  _TradePrice tP = serv.getLastTradePrice(tpr);
  float res=tP.getPrice();
  System.out.println(uriStr+"\n  ... says that "+sym+" price is "+res);
}catch(Exception ex){ex.printStackTrace();}
```

Compile everything and run. Nothing happens because we haven't deployed the service. And this is not a *.jws service type, so the deployment is not automatic.

## Web Services Deployment Descriptor (WSDD)

As we saw in the Generated Service Stubs section, Axis gives us two WSDD files for our StockQuoteService inside the com/example/stockquote_wsdl directory. Within that directory, we can simply say (as the deploy.wsdd file mentions, in a comment)

```
java -cp %CP% org.apache.axis.client.AdminClient deploy.wsdd
```

In this command, the classpath CP contains at least the axis.jar file. Assuming that the Axis service itself is running, this will deploy the service at /axis/services/ StockQuotePort and all will be well until you run the same command with the undeploy.wsdd file. The deploy.wsdd content has been added to TOMCAT_HOME/ webapps/axis/WEB-INF/server-config.wsdd, so whenever the server is restarted the redeployment will be automatic. (WARNING: This arrangement does not at present complain if the classes to be deployed are not on the classpath. The easiest way to include the expected service is to copy the generated directory webapps/ wsbk/axis/com into webapps/axis/WEB-INF/classes so that com/example/*.class. To make sure it worked, visit the http://localhost:8080/axis location and look at your deployed services.)

Let's look at the files. As you might expect, undeployment is a lot simpler than deployment. The content of undeploy.wsdd is shown in Listing 9-19.

*Listing 9-19. Undeployment WSDD File*

```
<undeployment xmlns="http://xml.apache.org/axis/wsdd/">
  <service name="StockQuotePort"/>
</undeployment>
```

The deployment has a parallel structure with a service tag in a deployment tag, but the service tag has a list of parameters and type mappings. The top level of the file is shown in Listing 9-20.

*Listing 9-20. Deployment WSDD File*

```
<deployment
    xmlns="http://xml.apache.org/axis/wsdd/"
    xmlns:java="http://xml.apache.org/axis/wsdd/providers/java">
  <service name="StockQuotePort"
        provider="java:RPC" style="document" use="literal">
    <parameter name="wsdlTargetNamespace" .../>
    <parameter name="wsdlServiceElement" .../>
    <parameter name="wsdlServicePort" .../>
    <parameter name="className" .../>
    <parameter name="wsdlPortType" .../>
    <parameter name="allowedMethods" .../>
    <typeMapping ...type="java:com.example.stockquote_xsd._TradePrice".../>
    <typeMapping ...type="java:com...._TradePriceRequest".../>
  </service>
</deployment>
```

The default namespace for all these tags is the `wsdd` namespace, but a few elements are in a `java` namespace. We're defining a `StockQuotePort` service that is provided as java-RPC. The server uses Java code that doesn't mention the intermediate XML at all, even though it is part of a service that uses the document/literal encoding, and the XML Schema definition of the documents goes both ways. However, there will be a list of parameters that will help Axis decide when to invoke this service and `typeMapping` elements to tell Axis how to convert between the XML documents on the wire and the Java objects in the service.

Listing 9-21 shows the parameters, which simply say that we're defining a `StockQuoteService at /axis/services/StockQuotePort` that is implemented by the `BindingSkeleton` class we've seen. The `PortType` defined in the `wsdl` was `StockQuotePortType`, and the `allowedMethods` of the service are "*", that is, any public methods of the service may be invoked by the client.

*Listing 9-21. Parameters in Deployment File*

```
<parameter name="wsdlTargetNamespace"
    value="http://example.com/stockquote.wsdl"/>
<parameter name="wsdlServiceElement" value="StockQuoteService"/>
<parameter name="wsdlServicePort" value="StockQuotePort"/>
<parameter name="className"
    value="com.example.stockquote_wsdl.StockQuoteSoapBindingSkeleton"/>
<parameter name="wsdlPortType" value="StockQuotePortType"/>
<parameter name="allowedMethods" value="*"/>
```

The two `typeMapping` elements are almost identical, so we'll only show
the `_TradePrice` mapping (see Listing 9-22). In effect, we are telling Axis that
when it encounters a `TradePrice` element with a `http://example.com/`
`stockquote.xsd` namespace, it should invoke the deserializer utility
`org.apache.axis.encoding.ser.BeanDeserializerFactory` to find out how
to convert it into a `com.example.stockquote_xsd._TradePrice` object. We
also tell Axis that if it encounters a `com.example.stockquote_xsd._TradePrice`
object that needs to be sent over the wires, it should invoke the
`org.apache.axis.encoding.ser.BeanSerializerFactory` utility to serialize and send.

*Listing 9-22. Type Mapping for Deployment File*

```
<typeMapping
  xmlns:ns="http://example.com/stockquote.xsd"
  qname="ns:>TradePrice"
  type="java:com.example.stockquote_xsd._TradePrice"
  serializer="org.apache.axis.encoding.ser.BeanSerializerFactory"
  deserializer="org.apache.axis.encoding.ser.BeanDeserializerFactory"
  encodingStyle=""
/>
```

This code relies heavily on the fact that Java beans can be constructed and
accessed by a program using the default constructor and get/set access methods.
The `typeMapping` element of `_TradePriceRequest` will be identical with this one
except for name substitution.

## The TCP Monitor on StockQuote

The StockQuote service is installed, it works, and all is well…for the moment. We can certainly get at it from an Axis-generated Java client, and we should be able to get at it from a client generated by some other system, such as .NET. Could we get at it by our xmlhttp methods in Javascript? Not very easily; we specified the XML input and output, but going from that specification to the actual data manually is rather error prone. However, with the client and server in place, we can use the TCP Monitor to look at the XML.

We start `tcpmon` as before but add a listen port of 54321. Then we invoke our `StockQuoteClient` as

```
java -cp %CP% StockQuoteClient MSFT
    http://localhost:54321/axis/services/StockQuotePort
```

We get the same response as before, except that the client says it's talking to 54321 instead of to 8080. Looking at the `tcpmon` monitor window, we can see that the request had a SOAPAction of `http://example.com/GetLastTradePrice` and the body as shown in Listing 9-23.

*Listing 9-23. XML Request (HTTP Body) for StockQuote*

```
<?xml version="1.0" encoding="UTF-8"?>
   <soapenv:Envelope
          xmlns:soapenv="http://schemas.xmlsoap.org/soap/envelope/"
          xmlns:xsd="http://www.w3.org/2001/XMLSchema"
          xmlns:xsi="http://www.w3.org/2001/XMLSchema-instance">
     <soapenv:Body>
       <TradePriceRequest xmlns="http://example.com/stockquote.xsd">
         <tickerSymbol xsi:type="xsd:string" xmlns="">IBM</tickerSymbol>
       </TradePriceRequest>
     </soapenv:Body>
   </soapenv:Envelope>
```

The body contains a `TradePriceRequest` that contains a `tickerSymbol` with the value of "IBM." Here you see standard namespaces for the SOAP envelope and for the data, and the `TradePriceRequest` has its own stockquote.xsd namespace. The `tickerSymbol` is not in a namespace. We can paste this into a Javascript function definition and use it to write a Javascript function invoking the service, just as we did in Chapters 1–3. The `doStockQuoteEnvelope()` function of the resulting Javascript client (shown in Listing 9-24) was created by copying and pasting from the `tcpmon` window.

*Listing 9-24. Javascript Client Excerpt for the StockQuote Service*

```
function doStockQuoteEnvelope(sym){
  showCallRequest=false; showCallResponse=false;
  var S='<?xml version="1.0" encoding="UTF-8"?>';
  S+='<soapenv:Envelope';
  S+='  xmlns:soapenv="http://schemas.xmlsoap.org/soap/envelope/"';
  S+='  xmlns:xsd="http://www.w3.org/2001/XMLSchema"';
  S+='  xmlns:xsi="http://www.w3.org/2001/XMLSchema-instance"> ';
  S+=' <soapenv:Body>  ';
  S+='  <TradePriceRequest xmlns="http://example.com/stockquote.xsd">';
  S+='   <tickerSymbol xsi:type="xsd:string" xmlns="">'+sym+'</tickerSymbol>';
  S+='  </TradePriceRequest>';
  S+=' </soapenv:Body>';
  S+='</soapenv:Envelope>';
  return S;
}
```

We now have two clients for the StockQuote service, and the service has no way of knowing which one invokes it because all it sees is XML on the wire, and it sends back an XML response such as in Listing 9-25 (also clipped from the `tcpmon` window).

*Listing 9-25. XML Response Body for StockQuote*

```
<?xml version="1.0" encoding="UTF-8"?>
<soapenv:Envelope
        xmlns:soapenv="http://schemas.xmlsoap.org/soap/envelope/"
        xmlns:xsd="http://www.w3.org/2001/XMLSchema"
        xmlns:xsi="http://www.w3.org/2001/XMLSchema-instance">
  <soapenv:Body>
    <TradePrice xmlns="http://example.com/stockquote.xsd">
       <price xsi:type="xsd:float" xmlns="">3.0</price>
    </TradePrice>
  </soapenv:Body>
</soapenv:Envelope>
```

Again, the body contains a TradePrice, which contains a Price, which is "3.0," and we can handle that (or a SOAPFault in case of error) in any language we like.

We recommend that you (for the most part) generate clients from WSDL even when you are working in a language like Javascript that does not have the equivalent of WSDL2Java. The procedure is to generate a Java client with WSDL2Java, trace the result with `tcpmon`, and then use that to write the client code just as we did in the first few chapters of this book. Still, when things go wrong, you'll need to have some knowledge of what the WSDL is saying, and sometimes you will want to publish a service. We don't want to write a lot of WSDL in this client-oriented book, but we do want to give you a start—and the start will be to edit existing examples. What we're going to do in the remainder of this chapter is to develop WSDL for DBAuthService so that WSDL2Java can be used to generate clients.

# Creating WSDL for DBAuthService

DBAuthService has a request message in which the Envelope contains a Body, which contains a DBServerCallParams element with one or more dbParam children of the form

```
<dbParam xsi:type="xsd:string">paramValueHere</dbParam>
```

That's the way we set up the DBServerCall SOAPAction in Chapter 4: its first parameter is the name of the query or update to be executed, and the rest, if any, are the arguments to those queries. Both kinds of parameters come out as dbParam elements in WSDL.

There are two kinds of responses: an updateCount message for updates and a resultset message for queries. That gives us three XML Schema definitions to write: one for requests, one for updateCount results, and one for resultset results. Just as we did with XSLT, we'll begin with the simplest one, updateCount.

## WSDL for Database Updates

Most of the WSDL file we need can be created by replacing stockQuote with updateCount in the example we've just seen. We'll start with the service element (shown in Listing 9-26), and we'll gradually unwind all the references in it.

*Listing 9-26. updateCount.wsdl for DBAuthService: The Service Element*

```
<service name="UpdateCountService">
    <documentation>The update part of DBAuthService</documentation>
    <port name="UpdateCountPort" binding="tns:UpdateCountBinding">
        <soap:address location="http://localhost:65432/"/>
    </port>
</service>
```

This refers to the `UpdateCountBinding`, which binds the `UpdateCountPortType`, which uses the `GetUpdateCountInput` and `GetUpdateCountOutput` messages, which refer to our defined types. The abstract `portType` is in Listing 9-27.

*Listing 9-27. updateCount.wsdl for DBAuthService: The* `portType` *Element*

```
<portType name="UpdateCountPortType">
    <operation name="GetUpdateCount">
        <input message="tns:GetUpdateCountInput"/>
        <output message="tns:GetUpdateCountOutput"/>
    </operation>
</portType>
```

If you compare Listing 9-27 to the corresponding definitions for `stockQuote` and `Factorial` (Listing 9-12), the pattern should be fairly obvious.

The binding element (see Listing 9-28) is an `UpdateCountBinding` for the `portType` of Listing 9-27. It has one operation that has a soapAction and a literal SOAP:body for both input and output.

*Listing 9-28. SOAP Binding (Document/Literal) for* `updateCount`

```
<binding name="UpdateCountBinding" type="tns:UpdateCountPortType">
    <soap:binding style="document"
      transport="http://schemas.xmlsoap.org/soap/http"/>
    <operation name="GetUpdateCount">
      <soap:operation soapAction="DBServerCall"/>
      <input>
          <soap:body use="literal"/>
      </input>
      <output>
          <soap:body use="literal"/>
      </output>
    </operation>
</binding>
```

The input and output contain `doSQLRequest` and `doSQLResponse`, respectively (see Listing 9-29).

*Listing 9-29. The Message Elements for Input and Output*

```
<message name="GetUpdateCountInput">
    <part name="body" element="xsd1:doSQLRequest"/>
</message>

<message name="GetUpdateCountOutput">
    <part name="body" element="xsd1:doSQLResponse"/>
</message>
```

This leaves us with the root element of the XML structure, which is the definition element (see Listing 9-30) whose start tag declares all the namespaces.

*Listing 9-30. The Root (Definitions) Element's Start Tag*

```
<definitions name="updateCount"
  targetNamespace="http://n-topus.com/DBS"
        xmlns:tns="http://n-topus.com/DBS"
        xmlns:xsd1="http://n-topus.com/DBS"
        xmlns:soap="http://schemas.xmlsoap.org/wsdl/soap/"
        xmlns="http://schemas.xmlsoap.org/wsdl/">
```

We use the same URI as a namespace ID for the targetNamespace, tns, and the xsd1 namespace, but we map them to different prefixes to help our human readers to keep the corresponding vocabularies apart. Using the same namespace results in a simpler code organization, WSDL2Java puts all the code into a single package, which will be called com.n_topus.DBS, and which will live in a directory com/n_topus/DBS. This directory will contain an UpdateCountServiceLocator class and the other classes that are generated as client stub code, but it will also include the files that correspond to our WSDL-defined types. These will represent an element named doSQLRequest (shown in Listing 9-31), which contains an element named DBServerCallParams, which contains a sequence of one or more elements named dbParam, each of which contains a string.

*Listing 9-31. Schema for doSQLRequest*

```
<schema targetNamespace="http://n-topus.com/DBS"
        xmlns="http://www.w3.org/2000/10/XMLSchema">
    <element name="doSQLRequest">
        <complexType>
            <all>
                <element name="DBServerCallParams">
                    <complexType>
```

```
        <sequence>
          <element name="dbParam" type="string"
                      minOccurs="1" maxOccurs="unbounded"/>
        </sequence>
      </complexType>
    </element>
  </all>
  </complexType>
</element>
```

The generated code therefore includes files named _doSQLRequest.java
and _doSQLRequest_DBServerCallParams.java, each of which is a bean with a no-
arguments constructor and set/get methods. In particular, _doSQLRequest.java has
a method setDBServerCallParams() shown in Listing 9-32.

*Listing 9-32. Part of Generated Java Code from Schema*

```
public void setDBServerCallParams(
  com.n_topus.DBS._doSQLRequest_DBServerCallParams DBServerCallParams) {
    this.DBServerCallParams = DBServerCallParams;
}
```

That's how we give the _doSQLRequest object the
_doSQLRequest_DBServerCallParams value it needs for the call. (We'll call that a
_DBServerCallParams object for short.) That subobject, in turn, has a method that
takes an array of strings as the sequence of dbParam values.

```
public void setDbParam(java.lang.String[] dbParam) {
  this.dbParam = dbParam;
}
```

It also has methods to get and set the array one string at a time. Both of
these classes have methods called equals() and hashCode() so they can be put in
hashtables effectively, and they have metadata used by the XML parsing process,
with lines like

```
elemField.setXmlName(
  new javax.xml.namespace.QName("", "DBServerCallParams"));
```

This is within _doSQLRequest.java. In effect, it's telling the XML parser to expect a DBServerCallParams element with no namespace. When the parser sees the DBServerCallParams element, it will refer to the rest of this metadata section and invoke the deserializer to produce the _DBServerCallParams Java object. That object will in turn contain metadata that specifies that the content of a dbParam XML element is a string. So each dbParam element in the XML will turn into a string object in Java that will be one item of an array within the _DBServerCallParams object, which will be a variable value within the _doSQLRequest object.

```
elemField.setXmlName(new javax.xml.namespace.QName("", "dbParam"));
elemField.setXmlType(new javax.xml.namespace.QName(
                      "http://www.w3.org/2000/10/XMLSchema", "string"));
```

The underlying parser for Axis' BeanDeserializer does not build a DOM document for the input; it traverses that input one element at a time and invokes whatever it's told to invoke as it begins and ends each element, or as it processes the text in between. This is SAX (Simple API for XML) event-driven XML processing, and it is somewhat faster and much less memory-intensive than DOM, but it is less flexible, as well. For example, you can't back up in a tree because there is none. This will become an important issue later in the chapter, but not within update-Count. doSQLResponse (see Listing 9-33) is even simpler.

*Listing 9-33. Schema for* doSQLResponse

```
<element name="doSQLResponse">
   <complexType>
      <all>
         <element name="span" type="float">
            <attribute name="class" type="string"/>
         </element>
      </all>
   </complexType>
</element>
</schema>
</types>
```

This generates a _doSQLResponse class with a getSpan() method, which returns the content of that span element.

```
public float getSpan() { return span; }
```

That's almost all we'll need to write the UpdateCountClient, build the request, and return getSpan() from the response.

# *The Code of the Database Update Client*

This is a fairly long piece of code, so we will present it in chunks, beginning with imports. A major problem in constructing the code is that DBAuthService requires a username and password for updates, so we have to figure out how to insert these into an Axis-generated Web Service call. If they were constant, we could ask WSDL2Java to do it, but we don't want that; we want them as command-line parameters. Fortunately, Axis provides a utility class called Options for parsing command-line parameters. We import this utility (see Listing 9-34) and also javax.xml.rpc.Stub so we can work with the properties of the client.

*Listing 9-34.* UpdateCountClient *Class: Imports*

```
import com.n_topus.DBS.*;
import java.net.URL;
import org.apache.axis.utils.Options;
import javax.xml.rpc.Stub;
```

There's a standard way to use an Options object: pass the command line to its constructor and it extracts the options it understands, after which you can ask it for the remaining arguments (those will be our dbParam values). This all happens in the main() method whose code begins in Listing 9-35.

*Listing 9-35.* UpdateCountClient *Class: The* main() *Method*

```
public static void main(String[]args)throws Exception{
  Options opts = new Options(args);
  args = opts.getRemainingArgs();
  if(args==null){
    System.err.println("Usage: [a usage explanation]");
    System.err.println("e.g. [a usage example]");
    System.exit(1);
  }
```

The host, port, and path arguments will be used to construct the URL we want to attach to. (Again, we are doing this explicitly so we can invoke tcpmon; otherwise we'd just attach to the service location as defined in the WSDL and carried over into the service locator's generated code.) The remaining command-line arguments now build the request object, one bean inside another (see Listing 9-36).

*Listing 9-36.* `UpdateCountClient` *Class: The* `main()` *Method Continued*

```
_doSQLRequest_DBServerCallParams dbcp =
      new _doSQLRequest_DBServerCallParams();
  dbcp.setDbParam(args);
  _doSQLRequest request = new _doSQLRequest();
  request.setDBServerCallParams(dbcp);
```

Now we try to locate the service.

```
try{
    UpdateCountServiceLocator sL=new UpdateCountServiceLocator();
    UpdateCountPortType serv = sL.getUpdateCountPort();
```

At this point, we might be tempted to start using the `serv` object, but there's a problem. `UpdateCountPortType` is, as we saw with StockQuote, an interface (see the section "Generated Client Package" earlier in this chapter). When we look at the interface all we see is the `getUpdateCount()` method; there are no methods for username or password. How do we add a password? Are we stuck? No, because we can look at the service locator class and see that it is actually returning an object of class `UpdateCountBindingStub` that implements the port type interface.

```
public class UpdateCountBindingStub extends org.apache.axis.client.Stub
                 implements com.n_topus.DBS.UpdateCountPortType {
```

We can expect the `client.Stub` class to provide a variety of methods for getting at the underpinnings if we need them, and concepts like username and password shouldn't be very far down. So we look at the Axis javadoc and see that indeed this class (and therefore our own `UpdateCountBindingStub` class) has what we need, and we can finish the `main()` method's code.

*Listing 9-37.* `UpdateCountClient` *Class: The* `main()` *Method Completed*

```
    UpdateCountBindingStub stub = (UpdateCountBindingStub)serv;
    stub._setProperty(javax.xml.rpc.Stub.ENDPOINT_ADDRESS_PROPERTY,
                      opts.getURL());
    stub.setUsername(opts.getUser());
    stub.setPassword(opts.getPassword());

    _doSQLResponse dsr=stub.getUpdateCount(request);
    System.out.println("The update count is "+dsr.getSpan());
  }catch(Exception ex){ex.printStackTrace();
}
```

The Options object puts the URL together from the command-line arguments. It picks out the user and password from the -u and -w options, and from there on it's straightforward. We can trace the process with `tcpmon` and we can see it all go in and out. Well, it's almost straightforward. In fact, the first time we ran this, DBAuth-Service complained about an invalid SOAPAction because the Axis-generated client was producing "DBServerCall" with quotation marks, and DBAuthService expected to see it without them. Having the Axis source code, we could fix that in the client code, but it seemed better in this case to fix the service. When you control the server, that's a judgment call, but it is usually much better to make your custom code conform to the standard tool, in this case Axis, than the other way around. (If you discover something actually wrong with Axis, and you're sure about that, you should document it carefully and report it. If you want to fix it, read the developer's guide, fix it, and submit the patch so other people can benefit.) Other than removing the quotation marks from the SOAPAction, we left the service code alone.

## WSDL for the Database Query Client

After getting the `UpdateCountClient` to run, we can take up `ResultSet`. resultSet.wsdl is pretty much a copy of updateCount.wsdl except for a case-sensitive global replacement of `updateCount` with `resultSet`, and of course the changed definition of doSQLResponse (see Listing 9-38). This time, the response element should contain a table, which contains a tr element. The tr element contains th elements that contain strings and a sequence of tr elements containing td elements that contain strings.

*Listing 9-38. XML Schema for* resultSets *from DBAuthService*

```
<element name="doSQLResponse">
   <complexType>
      <all>
         <element name="table">
            <complexType>
               <element name="tr">
                  <complexType>
                     <sequence>
                        <element name="th" type="string"
                           minOccurs="1" maxOccurs="unbounded"/>
                     </sequence>
                  </complexType>
               </element>
               <sequence>
```

```
                        <element name="tr" minOccurs="0"
                                maxOccurs="unbounded">
                      <complexType>
                        <sequence>
                          <element name="th" type="string"
                            minOccurs="1" maxOccurs="unbounded"/>
                        </sequence>
                      </complexType>
                    </element>
                  </sequence>
                </complexType>
              </element>
          </all>
        </complexType>
      </element>
```

This is verbose but readable, and we can pass it to WSDL2Java, but if we don't take a necessary precaution, we will overwrite the UpdateCount version of _doSQLResponse. The precaution is to invoke WSDL2Java with the option that specifies the package to place the code in: --package com.n_topus.DBS_RS. This overrides the default package naming option that simply copies the namespace. After doing this, the output goes into com/n_topus/DBS_RS and all is well except for a nasty little error message.

```
{http://n-topus.com/DBS}>doSQLResponse>table>tr already exists
```

Ouch. This means is when WSDL2Java is traversing the WSDL that describes the rows of data headed by tr elements and containing td elements, it wants to create a class that will be called _doSQLResponse_table_tr, but this class already exists. It was created just a few microseconds earlier to handle data headed by tr elements and containing th elements. The _doSQLResponse_table class wants to know what to do when it encounters a tr element. In principle, it could figure out that it should do one thing the first time and then something else for every time after that—this is what the WSDL says. However, WSDL2Java is not smart enough to handle this on its own. The table class just calls on its tr class, which knows what to do with th elements. What to do? Well, we have to inspect the generated code and see if we can fix it. Indeed we can, but we'll have to do a number of modifications to _doSQLResponse_table_tr.java.

## Modifications to Generated Code

Let's look at what happens with th elements; they go into an array of strings
(see Listing 9-39).

*Listing 9-39. Generated Code for* _doSQLResponse_table_tr *Class*

```
private String[] th;
public String[] getTh() {return th;}
public void setTh(String[] th) {this.th = th;}
public String getTh(int i) {return th[i];}
public void setTh(int i, String value) {this.th[i] = value;}
```

Now we want exactly the same thing to happen with td elements (see
Listing 9-40).

*Listing 9-40. Insertion into* _doSQLResponse_table_tr.java

```
private String[] td;
public String[] getTd() {return td;}
public void setTd(String[] td) {this.td = td;}
public String getTd(int i) {return td[i];}
public void setTd(int i, String value) {this.td[i] = value;}
```

We know that some rows are header rows that contain only th elements, and
others are data rows that contain only td elements, and there are no mixed rows
containing both kinds of elements. An array generated from a row is either an
array of td elements or an array of th elements, and we can test which one it is
by a Boolean isHeaderRow() method.

```
public boolean isHeaderRow(){
  return getTh()!=null && getTh().length > 0;
}
```

Because we now have two kinds of arrays, we have to modify the equals() and
hashCode() methods as well as metadata for serialization and deserialization. The
equals() method of the generated code compares one object to another object of
the same class and returns true if the following condition holds:

```
((this.th==null && other.getTh()==null) ||
 (this.th!=null &&
  java.util.Arrays.equals(this.th, other.getTh())))
```

We want `td` and `th` to be handled exactly the same way, so we make a copy of this expression, change `.th` to `.td`, change `getTh()` to `getTd()`, and let `equals()` return true if and only if both of these expressions are true.

Similarly, the `hashCode()` method builds up a `_hashCode` value, which has been initialized to 1, as follows:

```
if (getTh() != null) {
    for (int i=0;
            i<java.lang.reflect.Array.getLength(getTh());
            i++) {
            java.lang.Object obj = java.lang.reflect.Array.get(getTh(), i);
            if (obj != null &&
                !obj.getClass().isArray()) {
                _hashCode += obj.hashCode();
            }
    }
}
```

Again, we want `td` to be treated like `th`, so we make a copy of this block, changing `getTh()` to `getTd()` throughout, and insert it. On with the metadata! The metadata is held in an object of type `org.apache.axis.description.TypeDesc`. The constructor for the class takes an argument of our class that we are busy modifying. What happens in the constructor call `TypeDesc(_doSQLResponse_table_tr.class)` is shown in Listing 9-41. An XML type (with the DBS namespace) is defined for this class. It has a field named "th" whose XmlName is also "th" (with no namespace). This field's XML type is a standard XML Schema type, namely "string."

*Listing 9-41. Excerpt From the* `TypeDesc()` *Constructor*

```
typeDesc.setXmlType(
    new QName("http://n-topus.com/DBS",
            ">doSQLResponse>table>tr")); // note funny generated code
ElementDesc elemField = new ElementDesc();
elemField.setFieldName("th");
elemField.setXmlName(new QName("", "th"));
elemField.setXmlType(new QName("http://www.w3.org/2000/10/XMLSchema",
                            "string"));
typeDesc.addFieldDesc(elemField);
```

Again, we want td to be handled just like th, so we copy this block and change th to td and elemField to elemField2. All our modifications to _doSQLResponse_table_tr are now complete. We can proceed to ResultSetClient.

## The Database Query Client and Its Messages

The ResultSetClient class looks just like the UpdateCountClient class except that it will do its imports from com.n_topus.DBS_RS and pull out the arrays at the end (see Listing 9-42).

*Listing 9-42.* ResultSetClient *for DBAuthService*

```
_doSQLResponse dsr=stub.getResultSet(request);
_doSQLResponse_table table = dsr.getTable();
_doSQLResponse_table_tr[] rows= table.getTr();
for(int i=0;i<rows.length;i++)
 if(rows[i].isHeaderRow())showRow(rows[i].getTh());
 else showRow(rows[i].getTd());
```

The showRow() method (see Listing 9-43) is quite straightforward:

*Listing 9-43.* showRow()

```
public static void showRow(String[]row){
  if(row==null || row.length==0) return;
  System.out.print(row[0]);
  for(int j=1;j<row.length;j++)
    System.out.print("\t"+row[j]);
  System.out.println();
}
```

To see the SOAP traffic, we run ResultSetClient with via tcpmon.

```
java ResultSetClient -utjm -wtjm -hlocalhost -p54321 GETALL_AmaAuth
```

This connects to tcpmon's 54321 listen port, which tcpmon then connects to DBAuthService's own 65432 port. Our modified Axis-generated client produces a request, shown in Listing 9-44.

*Listing 9-44. Request from* ResultSetClient

```
POST /axis/servlet/AxisServlet HTTP/1.0
Content-Type: text/xml; charset=utf-8
Accept: application/soap+xml, application/dime, multipart/related, text/*
User-Agent: Axis/1.1
Host: 127.0.0.1
Cache-Control: no-cache
Pragma: no-cache
SOAPAction: "DBServerCall"
Content-Length: 451
Authorization: Basic dGptOnRqbQ==

<?xml version="1.0" encoding="UTF-8"?>
    <soapenv:Envelope
        xmlns:soapenv="http://schemas.xmlsoap.org/soap/envelope/"
        xmlns:xsd="http://www.w3.org/2001/XMLSchema"
        xmlns:xsi="http://www.w3.org/2001/XMLSchema-instance">
      <soapenv:Body>
        <doSQLRequest xmlns="http://n-topus.com/DBS">
          <DBServerCallParams xmlns="">
            <dbParam xsi:type="xsd:string">GETALL_AmaAuth</dbParam>
          </DBServerCallParams>
        </doSQLRequest>
      </soapenv:Body>
    </soapenv:Envelope>
```

The response from DBAuthService is shown in Listing 9-45.

*Listing 9-45. Response to* ResultSetClient

```
HTTP/1.0 200 OK
Content-Type: text/xml; charset=utf-8
Content-Length: 923
Date: Sun, 10 Aug 03 18:54:3 GMT
Server: DBAuthService 0.11

<?xml version='1.0' encoding='UTF-8'?>
    <SOAP-ENV:Envelope  xmlns:nns='http://n-topus.com/DBS'>
      <SOAP-ENV:Body>
        <nns:doSQLResponse>
          <table border='1'>
            <tr>
```

```
        <th>Asin</th>
        <th>Author</th>
    </tr>
    <tr>
        <td>0393047644</td>
        <td>Fareed Zakaria</td>
    </tr>
    <tr>
        <td>0465016154</td>
        <td>Hernando de Soto</td>
    </tr>
    ...
```

The output from the `ResultSetClient` is shown in Listing 9-46.

*Listing 9-46. Console Output from* `ResultSetClient`

```
Asin     Author
0393047644    Fareed Zakaria
0465016154    Hernando de Soto
```

This concludes our last WSDL example and the entire chapter, which happens to be the last chapter of the book. Time for conclusions on all levels.

## Conclusion

In this chapter, we worked our way through three Axis-framework Web Services and clients. The first and simplest one had its WSDL description and client code generated from the code of the service. The second one started from a WSDL description (from an example published by w3c.org) and used Axis tools to generate much of the code for both the service and the client. The third and most ambitious one developed a WSDL description to match an existing service—our own DBAuthService from Chapter 5. With a WSDL description in hand, we have again produced the client code using Axis tools, but this time the code needed more tweaking. We hope we convinced you that sometimes you don't need to fiddle with WSDL-generated clients very much, but if you do, on some occasions you may even want to go so far as to write your own serialization and deserialization classes. Almost always, some knowledge and understanding of WSDL is helpful.

The next Version 1.2 is at `http://www.w3.org/TR/wsdl12/`; it is in progress as we write this book (summer of 2003). It renames some components, introduces a few extensions (such as the use of James Clark's Relax NG notation for the WSDL, which will definitely make your life easier), and brings in a few restrictions (such as the removal of overloaded methods, which will prevent some problems).

# APPENDIX A

# Installation

DETAILED AND RECENTLY UPDATED installation instructions are in the readme.htm file of our code archive at `http://www.apress.com`. This Appendix gives an overview of the installation process. The basic installation logic is the same for Windows, Linux/Unix, and Macintosh OS X.

The main steps of the installation are as follows:

1. Download and install the free software packages that together form the framework in which our code operates.

2. Expand our code archive into appropriate places.

3. Register as a user with the Google and Amazon Web Services.

4. Place the registration keys from Amazon and Google into specific files in our code archive.

The first of these steps is the most time-consuming, but once you have installed the framework, it will serve you well in many projects in addition to this book. Chances are, you already have some of the components installed.

## Installing the Framework

Begin by making sure you have an adequate browser: Internet Explorer 6.0 for Windows, or Mozilla 1.4+ (`http://www.mozilla.org`) for Windows, Linux, or Mac OS X. Test your browser installation and turn on its Javascript debugging tool. (The Javascript Console in Mozilla's Tool/Web Development submenu is a major help.)

Next get your Java Development Kit (JDK), version 1.4.2 or later, from `http://java.sun.com/j2se/1.4.2/download.html` for Windows or Linux, or from `http://www.apple.com/java/` for OS X. Note the documentation available, which you can download or use from the site `http://java.sun.com/j2se/1.4.2/docs/api`. You can simply edit your Java files as text and then compile (and run) with the JDK as we usually do, or you can use a graphical programming environment. NetBeans works on all three platforms and is available from Sun's Java download page or directly from `http://www.netbeans.org`. (See `http://www.netbeans.org/kb/articles/mac.html` for specific OS X information.)

At this point, you could expand our code archive, register with the Google and Amazon Web Services, and work through the first three chapters before installing Tomcat. However, the installation is easier to describe if you do it all at once.

Next download the Tomcat Web server from `http://jakarta.apache.org/tomcat/`. Because this is pure Java, there should be no problem running it on any system. Installation for Windows and Linux is discussed on `http://www.apache.org`, and the OS X install is explained at `http://developer.apple.com/internet/java/tomcat1.html`. We'll assume the simplest installation, which has Tomcat running as a standalone server. Check the documentation directory, `http://jakarta.apache.org/tomcat/tomcat-4.0-doc`, for installation instructions. MySQL for all platforms is at `http://www.mysql.com/downloads/mysql-4.0.html`. This site has exhaustive documentation at `http://www.mysql.com/documentation/` but the OS X user may also find `http://developer.apple.com/internet/macosx/osdb.html` helpful. To use a database from within Java programs, you need a JDBC driver; a driver for MySQL can be found at `http://www.mysql.com/downloads/api-jdbc-stable.html` (Connector/J). After downloading the archive, put its jar file (currently named mysql-connector-java-3.0.8-stable-bin.jar but the version number will change with each update) in Tomcat's common/lib directory. (Whenever you add something to the common/lib directory or add a new webapp, you'll have to restart Tomcat.)

The `http://sourceforge.net/projects/jtidy` project is the Java version of Tidy. You should be able to expand the downloaded file (look at the documentation and examples) and use it. We sometimes get peculiar error messages that go away when we recompile it from the source. Download it, test it, and place the jar file in Tomcat's common/lib directory.

The last of the outside packages, `http://ws.apache.org/axis/`, is a framework for developing Web Services. Download it and put it as a webapp in Tomcat's webapps directory, as its installation instructions suggest.

## The Rest of It

Finally, it's time to install our code archive. Download it from `http://www.apress.com` and expand it. Copy or move the wsbk directory and the Axis directory into Tomcat's webapps directory. This will add a few files to your Axis installation. (Remember to restart Tomcat.) The `mysql/data` directory can be copied into your MySQL data directory; this will preload a wsbkdb database to mysql, though you have the programmatic tools to create this from scratch.

Obtain a Google registration key from `http://www.google.com/apis`, and an Amazon developer's token from `http://www.amazon.com/webservices`. Use these to replace the values in your TOMCAT_HOME/webapps/wsbk/utils/key.js file. The Google key is not used anywhere else, but the Amazon developer's token (D2Y0P98RA19J1K) used in developing this book is included as a constant in

XmlHttp.java and in a couple of XSLT files that have no easy way to import JS files. If you're going to use these more than a few times, or if a request is rejected because some other reader is using them, please replace the token with your own.

Within Tomcat, the start file for our code archive is `http://localhost:8080/wsbk`. As a local file, the start file is `TOMCAT_HOME/webapps/wsbk/index.html`. Depending on your security settings, you may find that local file access is more trusted than the HTTP access, so you may prefer to use the local file access for the first few chapters. The later chapters require Tomcat, but they won't raise the security issues because they don't use applets. The choice is yours. Point your browser toward the start file, and open to Chapter 1.

# APPENDIX B

# Troubleshooting

THINGS GO WRONG OFTEN, and when they do, we get error messages. For Javascript, you can set both Mozilla and IE to produce error messages and help debug them. (We like the Mozilla Javascript console a lot, but we do try to debug all code in both.) For Java applets, there's the Java console; for command-line Java applications there's the regular console. For apps running in Tomcat, you may have a visible console or just the log files in TOMCAT_HOME/logs. Between your error output, the availability of the source (including the full Tomcat source, Axis source, and Tidy source), and the online documentation, you have a lot to go on.

There is, however, one major source of trouble for experienced as well as inexperienced Java programmers. A large fraction of the problems you will encounter when running or recompiling our code are classpath problems. The classpath is a system variable; that is, a list of directories and .jar files where Java looks for classes. Say you are invoking a library in a .jar file, but Java or Javac can't find it. If you get a "Class Not Found" exception, you probably have to add something to your classpath. Worse, when you invoke a library in a .jar file, Java finds the wrong version of the library. For example, you may have several copies of xerces.jar (an XML parser) or tidy.jar on your classpath, and Java takes the first copy it finds. The situation is better than the DLL hell, but to make problems less likely, we simplified it further by putting all our jars into TOMCAT_HOME/common/lib so Tomcat adds them to the classpath automatically. Still, you should be aware of possible problems. If you see a "Package Not Found on Import" error or a "Cannot Resolve Symbol" error, it's quite likely that a jar is in the wrong place or that you have not restarted Tomcat since putting it in the right place.

To find which jar or jars have definitions for a given class, it helps to understand that a .jar file is a zip archive, a compiled Java class or interface is a .class file, and filenames are stored in uncompressed format. To find which jars have definitions of the Node interface, you can search (with grep on Linux or Control-F on Windows) for .jar files containing the string Node.class or even, if you know specifically that you are looking for org.w3c.com.Node, for the string org/w3c/dom/Node.class. You probably have a fair number of these; most of them are probably copies of xerces.jar or xalan.jar. Look at dates and sizes to see which one you want (usually the latest), put it ahead of the rest of them on the classpath, and perhaps remove the rest from your system. If you have an old copy of a .jar file (let's say a servlet.jar) in your JDK's jre/lib/ext directory, the new copy in common/lib is not going to be seen. You can usually think of the `jre/lib/ext` directory as though everything in it were put in the front of the classpath.

Usually, especially with our usage of `common/lib` (all required jars are in one flat directory), that's enough. Sometimes it's not, though, because the term "classpath" is really a misnomer. The term actually refers to a hierarchy of class loaders that invoke each other, and the top class loader (for our purposes, the one that loads all jars in your jdk's `jre/lib/ext` directory) is visible to all others, but not necessarily vice versa.

Similarly, you should be aware of the possibility that Tomcat's common libraries in `common/lib` are visible to your webapp's libraries, but not vice versa. This is a good design principle: each class loader effectively defines an extension to the Java language. Usually it doesn't cause any problems—for example, your own `WEB-INF/lib` and `WEB-INF/classes` directories can contain classes that come from `common/lib/xalan.jar`. However, if you see a "Class Not Found" exception and you believe that the class is on the classpath, you may have to start thinking about hierarchies of class loaders, and you may well end up using more than one copy of some of your .jar files.

# APPENDIX C

# Online Resources

WE GROUP ONLINE RESOURCES into two categories: Standards and Sources of information. For sources of software, refer to Appendix A.

## Standards

None of the XML-related "standards" are literally so; they have not been approved by any standards organizations such as ISO or ANSI. They are all de-facto standards produced by industry consortia. The most important consortium by far is the World Wide Web Consortium, W3C.

## *W3C Technical Reports*

All W3C technical reports (Recommendations, Candidate Recommendations, Working Drafts, and Notes) can be found at `http://www.w3.org/TR/`. You can also find any W3C technical document by searching through that page. You can form an individual document's URL by attaching an identifying string; for instance, *Extensible Markup Language (XML) 1.0 (Second Edition)* is found at `http://www.w3.org/TR/REC-xml`. Here are some of the URLs that are used in this book; we provide a title and the string to attach to `http://www.w3.org/TR/`:

- Extensible Markup Language (XML) 1.0 (Second Edition): `REC-xml`

- Namespaces in XML: `REC-xml-names/`

- XSL Transformations (XSLT): `xslt`

- XML Path Language (XPath): `xpath`

- XML Schema Part 1: Structures: `xmlschema-1`

- XML Schema Part 2: Datatypes: `xmlschema-2`

- WSDL Version 1.1: `wsdl`

- WSDL Version 1.2: `wsdl12`

- SOAP Version 1.2 Part 1: Messaging Framework: `soap12-part1`

In addition to technical reports, W3C is a source of WWW, HTML, and XML news, information, and public domain software. It also maintains a number of public mailing lists on its activities, found at `http://www.w3.org/Mail/Lists.html`.

## OASIS Technical Committees

Another source of XML standards that is becoming increasingly important is OASIS (Organization for the Advancement of Structured Information Standards), found at `http://www.oasis-open.org`. OASIS also provides a home for the Cover pages and `xml.org`, two important sources of information.

## Other Consortia

It seems that a business consortium has become a well-developed mechanism for creating de-facto standards. We will mention a few:

- UDDI.org, for developing UDDI, as described in Chapter 9.

- Web Services Interoperability Organization (WSIO), to ensure interoperability of Web Services based on the SOAP, WSDL, UDDI protocols. (See `http://www.ws-i.org/`.)

- DAML.org, a non-industry consortium of a number of academic and research institutions, funded by DARPA and committed to the vision of the Semantic Web.

## Sources of Information

Our book touches upon several large topics: XML; Java XML processing; JSP and Web applications; and Web Services. Resources in the next section are grouped according to these topics.

Big companies (IBM, Microsoft, and Sun) have large stores of information on these topics. We particularly mention the following in this book:

- IBM Developerworks: `http://www.ibm.com/developerworks/`. This site has many tutorials, often with links to IBM alphaworks sites for free software. (IBM free software is not necessarily open-source.)

- Microsoft Developer Network (MSDN): `http://www.msdn.microsoft.com/`, and especially `http://www.msdn.microsoft.com/xml` and `http://www.msdn.microsoft.com/asp`.

- Sun's Java site, `http://java.sun.com`, and especially `http://java.sun.com/xml`, `http://java.sun.com/jsp` and `http://java.sun.com/j2ee`, all with links to developer sites. There is also interesting software at `http://wwwswest.sun.com/xml/`.

## XML Resources

The Cover pages (`http://xml.coverpages.org/`) is the oldest source of information on XML and, before it, SGML. It is maintained by Robin Cover (hence the name) and hosted by OASIS. It is a huge and diligently maintained resource; Robin Cover's summaries frequently provide useful insights.

While you are at or near OASIS, visit `http://www.xml.org/xml/xmlfaq.shtml`. It has links to several XML and XSL FAQs as well as FAQs for XML Schema, SOAP, and UDDI. It is also home to xml-dev mailing list, at `http://www.xml.org/xml/xmldev.shtml`. Another very active XSLT mailing list is at `http://www.mulberrytech.com/xsl/xsl-list`.

Several XML-related resources are maintained by the O'Reilly network. The most important one is `http://www.xml.com`. It serves both as an online journal and a repository of information, with links to tutorials, reviews, and software.

For Microsoft's coverage of XML, go to `http://www.msdn.microsoft.com/xml`. There is an abundance of information there, some of it Microsoft-specific, some of general interest.

## Java XML Processing and Web Services

At Sun, there is a Java XML page, `http://java.sun.com/xml/`, and a Web Services page, `http://java.sun.com/webservices/`.

## Web Services

All the major sources of XML ideas or software are involved with Web Services one way or another. Here is a brief listing:

- W3C is working on standards for SOAP, and more broadly, for XML protocols. W3C also has a Note on WSDL and is actively working to position RDF as a Web Services description language. The W3C page on semantic Web Services resources is found at http://www.w3.org/2001/11/11-semweb-webservices.

- OASIS is working with UN/CEFACT (United Nations Centre for Trade Facilitation and Electronic Business) on XML messaging and a number of other projects within its ebXML initiative. Don't ask us how or why but ebXML stands for Electronic Business using XML. There is a dedicated website at http://www.ebxml.org.

- Microsoft, IBM, Sun, Oracle, and Hewlett-Packard all work on various aspects of SOAP, WSDL, and UDDI. In addition to individual companies' sites, there is also http://www.UDDI.org and http://www.WSIO.org.

## Keep Looking

Any static page on Web resources, especially printed in a book, is going to be obsolete and incomplete soon. Keep looking through Google, AltaVista, and AlltheWeb for other tutorials, code collections, or interesting developments. Visit xml.com and w3c.org once a week and subscribe to the xmlhack.com newsletter. Things are moving fast, and they keep moving faster. Last but not least, check our own website http://www.n-topus.com/AmaGoogle/ for updates!

# Index

# forums.apress.com
## FOR PROFESSIONALS BY PROFESSIONALS™

JOIN THE APRESS FORUMS AND BE PART OF OUR COMMUNITY. You'll find discussions that cover topics of interest to IT professionals, programmers, and enthusiasts just like you. If you post a query to one of our forums, you can expect that some of the best minds in the business—especially Apress authors, who all write with *The Expert's Voice*™—will chime in to help you. Why not aim to become one of our most valuable participants (MVPs) and win cool stuff? Here's a sampling of what you'll find:

## DATABASES
**Data drives everything.**

Share information, exchange ideas, and discuss any database programming or administration issues.

## INTERNET TECHNOLOGIES AND NETWORKING
**Try living without plumbing (and eventually IPv6).**

Talk about networking topics including protocols, design, administration, wireless, wired, storage, backup, certifications, trends, and new technologies.

## JAVA
**We've come a long way from the old Oak tree.**

Hang out and discuss Java in whatever flavor you choose: J2SE, J2EE, J2ME, Jakarta, and so on.

## MAC OS X
**All about the Zen of OS X.**

OS X is both the present and the future for Mac apps. Make suggestions, offer up ideas, or boast about your new hardware.

## OPEN SOURCE
**Source code is good; understanding (open) source is better.**

Discuss open source technologies and related topics such as PHP, MySQL, Linux, Perl, Apache, Python, and more.

## PROGRAMMING/BUSINESS
**Unfortunately, it is.**

Talk about the Apress line of books that cover software methodology, best practices, and how programmers interact with the "suits."

## WEB DEVELOPMENT/DESIGN
**Ugly doesn't cut it anymore, and CGI is absurd.**

Help is in sight for your site. Find design solutions for your projects and get ideas for building an interactive Web site.

## SECURITY
**Lots of bad guys out there—the good guys need help.**

Discuss computer and network security issues here. Just don't let anyone else know the answers!

## TECHNOLOGY IN ACTION
**Cool things. Fun things.**

It's after hours. It's time to play. Whether you're into LEGO® MINDSTORMS™ or turning an old PC into a DVR, this is where technology turns into fun.

## WINDOWS
**No defenestration here.**

Ask questions about all aspects of Windows programming, get help on Microsoft technologies covered in Apress books, or provide feedback on any Apress Windows book.

## HOW TO PARTICIPATE:
Go to the Apress Forums site at **http://forums.apress.com/**.
Click the New User link.